❀

Ideology in Cold Blood

IDEOLOGY IN COLD BLOOD

A Reading of Lucan's *Civil War*

SHADI BARTSCH

HARVARD UNIVERSITY PRESS
Cambridge, Massachusetts
London, England
1997

Library of Congress Cataloging-in-Publication Data

Bartsch, Shadi, 1966–
Ideology in cold blood :
a reading of Lucan's Civil War /
Shadi Bartsch.
p.   cm.
Includes bibliographical references and index.
ISBN 0-674-44291-1 (alk. paper)
1. Lucan, 39–65. Pharsalia.
2. Rome—History—Civil War, 49–48 B.C.—Literature and the war.
3. Epic poetry, Latin—History and criticism.
I. Title.
PA6480.B374 1998
873'.01—dc21   97-18200

For my husband, Robert,
benigno et lepido et comi

Contents

Preface

THIS IS A little book, but I had more people to discuss it with than ever before. So I would like to thank, in alphabetical order, a roster of excellent friends and colleagues: some directed me to important reading material, others had the patience to discuss the most embryonic of ideas, and still others listened to conference talks and other presentations and offered valuable feedback. They are W. S. Anderson, Carlin Barton, David Cohen, John Henderson, Tony Long, Kathy McCarthy, Charles Murgia, Ramona Naddaff, James O'Hara, Jay Rynek, Dalya Sachs, Charles Segal, Zeph Stewart, Ron Stroud, Richard Tarrant, Kate Toll, and Cal Watkins. I am also indebted to Harvard University Press's readers for their suggestions for revision, and especially to John Henderson, whose painstaking criticism and thoughtful questions made this a better book. As for the faults that remain, many in disregard of friendly advice: it must be said that they are all my own.

Institutional appreciation is due as well: I finished this book as a Berkeley Humanities Fellow in 1995–96, and owe thanks to the Departments of Classics and Rhetoric at the University of California, Berkeley, for letting me continue to prowl the hallways during my sabbatical, and without any snares of administrative birdlime. I also want to express my gratitude to Peg Fulton, my editor at Harvard University Press, who supported this project when it was barely an idea; and to Ann Hawthorne, who edited the final version of the manuscript and whose diligent eye saved me from many an error.

A few scholarly annotations: The passages quoted from the *Bellum Civile* are taken from Housman's text except where indicated. Translations of Lucan are mine, as are the quotations of secondary material originally in French, German, or Italian; in the notes I have let the original languages stand. The Latin texts are not reproduced except where crucial to the discussion. Periodical abbreviations are used in the bibliography where they are readily recognizable, and standard abbreviations for Latin works throughout. I have consistently used the title *Civil War* or *Bellum Civile* to refer to Lucan's epic, but do not change the alternate title *Pharsalia* when citing secondary sources who have used it; readers interested in the plagued question of Lucan's original title may consult *(inter alia)* F. Ahl's *Lucan: An Introduction*, pp. 326–332. There are other issues too that this book does not touch: it is not meant to be a comprehensive treatment of Lucan or an introduction of any kind. I hope, simply, that it will make some readers think.

At the end of everything, a big thank-you to my husband, Robert K. Innes, who was always full of encouragement and praise, listened to interminable paragraphs about detachment and dismemberment, and never objected to the dedication of this sometimes rather grisly piece of prose. Writing may be a solitary activity, but his presence has always made a difference

Berkeley
July 1997

Ideology in Cold Blood

Introduction

THIS BOOK is meant to unfold as a movement in time. It starts from the figure of the Roman poet and senator Marcus Annaeus Lucan as he has appeared in recent scholarship, but builds on this interpretation to argue for a more nuanced writer than this Lucan we know—to argue for an author, that is, whose opus enacts for us the startling conditions for the existence of political idealism in the first century A.D. at Rome. As a period in which the problems of political involvement and political efficacy loomed larger and presented greater dangers than ever before, at least for the upper classes who had traditionally participated in the business of government, the transition of the Roman Republic into a principate and eventually an empire changed the terms for senatorial conduct both in and out of office; it precipitated philosophical discussions about the morality of affiliation with a tyrannical government as well as literary probings into the ramifications of criticizing such a regime. Against this background, Lucan, originally friend, then foe, of his near age-mate Nero, writes an epic on the civil war between Gnaeus Pompey and Nero's ancestor Julius Caesar, describes Caesar's whirlwind triumphs and Pompey's final defeat and death—and then himself is put to death for taking part in a plot to assassinate his emperor.

Lucan's tendentious poetic history of this civil war, a struggle that eventually brought down the curtains on the Roman Republic despite Brutus' and others' brief attempt at its restoration, has often evoked contradictory reactions among its readers. Indeed, it presents notorious cruxes for interpretation. The epic claims to represent a historical event, and yet its account often veers into the purely fictional. In some ways its vision of warfare and loss is tragic, but more often it seems merely grotesque. None of its protagonists are particularly likable or even admirable, from the ineffectual Pompey to the despotic Caesar and the self-righteous Cato. And strangest of all, the poem's narrator himself, who portrays Rome as a state completely immolated on the altar of war and proclaims the hopelessness of any future, seems a man both cynically detached from history and deeply embedded in its possibilities: his ill-fated protagonist Pompey, supposed defender of the Republic, thus emerges in a dual light as Caesar's equally selfish rival and yet a man for whom the narrator himself enacts a fervent advocacy.

These paradoxes are easier to think about if we sensitize ourselves to the double movement of the poem's story. In terms of history and plot, of course, the epic begins with Caesar's crossing of the Rubicon and stops short inconclusively in Egypt, where Caesar and Cleopatra are at war with Ptolemy XIII. In between are all the events of 49–48 B.C.: Caesar's march down the Italian peninsula, Pompey's panicked crossing to Greece, confrontations between the two sides at Massilia and Ilerda, both ending with victory for the Caesarian forces, and Pompey's climactic loss at Pharsalus on 9 August 48. After this, Pompey's flight and death at the hands of the faithless Egyptian Pothinus, his ally Cato's Stoic march across the Libyan desert with his troops, and Caesar's arrival in Egypt. Where the epic was to end, nobody knows: possibly with Cato's suicide at Utica in 46, possibly with Augustus' victory at Actium in 31, and probably *not* with Caesar's assassination in 44—too hopeful a terminus for a poem so insistent, in its *narrative* progression, on the bleakness of what had become of Roman history.

But even as these events follow their predestined path, another story is unfolding in the *Civil War,* the "story" of the narrator. Originally a figure who steps into the text to decry with equal cynicism the tyrannical ambitions of both Caesar and Pompey, by the end his voice evolves into that of a Pompeian sympathizer: our poet seems to have moved from extreme political cynicism to the adoption of a distinct political choice. The reason for this change, which is crucial to our understanding of this Protean piece of writing, is the subject of this book; indeed, the account I provide in the following chapters mirrors Lucan's own move from detachment to engagement to a juxtaposition of the two. I start with a very grisly species of detachment: the fate of the soldierly bodies of Lucan's epic, whose torn and bleeding forms he seems intent on exposing to our view as a metaphor for the collapse of the self in civil war, and whose destruction he repeats in his' collapsing of conventional forms of expression throughout the poem. But I end with a consideration of the redemptive power of storytelling and interpretation for those confronting such a specter of nothingness.

My reading of Lucan's *Civil* War, like *his* reading of Caesar and Pompey's civil war, is a self-avowedly engaged one. It advocates a model of reading that I argue Lucan himself endorsed and that I enact by my necessarily tendentious interpretation of the poem. The Lucan I present here is an author who presents us with two incompatible possibilities for our relation to political belief and political hope and who forges a position for himself out of the clash of the two. Like the extant views of the poet himself, which I discuss in more detail below, one of these positions is cynical and nihilistic, the other fiercely committed to the possibility of making the good choice in life and acting upon it. It is their unlikely combination in one work that opens up a different space for thought. Obviously, I make no claims to a corner on the whole truth—and I argue that Lucan too would reject such claims as inimical to the spirit of his project. If it is true that some readers may find this book's version of the poet and his work to be too well-tailored to the postdeconstructive atmosphere of the academy today, I acknowledge this risk and, indeed, publish it: like Lucan's own epic, what the reader is about to peruse may be a construct of our own times.

Lucan's *Civil War* is a hard poem to read. Its forays into deviant syntax and dismembered bodies, the stridency of its narrator, and the apparent laxness of his historical objectivity are part of the problem; Lucan seems to have taken no steps to render his subject matter or his style palatable to his (modern, at least) interpreters. To be sure, some readers have managed to overlook these difficulties by applying to them a blanket diagnosis of "rhetoric" and thus eliminating them from consideration as part of the meaning of the poem. For such readers, Lucan's rhetorical excesses are as cankers on the body of the text, and a little minor surgery lets us through to the poet's actual message—unfortunately, as it turns out, a rather predictable admonition that civil war is bad and Julius Caesar, its architect, even worse. This idea of rhetoric in the derogatory sense has often obscured our view of the real poet in explaining away the features that apparently mar his creative activity and sense of proportion, and in locating the origin of the disease in the tastes of his times. A versifier and rhetorician of the notoriously "silver" first century A.D., a quondam friend of Nero and dead before age twenty-six to boot—what else would we expect but the fascination with bodily vicissitudes, the interest in linguistic play, the high emotional pitch of the public speaker, and the pliant treatment of facts?

But it is not these traits—although they may have contributed little to the poem's place in the canon—that block, in the end, the readerly project of making sense out of the poem. We may admit that there are stridency, lying, and gore, but ask why instead of condemning them; and a number of recent critics have been willing to do just this, leading to insightful work on Lucan's relationship to ancient literary criticism, historiography, natural history, and other topics. Even so, however, the poem seems unwilling to yield itself up to any single persuasive account of its literary mission. Especially when we stand back and view the work in its entirety, it is hard to know what to make of this epic; a little distance lets us see the central fault line in Lucan's representation of the disintegration of the Roman Republic and makes coherent explanation of it difficult. I am referring, once again, to the systematic clash in the *Civil* War between detachment and engagement as a stance toward disaster.

This fault line is replicated in the two major camps of scholarship on Lucan, each critically persuasive on grounds justified by the epic's own material—its tormented linguistic style, the presence of the poet's Republican voice. There is the school that brings biography to the aid of interpretation, calling to witness the *Vitae* of Vacca and Suetonius and what little else we know of Lucan's life and death to read the poem in political as well as literary terms. In this perspective, the poet's so-called quarrel with Nero and his eventual participation in the Pisonian conspiracy provide an interpretive background that highlights his anti-Julio-Claudian stance in the poem, his nostalgia for the Republic, and his favorable portrayal of Pompey, historical leader of the Senate's cause. This approach to the poem is readily invited by the narrator's own strong participation in his work, exhorting us with apostrophe and outrage to look upon the death of freedom; and the epic thus emerges as a highly political piece of writing, perhaps slightly naive in its partisanship of the flawed figurehead Gnaeus Pompeius and certainly a bit too overwrought to win many modern converts to its point of view, but in any case a heartfelt testimony to the poet's political beliefs. Or even his philosophical beliefs; for I would include within the "sincere author" group those who argue that Lucan's main concern was less political than personal, that his epic is an exhortation to Stoic endurance and self-control in the face of all political opposition.

Another school of thought concentrates on an altogether different aspect of the epic: its medium. For these critics, it is the war within the text that emerges as the poem's defining trope, the twisted plays of paradox, exaggeration, inversion, and sheer falsehood that deny the epic its place in generic tradition and seem to proclaim the invalidity of all claims to cohesion. For this group, the very language of the epic (aided by the poet's own dark vision and his sporadic cries of despair) provides a self-conscious testimonial to Lucan's belief in—*nothing*. The poem is about the collapse of the Roman Republic and, with it, the only world in which meaning, ideology, belief, and hope had a chance; without this world, no coherent belief system is possible. Epic values are set up to be knocked down, narrative gives way to fragmentation, and both Pompey and Caesar invert the ideal of the *dux,* as the civil war makes a mockery of any political ideology. The poem is a poem of cynical despair and the work of a nihilist: and as W. R. Johnson (1987: x) has eloquently put it, "The *Pharsalia* . . . has no privileged center except for the energetic, bitter, and witty skepticism that devotes itself to demolishing the structures it erects as fast as it erects them; Lucan's heroes lend their zestful assistance to this demolition, and that is their chief function."

There are names and methods to go with the two stances. The legion of scholars who have addressed interpretive questions such as the sincerity of the prologue in praise of Nero, the separate publication of books 1 to 3 prior to the poet's reported quarrel with the emperor, the identity of the poem's "hero" (Cato? Pompey, in defeat?), and the general tides of Lucan's political fortunes fall into the former of the two camps I have roughly outlined above. More prone to engage in New Critical interpretation of the poem's remaining passages and to treat its "problems" (such as those mentioned above) as flaws rather than as sources of meaning, their approach characterizes most of the criticism published before 1980. F. M. Ahl's important monograph *Lucan: An Introduction* (1976), as well as the valuable work of Berthe Marti, M. P. O. Morford, E. Narducci, and many others, provide examples; nary a deconstructionist to be found in *this* group.

On the other hand, writers such as Ralph Johnson in *Momentary Monsters* (1987); Jamie Masters, author of the recent *Poetry and Civil War in Lucan's Bellum Civile* (1992); and John Henderson, whose challenging 1987 article "Lucan/The Word at War" is only now winning the recognition it deserves, fit more comfortably into the latter of these two camp. Masters' and Henderson's deconstructionist analysis of Lucan's poetic style *as* civil war (together with Masters' thesis of the narrator's "fractured voice," which enacts the collapse of authoritative perspectives per se in such a mess as civil war) lucidly illustrate the impossibility of reading this poem as a simple exercise in ideology, and indeed, expose the hash it makes of the very idea of ideology. An epic that emphasizes the destruction of the material of bodies and the fabric of language is not the site for idealistic beliefs. Masters' 1994 article goes even further in this vein, suggesting that the whole poem is in fact a *reductio ad absurdum* of any ideological stance, an elaborate joke to show the pliability of history in any indoctrinated mind.

The question here is what we are to make of these two tendencies. Is the *Civil War* an example of ideological poetry at its most flagrant or a work that despairingly proclaims the meaninglessness of life and ideology and works to deconstruct the viability of any linguistic and political system? Or is there a third possibility? To be sure, these two are not normally reconcilable perspectives; yet fully understanding this poem surely necessitates making sense of this problem that has made the epic so difficult to reconcile with itself. While I have no interest in denying the validity of either interpretive school's insights into Lucan's poem, I would suggest that the *Civil* War, in some way, encourages both interpretations simultaneously, and it is in their juxtaposition that we should look for a more comprehensive reading of the poem. In other words, Lucan's project as poet is precisely to provoke (as he clearly does) and then reconcile these two possibilities for understanding. So far we critics have done half the critical work: we have laid bare the poem's two faces. But as the scholarship now stands, each interpretation eclipses its rival and, with it, the kernel of the poem. This book is an attempt to change the status of affairs.

Pompey is the pivot in this process. It is around his character that the two sides of the *Civil War* formally join battle: or rather, around his characters, for there seem to be two Pompeys in the epic. One is Caesar's rival for Roman supremacy, a man as greedy for *regnum* as his energetic father-in-law; even in death he is excoriated by Cato as a grubber after power, a would-be *rex,* a *tyrannus* rather than a martyr. The other is Pompey the hero, the man some critics have seen as a Stoic *proficiens,* certainly not perfect but a figurehead for his times and the last defender of the Roman Senate. One Pompey for the cynic, one for the idealist. The key lies in the lens through which these Doppelgängers emerge. One Pompey is more or less the narrator's creation; his presence relies on the frequent intervention of the narratorial voice to praise his achievements and his character and to paint them in as tragic a light as possible. For the narrator, Pompey is in the end a hero and Rome's darling; his death is the last gasp of the moribund Republic.

The other Pompey emerges more naturally from the text of the poem itself. What we read of his actions, what the other characters have to say of him, and the knowledge evoked by the poem's glances at history provide a background against which we find ourselves tempted to question the narrator's uncritical partisanship. What we end up with is a question about the poet rather than the narrator: why use a narratorial voice that so unsubtly and unjustifiably favors Pompey that it alienates, rather than persuades, his readers? For this he does: in perhaps the most famous passage in the epic, the narrator *tells us* how we, his future readers, will respond to his text: we will favor Pompey. Perhaps, he says at 7.207–213, I too, by writing this epic, will be able to offer assistance to great names, *magnis nominibus* (the echo of *Magne* at 212 is not fortuitous), and as future generations read my work, they will still favor you, Pompey. He thus dictates our response at the same time that he problematizes our ability to provide it: for it was *Lucan's* choice, of course, not to make Pompey more admirable.

The very fact that the narrator chooses to enact belief in a hero in a context in which the poet has undermined all grounds for believing in the possibility of heroism and in which meaning is gone from politics as from life, is the striking development that makes the *Bellum Civile* more than it seems to be—more than an ill-executed excuse for an undeserving figurehead, more than a final groan into the darkness of the Roman Empire. Instead, the paradox at the epic's core puts it on a par with other explorations of the central paradox of man's basic need to believe: it brings us face to face once again with the idea that we are both condemned and blessed by our own enduring search for transcendent values in a world that cannot provide them.

Most important in all this is to remember that Lucan's *Civil War* self-consciously tells a *story,* and that, as Lisa Jane Disch (1994: 4) well remarks, "to tell a story is to break the usual 'rules of caution' and refrain from the rhetorical moves that would give one's position the appearance of unquestionability." Lucan refuses to hide behind a veil of objectivity; he reminds us constantly of his involvement in the act of narration and his construction of that narrative out of the fragments of a history no longer fully accessible to anyone. Like the mysterious guide among Troy's ruins who, in book 9, makes meaning out of rubble for the tourist Caesar, Lucan self-consciously steps into his text to remind us who is creating it, a strategy that points both to the subjective position behind the text and the flaws in that voice. I would suggest, borrowing from Hannah Arendt, that we should try to see such storytelling "neither as a vehicle for the authentic critical voice of the oppressed nor as a means by which endlessly to postpone the authoritative moment that is necessary to criticism and to action" (Disch 1994: 2). To pick either of these options is to side with one of the two Lucans of scholarship: the poet as rebel and the poet as nihilist. And so in the end I will return to Lucan the storyteller: not the impassioned marginal voice trying to undercut official "truths," nor the self-undermining repudiator of any point of view, but a figure who has come to terms, squarely and paradoxically, with what political engagement must be in the 60s A.D.

ONE

The Subject under Siege

I do not know if it has ever been noted before that one of the main characteristics of life is discreteness. Unless a film of flesh envelops us, we die. Man exists only insofar as he is separated from his surroundings.

—*Vladimir Nabokov*

Aᴛ ᴛʜᴇ sɪᴛᴇ of the human body, a group of our most common abstractions finds a material convergence point: the concepts of nation, identity, church, even the growth of civilization, are all resurrected in the flesh and blood of the discrete and self-contained human subject, writ small on the complex but coherent text of the living individual. The analogic role of the body seems to span cultures and times, surfacing repeatedly as a metaphor that suggests the organic unity of anything perceived as bounded, whether it be the political state or the human psyche; similarly, the body's vulnerabilities can reflect the susceptibility to wounding or dismemberment of the other "bodies" at stake. The examples are familiar to us from a range of disciplines and institutions: in politics and theology, the secular monarch was often figured as head of the body politic, the Church as the mystical body of Christ. Literary critics have observed that the classical notion of the decline of civilizations arises from "that still persistent analogy . . . between the body's destiny and that of societies and institutions" (Gilman 1975: 42), while some anthropologists, in contrast, compare primitive cultures (wrongly or rightly) to infantile stages in human development, and in psychology, as Armando Favazza (1987: 233) comments, the integrity of the individual body seems to go hand in hand with the "psychological, social, cultural and physical integrity of the 'communal' body."[1] Even the literary text—in prescriptions from Aristotle's *Poetics* to the New Criticism in general—falls prey to the influence of this analogy, so that the failed story, the inferior plot, is the one that is not organic, intact of limb, and well proportioned.[2]

On the other side of the coin, the violation of the body's boundaries—the penetration of human flesh from the outside or the ejection of what is already inside the body—is put to equally busy symbolic work. A powerful modern example is provided by the published opposition poetry of Vietnam GIs, which focuses on the violent fragmentation of the soldier's body as a way to articulate resistance to the political imperatives and hierarchical structures of wartime authority—because it demonstrates so graphically the bloody outcome of ideological clashes played out on the battlefield, but more importantly because the soldier's body is made to stand in for the military "corps" itself. Such poetry aims at exploding the military's control over the official (and optimistic) narrative of events as it describes in stomach-churning detail the destruction of human flesh, so that "the graphic portrayal of mutilation, of bodies penetrated, lacerated, blown apart, torn open" has the effect of blasting apart military rhetoric and hegemony, sources of the suppression of true fatality figures and of the elision of human suffering.[3] Metaphorical uses of the body can also refer to healing processes, of course: Favazza (1987) documents the symbolic purpose of self-mutilation across a number of aboriginal cultures, such as the Abidjis of the Ivory Coast, who mutilate themselves for a new year's festival by plunging knives into their abdomens: here the violence is directed against the self, not inflicted from without, and the healing of the wound is thought to demonstrate the community's capacity for social healing.[4] On a different note, M. M. Bakhtin's famous study of Rabelais (1968) puts this economy of the body to work in the service of the carnivalesque, so that the gargantuan effluxes of bodily wastes and the focus on the lower body over the mind and head are shown to point to a reversal of theological casuistry and otherworldly ideology. In short, just as the physical body can stand as a metaphor for the stability and coherence of other less palpable bodies, so too we can say of its violation that these transgressions of bodily boundaries reflect alterations "of the psychic economy, of spatial division, and of the hierarchies of the social formation" (Stallybrass 1990: 16).[5] And as this short list of examples should illustrate, the relationship between the body, the "psychic economy," the state, and society is both symbiotic and multifaceted: changes wrought on the body can stand as performative attempts to alter social hierarchies, reactive responses to changes already at work in the political or psychic world, or in turn part of a still larger metaphor in which body and society together reflect the alteration of old ways of looking at the meaning of human existence.[6]

I have started with this gesture toward the metaphorical uses of the human body precisely because its vicissitudes exert a compelling fascination on the first-century A.D. poet Lucan, whose epic, the *Civil War,* is violent to a degree shared but not rivaled by other Roman writers of his time. Reflecting on the disintegration of the Roman Republic in the wake of a series of internecine conflicts—and writing of it over a century later, under a regime marked by the ongoing oppression of the upper classes—Lucan expresses the folly of civil war in a language that focuses sharply on the violation of soldierly bodies through the death-dealing wounds inflicted by their fellow Romans. In some ways his epic seems the prolonged expression of a crisis around the body, or rather the boundary that separates men from what is pointedly not-man, from the inanimate and the environment—a boundary which the weapons of civil war physically violate by spilling human blood and guts on the field of war and which the intrusive imperial government that the war spawned would violate too, if in another way. It will be my purpose in this chapter to explore these and related issues that jump out at us from the *Civil War:* the critical state of the human body and the other bounded entities with which it shares a symbolic relationship, the effect of this boundary crisis on the agency and autonomy of the Roman subject, and the concomitant blurring (and its significance) of the distinction between the animate and the inanimate, the self and the not-self. Lucan as author enacts these crises in the subject matter of his epic and in its very syntax, so that his writing constantly brings home to us the violation of the normative that civil war forces upon its participants: catachrestic twists on subject-object relations in the poem's syntax only intensify the confusion visited upon the concept of the contained and instrumental self in the poem's content. But the human players of Lucan's verse, spitted on spears and distorted in syntax, are not the only actors and speakers in his poem: there is also the narrator himself, and his fate is a very different one. In this chapter I will be looking only at the fortunes of the victims of civil war, the objects of its violence: the men whose lacerated bodies the narrator describes with such apparent fascination. Later, as we turn to the voice behind these victims, the impassioned character played by the narrator himself as he tells the tale of Rome's self-destruction, we will have cause to see a different development in the status of the human self. The argument of Chapter 1, in other words, is part of a dialectic and not the whole story. In the end, our movement will be from the violation of human bodies, a topic that has spurred the interest of much recent Lucan scholarship, to a prescription for the human psyche.

Recent scholarship, especially the excellent work of John Henderson (1987) and Jamie Masters (1992), has correctly noted the obsession with boundaries that pervades Lucan's work.[7] His view of civil war relies on the notion that such conflict is best characterized as the violation of the most important boundaries that constituted human society at Rome before the fall of the Republic: the boundaries that separated Italy from its provinces and regions further afield; that distinguished family members from strangers and friends from enemies, citizens from aliens and patriots from traitors; that gave meaning to ethical terms such as virtue and evil, heroism and cowardice; that made possible the old social rankings of the Republic, in which senators and slaves stood on either side of an all but impassable gulf; even those that marked the dermal limit where the human body stopped and its immediate environment began—boundaries once inviolable by the whims of power, at least for citizens, at least in theory. For Lucan, Pompey's loss against Caesar at Pharsalus in 48 B.C. would cause the demolition of yet another boundary, that which separated the Republic from dictatorship, principate, and empire; and as he looks back from his own time in the 60s A.D. he has clearly in mind (whether for the purposes of history or propaganda) the inversions that loss engendered: ex-slaves in office, foreigners as Romans, the senatorial body, both physically and institutionally, compelled to self-slaughter by imperial paranoia and greed. And more, of course: the laws, the constitutive boundaries of human society, dissolved at need by a greater power; the magistrates stripped of their true powers of agency; and the Roman (upper-class) subject as he used to be slowly disappearing, together with his civic and legislative responsibilities. As Tacitus would bitterly summarize Caesar's encroachments on these rights in *Annales* 1.2, "little by little he pushed ahead, taking over the functions of the senate, the magistracies, the laws."[8]

The act that sets the poem in motion, the reason for its existence, is the greatest violation of them all: Caesar breaches the frontier of Italy with his army and thus, in January of 49 B.C., begins the civil war by an act that transgresses both law and nation.[9] So much for the defining power of the river Rubicon to distinguish between Italy and not-Italy: it is a landmark that Lucan ironically identifies as the "fixed boundary" between Cisalpine Gaul and Italy just as it fails in its function of "marking off" or "separating" ("Gallica certus / limes ab Ausoniis disterminat arva colonis," 1.214–216).[10] In fact Lucan's focus on boundaries at this crucial moment provides the climax to a theme already introduced in his exploration of Caesar's act. First is the death in 53 B.C. of M. Licinius Crassus, pictured as a buffer between Caesar and his son-in-law Pompey in the first triumvirate:

"for Crassus, standing in the middle [*medius*], was the only obstacle to future war" (1.99–100). Lucan compares him to the Isthmus of Corinth, a narrow strip of land that prevents the violent clash of the Ionian and Aegean seas; when Crassus dies at Carrhae—"Crassus, who kept apart the brutal weapons of the two leaders"—this death lets loose all the force of the Roman world against itself (1.103–106). Just before these lines we have traveled still further back in time, for Lucan indicts the folly of these three men in ever combining their strengths as one and sharing the world between them, as they did from 70 B.C. onward: such an alloy leads only to war (1.87–89). And now Lucan invokes the original Roman sin, the Cain and Abel of Rome's founding days: the walls of the city's first site ran with a brother's blood after Romulus killed Remus for jumping over them— for undoing, in other words, the first attempt to mark off the boundaries of Rome (1.95).[11] When a happier moment in Roman history is glanced at, it is precisely in terms of a boundary *that held:* the Sabine women, who once stood between the advancing battle lines of their husbands and their fathers and prevented a similar war of sons-in-law and fathers-in-law (1.118). Again, such an intervention is what the death of Julia, Pompey's wife and Caesar's daughter, rendered impossible: in Lucan's aetiology, another boundary lost, another step toward civil war (1.111–117).

Once the struggle between Caesar and Pompey has passed over into full-fledged war, the imagery of boundary violation becomes grimmer and more startling as human bodies are used as the medium for its expression. It may be no news to Lucan's readers that such a war pits brothers and citizens against each other and thus rips apart the social fabric by rending the mores that make it possible; but if we are not surprised to see the poet evoking such unholy mixings as an army in the forum (1.320) or the *potentes* mingling with the plebs (1.101, 271), we are surely startled when an elderly Roman, anticipating the horrors of the coming civil war, evokes the horrors of the recent struggle between Sulla and Marius in terms too anatomically correct for comfort. Among the many victims whose fate he recalls, one Baebius is ripped apart at the joints and the pieces scattered through the debris of his own guts (2.119–121); the entire family of the Crassi are cut down to *trunci* (2.124); the pontifex Scaevola is sacrificed like an animal (2.126–129); brothers struggle for the privilege of beheading a parent (2.150–151); and a huge heap of lacerated body parts is the main product of war (2.160–165). Even the speaker's own brother is no longer recognizable; what used to be his face is now a shapeless mess (2.169–170). The ill-fated M. Marius Gratidianus, adopted member of the family of Sulla's foe, provides the climax to this roll call of the truncated (2.181–190):

> His arms, ripped off, fall to earth; the tongue is lopped, squirms on the ground, and beats thin air in silent motion. One man amputates his ears, another the nostrils of his hooked nose; a third scoops the orbs from their hollow sockets so that the eyes, dug out last, can see the severed limbs. It is hard to believe in so savage a crime, or that one life could endure so many tortures. Thus are limbs mangled under the massive weight of a collapsed and ruined building; headless bodies washed onshore are equally formless, and the bodies of men who have perished far out to sea.

In short, Sulla's surgery on the state was marked, paradoxically, by an excess of damage to the patient: "He drained what little was left of the city's blood; and while he was cutting off too zealously its overputrid limbs, the surgery exceeded all proper limit, and his operating hand followed too far where the disease led it" (2.140–143). The state in civil war becomes a mutilated body parallel to those of its citizens[12]—which gives Lucan fodder for a gruesome pun after Pompey's defeat and murder, when Gnaeus Pompey inquires unknowingly after his decapitated father, "Is he still the head of the world, the *caput mundi?* (9.123–124)."[13]

And this is only the beginning. Books 3, 6, 7, and 9 continue the orgy of headless trunks and trunkless heads, airborne limbs and squashed vitalia, now as the by-products of the civil war that Lucan himself is documenting and not its precedent in the 80s B.C.[14] The sea battle at Massilia in book 3 depicts another prolonged metamorphosis of bodies into fragments. One daring Massilian catches hold of a Roman boat from his own deck, only to get his right hand, then his left hand, then his entire left arm lopped off; undaunted, he uses the mutilated trunk that remains as his last weapon (3.603–626).[15] Unhappy Lycidas, next in line, is torn in two, and oddly enough his upper half lives on beyond his lower half, at least until death finally gets the better of the still-working lungs and heart and takes the whole body as its trophy (3.635–646); meanwhile a third sailor's bones are ground to powder between the prows of two ships (3.652–661). As other bodies come apart, the book closes with the fathers and wives of the combatants mourning over the headless bodies and featureless faces of those they suppose (not always correctly) to be their lost sons and husbands (3.756–761).[16] And so it goes.[17] There is no need to document further, perhaps literally ad nauseam, the mutilations that pervade the epic: it should be clear that the wholeness of the body is rudely and graphically violated as a principal casualty of civil war.[18]

The scope of this violation of boundaries extends outward to the universe as it extends inward to the body; microcosm and macrocosm reflect the dissolution of all normative limits.[19] As departing Roman legions leave the known world exposed to foreign tribes (1.465), the gulf between life and death, earth and sky, land and sea, even chance and fate, dissolves and brings on the strangest of chaos. Civil war makes the living hide in the tombs of the dead and corpses mingle with the quick (2.152–153); dead bodies stand upright in battle because there is no room to fall, and crush the living with their weight (2.203–206, 4.787). On several occasions the earth, the heavens, the oceans foam together in an unholy mixture, while daylight becomes darkness and the moon is dim by night. A storm in Spain confuses the very markers that keep separate the elements of the world ("rerum discrimina miscet / deformis caeli facies," 4.104–105),[20] and nature in general overturns the laws and limits of the world (2.2–3). And even the course of history may or may not be bound by fixed limits (2.10–11);[21] civil war makes it impossible to tell. Indeed, the sudden ending of the epic, deliberate or not, plays nicely into this chaos. As Masters (1992) discusses in the concluding chapter of his book, even the limit to the written *Civil War* is lacking: the epic has no end on paper, just as there is no *finis*—no boundary/end—to civil war.

Somatic, natural, political, and legal: the demarcations that make things what they are clearly under siege in the *Civil War*.[22] What are we to make of this? Certainly David Quint has forged one striking link between boundary violations and the narrator's world view; taking into account the episodic nature of Lucan's writing, he sees both bodily and narrative fragmentation as the sign of a breakdown in historical coherence:

> The vicissitudes of the body in the *Pharsalia* . . . reflect the shapelessness of recent Roman history as the poem conceives it, and as it imagines and portrays that history through a narrative of episodic disunity. The epic narrative, which classical literary theory describes with the metaphor of the whole, well-knit body, is deliberately fragmented by Lucan to depict a world out of joint . . . To portray history from the perspective of the lost republican cause and to counter the unifying historical fictions and narratives of imperial ideology, both bodies and poems must fall into pieces. (1993: 147)[23]

Glenn Most's excellent 1992 essay makes a related point, linking human bodies to the written corpus and to literary stylistics but also stepping beyond this to speculate that the widespread mutilation of humans in the gladiatorial shows brought them uncomfortably close to animals, which are routinely dismembered before or after cooking.[24] And he adds a further point, this one linked to the notion of personal identity. Citing the Stoic view of soul as spread throughout the body, or rather emanating from the heart and endowing the rest of the body with motion and sensation, he suggests that the natural result of such a view would be to ponder at what point the mutilation of a body led to "the loss of personal identity of that body's owner" (1992: 406).

Most in the end moves away from such speculations, reminding us that Lucan is a poet and not a philosopher, but I think there is more to be said where he left off. I would like to build on these insightful connections between body, text, and history, but in a different direction: not from the body outward to text and history, but rather inward to identity and personhood; and focusing not on Stoic notions of the dimensions of the soul but more generally on concepts and anxieties about the nature of the self that cut across cultures. I take my starting point from Julia Kristeva's useful notion (1982) of the *abject*—a bodily part or product that both is and is not identifiable with the self, a thing that is ambiguously positioned between self and other because it has been severed or separated from its origin. The abject thus includes all bodily emissions, all substances that pass from being part of us to being (usually) waste or filth, "other," and often taboo; Kristeva focuses in particular on human waste, semen, menstrual blood, mucus, nail parings, and the like, but the concept covers everything that belongs in the body and can under certain circumstances make its way outside—internal organs, blood in general, brain matter. But even in the case of nail parings and mucus, the abject is instinctively repugnant. From the point of view of the individual, it is neither subject (me) nor object (part of the outside world), but something in between; it disrupts our most basic conceptual categories, and our response is distaste. The disturbing quality of the abject arises precisely from this uncertain status, for it necessarily confuses our sense of the limits that define us against that which is not-us; it throws into disarray the boundary markers we use to establish our relationship to the world and especially those with which we satisfy our need to mark ourselves off from what is not human.[25] "The abject is undecidedly inside and outside the body . . . dead and alive (like the corpse), autonomous and engulfing. It is what disturbs identity, system and order, disrupting the social boundaries demanded by the symbolic" (Grosz 1990: 90).

Curiously enough, it is the *symbolic* realm that suffers most from the abject's grotesquely material effusions. Its impact on the binary concepts we think with extends beyond self and other: mind/matter, body/waste, inside/outside, cleanliness/corruption are all victims of the abject's transgressive nature and its confusion of the divisions with which we keep our world under control. As Elizabeth Grosz (1990: 89) puts it,

> Abjection is the underside of the symbolic. It is what the symbolic must reject, cover over and contain. The symbolic requires that a border separate or protect the subject from this abyss which beckons and haunts it: the abject entices and attracts the subject ever closer to its edge. It is an insistence on the subject's necessary relation to death, to animality, and to materiality, being the subject's recognition and refusal of its corporeality. The abject demonstrates the impossibility of clear-cut borders, lines of demarcation, divisions between the clean and the unclean, the proper and the improper, order and disorder.

Most important of all is its effect on the subject: for if what is *in* the body forms the subject and what is outside the object, then that which is abject upsets the integrity of the human subject by muddling subject-object relations, so that that integrity itself is put into question with the grisly, messy exposure of what "self" is made up of. If we identify ourselves with the coherent and nonpermeable boundaries of our body, what becomes of this understanding when these boundaries fail? Or, to put it oversimply but compellingly, is the self merely guts in a skin bag? Michael Bibby, who adapts the work of Kristeva and Grosz to the grisly verse of the Vietnam GI poets mentioned above, suggests that our recurrent fear is that the answer to this question may be yes. Bibby takes it as a given that the stability of the ego, our ability to form a distinct and coherent notion of who we are as individuals, is inextricably tied up with our corporeal coherence, the closed unit that we identify as our body and which allows us to formulate boundaries between self and not-self, animate and inanimate, person and environment. But these categories collapse when the body is opened up and its contents spill out, when the wounded soldier looks down at the spillage of his own intestines and, in horror, tries to push "himself" back inside: "the involuntary emergence of bodily contents radically threatens the subject with the im-

possibility of self . . . The laceration of a body by shrapnel, for example, exposing tendons, muscles, veins, blood exposes the disorder
the undamaged body seems to contain; it dramatizes the horror of
the body's otherness. The mangled corpse, especially, epitomizes the
intolerability of the abject" (1993: 33).

We could sum up the gist of this discussion with a single quotation
from Lucan: when a soldier in the Libyan desert has his skin melt
away from the alarming effects of a single snakebite, the poet lists all
the organs now showing—viscera, lungs, muscles, and sinews—and
comments with pointed paradox, "Whatever a human is, the ghastly
nature of this sickness showed" (9.779).[26] Indeed, the whole purpose
of the reptilian onslaught in book 9, which I discuss later in this
chapter, seems to be nothing other than a graphic illustration of the
physical disintegration of human limits, the metamorphosis of men
into nothing but their own viscera and blood. Here as elsewhere
Lucan graphically foists the abject upon us and forces us to confront
its truths. And in general, Lucan's focus on the blood and guts of
bodies violated in war points us exactly in this direction: his epic likes
to dwell on the abject, the by-product of transgression, such as the
ligaments and bowels that trail upon the ground (4.566–567, 7.620,
9.770 ff.), the severed tongue that cannot speak (2.181–182), the guts
that must be held in with a hand (3.678), the fetus stolen from the
womb (6.557–558), the brain that spills from the fractured skull
(6.176–178), the eye that is trod underfoot (6.218–229), even the putrid
decay of the lifeless body (6.88 ff., 6.543 ff., 7.789 ff.)—the stage of
death that lingers unpleasantly in the boundary between the living
body and the purified skeleton, a stage which cultures in general
"strain to mask and deny" (Bynum 1992: 295).[27] For as we read, we
find that clean deaths are quite a rarity in the *Civil War:* either cre-
mation is refused (Pompey's troops after Pharsalus), or corpses are
only half-consumed by the pyre (Pompey himself), or rotting corpses
are brought back to life (the witch Erictho's specialty); there can be
no clear-cut division between life as presence, death as absence.[28]

Lucan's interest in these manifestations of the abject provides us with a way of building upon the notion of boundary transgression to incorporate challenges to the integrity of the psychological person as well as the physical one; as Bibby (1993) points out, the abject, whose relation to us we need to deny in the interests of maintaining the physical integrity of the body, presents a certain challenge to the Cartesian ego.[29] We like to imagine that we think, therefore we are, but what the physical disruption of the body's boundaries illustrates instead is that even the ego, our self-understanding and self-awareness, is dependent upon matter: the mind may be conceived as a vehicle for transcendent thought and the site of our real identities, but its physical leakage through the skull eliminates consciousness altogether. When the body is violated, that abstract "I" can be boiled down to gray matter and internal organs, and, as Bibby (1993: 34) well remarks of Basil Paquet's war poem "In a Plantation," "the once sentient brain tissue exists only as an abject sign of the body's violation":

> The bullet passed
> Through his left temple,
> His left side
> Could not hold
> Against the metal,
> His last "I am" exploded
> Red and gray on a rubber tree.

It might seem nonetheless farfetched to think of the *Civil War* as concerned with the abject *qua* abject. We can grant that Lucan is grotesquely obsessed with people's insides, but is he really evoking our interest in everything that "threatens the subject with the impossibility of self" by attacking the very categories that make up "self," or with everything that merges the self with the other by failing to demarcate a line between human subject and inanimate object?

Our answer, I think, is yes, but it comes from an unexpected quarter. It is revelatory that a recurrent trope in Lucan's writing is precisely the *confusion of subject-object relations,* a phenomenon he sees as a constituent element (like boundary violation) of civil war. We find inverted subject-object relations in the reversal of various geographic and other natural phenomena, and more startlingly yet between the animate subject-person and the inanimate object-thing. So pervasive is this play that it extends to the level of the poem's syntax, where Lucan's writing is often marked by an inversion between the natural subject of a sentence and its object. The actor and the acted-on, the animated and the inert, the killer and the victim oddly change places in Lucan's topsy-turvy rendition of action and even intentionality. The subject of an act becomes its object; that which is other is equated with that which is its opposite; and the principle of identity is thus rendered problematic in both its aspects: the abstract idea of sameness and the concrete human subject.

At the level of syntax, Lucan shows particular fondness for the figure that U. Hübner in several studies has identified as "hypallage." In his terms, this is a reorientation *(Umorientierung)* of the normative syntax so that "the concept that is the logical object becomes the vehicle or medium for a process raised to the status of grammatical subject" (1972: 577). The verb that would normally go with the object is bestowed instead upon the subject, and an unusual quality is thus imparted to this sentence-subject. Elaine Fantham (1992a: 37) notices Lucan's fondness for this figure but modifies the definition; hypallage renders "the psychological focus of a sentence its syntactical subject." I am not entirely comfortable with this terminology; the name "hypallage," which is derived from ancient rhetorical theory, encompasses in classical rhetoric any interchange of syntactic relations in a sentence and is sometimes used to refer to another trope altogether.[30] I prefer, then, to avoid the term and will more simply address the inversion of subject-object relations.[31]

This figure, not coincidentally, is most conspicuous in the language of wounding; Henderson (1987: 139) sensitively links the figure to the subversion of "Military Narrative, that oldest story of misappropriation"; I would add that its generally violent context suggests its implication in the physical and psychological brutalities of war.[32] We find, in this upside-down world, that chests and bellies attack the spears and javelins of the battlefield, as if the former were the weapons, the latter the pierced flesh. On the suicide raft of Vulteius and his men, for example, the swords' steel is struck by human breasts, and the men's throats press down on the hand that carries the blade ("percussum est pectore ferrum, / et iuguli pressere manum," 4.561–562). Scaeva's frenzied address to his fellow soldiers at Dyrrachium urges a similar path: "Shatter their swords with the thrust of your chest, blunt their steel with your throats!" ("confringite tela / pectoris impulsu iugulisque retundite ferrum," 6.160–161). And Caesar, rebuking his mutinous soldiers, tells them that the weapons they abandon will find hands to hold them; Fortune will give him the men to "go round" the weapons (5.326–327), instead of vice versa.[33] The underlying reversal that the figure enacts continues even when the syntax itself is normal, so that (for example) at the sea battle off Massilia, we find bodies protecting shields instead of vice versa (3.619–620), and during Sulla's proscriptions, the gushing blood of the victims thrown in the Tiber undoes the clogging effect of their bodies (2.209–220).

This use of subject-object reversal receives such syntactical stress in Lucan because it is the perfect expression for the paradox of civil war, in which to distinguish between subject and object of any act of aggression makes little sense: on both sides, the citizen.[34] From here also comes Lucan's image of civil war as a senseless manifestation of self-slaughter: suicide and the act of self-sacrifice are paradigmatic cases of the melding of subject and object, since the murdered and the victim, the priest and the offering, are one and the same.[35] It is no accident, then, that the poem pivots on this image: suicides abound, from Vulteius' raftful of fanatics to the unfortunate Marius Gratidianus, who is said to carry out an unspeakable sacrifice to the ghost of Catulus: the offering being his own life, *he is both subject and object* of this sentence ("Marius . . . pendit . . . non fanda piacula busto," 2.174–176).[36] From the repeated opening image of the nation that chooses to plunge its victorious armed hand into its own intestines (1.2–3, 23, 32), to the idea that Rome's own great weight has caused her to collapse upon herself (1.71–72),[37] to Lucan's lament throughout book 7 that Pharsalus as a battle was an act of national self-immolation, the end of the real Romans, the message is forced home: Rome's victim is herself, or, as Charles Martindale (1993, 480) puts it, the *Civil War* is "a poem which might well be read under the sign of self-slaughter, both individual and collective."

The category violations of civil war are flaunted here: the enemy and object of attack is no different from the patriotic subject wielding arms for his country, and *everyone is guilty*. As Lucan puts it at 2.144: "The guilty perished, but now there were only the guilty to survive." For all the citizens, to kill an enemy is to murder a brother, to show *virtus* is to be implicated in a *crimen*, and even to ask which side is more justified is *nefas*. Hence, perhaps, the shift into syntax for the transmission of this crucial message. Merely to *describe* abjection is to resist it, to trust in the orderly capacity of language to express the dissolution of conventional categories even as one relies upon them for the transmission of a meaning; but to destroy normative syntax is in some measure to enact the abjection that pervades civil war, to show oneself as corrupted by chaos as the world one describes.

To bring home this confusion of subject and object, to continue the abuse of syntax-as-semantics, Lucan goes further and collapses the *agency* and *animation* of living beings. The categories of "alive" and "lifeless" become all but meaningless where action and intentionality are concerned: subjects-become-objects are no longer imbued with agency, while objects-become-subjects suddenly acquire animation. This issue of agency is crucial to our topic, raising as it does the question: what becomes of the idea of the human subject when agency is stripped of it? The problem is a crux for thinkers ancient and modern alike, for whom selfhood is often conceived as being in some measure dependent on agency—a strain of thinking present in early Stoic philosophy and later taken up vigorously by Nietzsche and other modern philosophers. As Thomas Rosenmeyer well remarks of the extant evidence from the early Stoics, "Their concept of body does not turn primarily on dimensions or solidity.

Rather, it is talked about in terms of acting and being acted upon; it is action that authenticates body. In Seneca's own words, *quod facit, corpus est*" (*EM* 106.4; however, on the Stoic emphasis of the passive side of this dual formulation under the Empire, see below).[38] In this kind of thinking the subject becomes the product of the pursuit of an end, or, as Nietzsche claimed, a construct shaped by the simultaneity of the doer and his body:

> Psychological history of the concept *"subject."* The body, the thing, the "whole," which is visualized by the eye, awakens the thought of distinguishing between an action and an agent; the idea that the agent is the cause of the action, after having been repeatedly refined, at length left the "subject" over.[39]

The subject becomes aware of his identity and distinctiveness by initiating a change in that which is other than himself—his environment. The object of his action changes, but the originator remains the same, so that agency mediates between the very notions of subject and object by establishing their difference. The idea is an intuitive one, not the product of experts in cognitive science; it is shared by Aristotle, Hume, Coleridge, Nietzsche, and there certainly seems to be a strain of it in Lucan and in the psychology of late Republican Rome, where, as Barton (1995: 5) has argued, "The absence of energy *(inertia, desidia, ignavia, socordia)* was non-being. In inactivity the spirit froze."[40] In other words, it seems that to tamper with agency is to tamper with one of the constitutive elements of (Roman) selfhood.

Once again, Lucan's favorite (but not exclusive) context for this kind of play is that of the battlefield—perhaps because, as Bibby (1993: 34) suggests, soldiers are normally agents par excellence, representatives of the myth of military power to act: "The soldier's body ... emptied of the content which makes subjectivity possible (i.e., the brain) ... lacks identity, totality, agency, or will and has been rendered utterly alien, other, abject. The representations of mutilated soldiers in these poems subvert the cultural norms of soldiers as active, self-reliant, endowed with certainty of will." And so, in Lucan's reversals, lifeless corpses can kill the living (2.205–206, 3.719–721, 6.170 172). At Pharsalus, one side of the battle is "waged" with throats, a strange attribution of agency to the object of action ("hinc iugulis . . . bella geruntur," 7.533),[41] while men on the receiving end of spears or swords will paradoxically take on the agency of the weapons, and "run through" the weapons or "propel" them through their own bodies ("per ferrum . . . exit," of a lion at 1.212; "pectore tela transmittant," 7.623–624).[42] At Dyrrachium, dead bodies "move" a wall to the level of the earth, a twisted idiom for the way a growing heap of corpses slowly rises to the height of the city's defenses ("cumulo crescente cadavera murum / admovere solo," 6.180–181). Here, not only are the cadavers the active subjects of the verb *admovere*, but they are said to move a wall that is in fact constituted of nothing but themselves: the dead are subject and object of their own impossible action. And even the sea, in the wake of earlier missiles, is "sent through" his body's wounds by a waterlogged corpse yielding to a moment of grammatical resuscitation (3.660–661). The dead take action; the living are equated with the inanimate instruments that pierce them. And these reversals of agency extend beyond death and violence to encompass geography, society, and *moral responsibility:*[43] the crucial debate between Cato and Brutus in book 2 revolves around the question of whether civil war will "make" Cato guilty ("facient te bella nocentem," 2.259), and Pompey voices the same concern about himself to the citizens of Mytilene (8.137). As R. Mayer (1940 ad loc.) appositely comments, "the phrase *facere nocentem* is somewhat paradoxical, in that the *nocens* is usually the agent of the crime, but this phrase rather implies that he is passive."[44]

Where is the boundary line here between the animate and the inanimate?[45] It disappears: the body becomes a lifeless machine, while detached body parts take on a curious life of their own and thus make a mockery of the bond between agency and personhood.[46] Oddly, the gruesome mutilations and truncations documented above seem to have little effect on the those who sustain them; the pain and fear of the victim are completely elided, as if nonexistent, while the victim's body soldiers on impervious to its fragmentary status. For the reader, this has the effect of rendering the body a mere tool for battle; the subjectivity of the victim *qua* victim never enters into play. Consider one Tyrrhenus, who gets a lead slug through the temples during the naval battle at Massilia; his eyes pop out from the impact, and presumably his brain is not in mint condition, but once he realizes death is not quite upon him he decides to put to use his own near-corpse: "Hey you! comrades!" he calls out, "arrange me upright like you do with catapult machines, in the position for hurling missiles." And then to himself in a similarly dehumanizing vein: "This corpse, mostly dead though it is, can carry out the main work of a soldier: you, instead of the living, will be hit" (3.716–721). Human decoy and military machine, he disappears from the narrative, but not before he dispatches one Argus through the groin. When Argus' father in turn finds him still alive, it is not his son he finds but "breathing limbs," once again suggesting the terrible interchangeability of the person *qua* person with his body parts ("spirantesque invenit artus," 3.732).[47] After all, it would be more natural to find *Argus* breathing, however wounded; to find his limbs alive forcibly raises the question of who Argus, or anyone, "is": just a pile of breathing limbs?[48] And similarly with the young Massilian who loses first his right arm, then his left: nothing daunted, "the noble torso shows more anger" ("plus nobilis irae / truncus habet," 3.614–615).[49] Person and corpse are so confused that we start to approach a state in which the former can put to use the latter even when the corpse is his own. The link between self and body is put into turmoil; the two merge into each other; we are not allowed to distinguish between an Argus and an assemblage of living limbs, a Massilian and a torso. What does constitute the person? In the *Civil War,* the concept is under constant assault as the narrator wreaks havoc with all the parameters society has set up for establishing its existence: its physical boundaries, its bodily integrity, its unique possession of agency, the fact that it has life, that its sum is greater than its parts. To force the point tastelessly, if an amputee's leg got off the operating table and ordered a cheeseburger for the road home, its owner might reasonably wonder who was "he." So it is with the throats waging war.[50]

The infamous "snake passage" of book 9 provides a good test case for the suggestions made above, precisely because it involves an apparently gratuitous assault on the integrity of the body. Here Cato and his men, trudging with Stoic endurance across the Libyan desert in the gloomy wake of Pharsalus, stumble onto an ophidian posse. Attacked by snakes that make them dissolve to a puddle, inflate to explosion, guzzle their own blood, or metamorphose into one large clot, the soldiers suffer grotesquely comic fates until the native Psylli come to their rescue with antidotes and spells. This, after the tragic death of Pompey has plunged Roman history into dark times indeed, and only Cato stands uncorrupted at the helm Pompey abandoned. As Ralph Johnson (1987: 51–52) wryly asks, "If Lucan is really serious about his Cato [and indeed, his epic!], does he really expect these ridiculous serpents to enhance his picture of Cato's perfected virtue? If we answer yes to this question, we are admitting, I think, that the snake segment is a huge and embarrassing failure in the poem, and we can see why it is that even Lucan's strongest champions tend to circumvent it in virtual silence." And indeed, the critics generally avoid this passage, mostly because it confounds all criteria for intelligent criticism. Frederick Ahl, whose important monograph on Lucan was something of a catalyst for the poet's critical resuscitation, has his bit to say on "the failure of the snake episode": Lucan, showing lack of "poetic common sense," produces a swarm of snakes that are "real enough to have zoological names, fanciful enough to be preposterous." Lucan's attempt to give Cato an *aristeia* is a flop, a stab at heroic pretensions that founders on this multitude of outlandish reptiles (Ahl 1976: 74).[51]

Ahl and other critics are responding to several factors here, I think: the merging of the disgusting with the comic, for one, which is fed by the ludicrous nature of the wounds the snakes inflict and the complete lack of affect on the part of the victims; the sheer unbelievability of the passage, all the more surprising in a poet who generally disavows the fantastic and mythological; and finally the sense that Cato, as possible candidate for the role of Stoic hero, comes out of the episode rather badly, confounding critical attempts to portray him as a sage on the path to virtue against incredible odds. As Johnson points out, if Lucan's goal here *is* to give Cato a kind of Stoic *aristeia*, he has badly miscalculated: if anything, we are likely to throw up our hands and complain that this time it is really all too much. Even if we are inured by now to the redoubled attention to violations of the human form, why the preposterous snakes? Consider Nasidius, bitten by a prester, who literally disappears within the frame or limit of his own body as it swells to gargantuan proportions (9.790–798, 801):

> A burning prester bit Nasidius, a farmer of Marsian soil. A fiery redness ignited his face; a swelling stretched his skin, merging his parts as his outline disappeared; he is larger than his body, distended beyond human limit [*humanum ... modum*]; contagion spreads everywhere as the poison goes to work. The man himself hides, deeply ensconced in the swollen body; his breastplate cannot hold the bulging of the distended chest ... And now the shapeless mass and unsteady trunk can hold no longer the swollen limbs.

If Nasidius seems not quite human here, in fact he is not: his body has literally transgressed the *humanum modum*. In the end, the other soldiers flee, leaving Nasidius still swelling beyond all standards of obesity but already quite dead.[52] Such a snake exists not even in Lucan's zoological sources, which he has adapted rather drastically to his purposes.[53] Another hair-raising example: Sabellus, who is bitten by a seps and promptly dissolves onto the desert floor as his skin spectacularly fails to keep what's inside in (9.767–774, 779–780):

> The skin closest to the wound broke and shrank all around, and exposed the white bones; the hole increases, pure wound without body. The limbs swim in gore, calves melt, the knees have no covering, all

the thighs' musculature is liquefied, the groin drips with black pus. The membranes holding in the stomach snap, and the guts spill out ... Whatever man is, the ghastly nature of this sickness showed: The ligaments of the sinews and the framework of the lungs and the hollow chest and everything hidden by the living viscera—all lie exposed in death.

Again, the bite of the seps normally causes a putrefying sore followed by mortification, while Lucan gives it the power of a bath in sulphuric acid.[54] Thanks to such features, what the snake episode is clearly *not* doing is making it easy for us to imbue it with any serious *narrative* purpose—aggrandizing Cato, having an effect on the course of the war, and so forth. The effect it does have is to play into the pervasive obsession with boundaries, while grotesquely mixing the disgusting and the ridiculous in a manner that successfully keeps readers at a distance. To take the passage seriously, on the one hand, is nearly impossible; if we do so, we must suggest that Lucan had no control over his own rhetorical pyrotechnics, and that the compassion he wanted us to feel is difficult to summon. To dismiss the episode as entertainment, however, is an equally inaccurate rendition of our response to it: while we might snicker at the grotesque ends the soldiers meet, the passage is not purely funny; it is too disgusting for that. In the end we seem to let the two reactions of horror and humor reside in a *concordia discors*—like that of Caesar and Pompey at 1.98. The ultimate result is a certain alienation from the text and its characters even as the violence it depicts provokes visceral reactions. Distance and involvement: here as elsewhere, Lucan will have his reasons for evoking both stances from his readers simultaneously.

The real answers to the perplexed question of why Lucan invented this strange episode, however, must come from the nature of its participants. Why *snakes* for this coup de grâce in the Libyan desert? Why *Cato* as the beleaguered leader? It must be granted that literary history is partially responsible, though not in the history of the civil war, where Cato's march across the desert was certainly not accompanied by killer snakes. The detailed study by R. B. Kebric (1976) suggests that Lucan's precedents lie in the march of Ophellas in Diodorus Siculus 3.10.1–6 and the earlier source Duris of Samos.[55] Mark Morford (1966) thinks the passage is based on Marius' *labor* in the African campaign, and adduces parallels from Sallust *BJ* 85, such as the presence of snakes and the program of hardship. Ignazio Cazzaniga (1957) traces the snakes back to the didactic tradition of Nicander's *Theriaca*. And Werner Rutz (1970a) suggests that Lucan borrowed from various Alexander-narratives, and finds similarities in Arrian's account of Alexander's march to the temple of Ammon in Arrian 9.23.2–3 and Plutarch's *Alexander* 26–27.

But I would argue that the greater part of the answer lies precisely in the combination of *Cato* and *snakes*. Cato as Lucan portrays him to us is above all a man who is fighting, amid the debris of the falling Republic, to keep things in their place. Cato, in other words, is Rome's last hope for the possibility of keeping apart the unholy mergings that signal civil war. Introduced in book 2 as a rigid maintainer of the ethical and political structures of Roman society—"Such was the character and the fixed practice of stern Cato: to observe the limit, to keep in place the boundaries" ("Hi mores, haec duri inmota Catonis / secta fuit, servare modum, finesque tenere," 2.380–381)—what he wants to do in the upcoming battles of the civil war is *stand in the middle*, literally enacting a boundary between Pompey's and Caesar's forces—like Crassus, like the Sabine women (2.310–311). And Cato above all others stands for the maintenance of kinship relations, already so cruelly violated by the exigencies of war:[56] while fathers and sons elsewhere are vying to decapitate each other, Cato emerges as true father of his country (2.388), and sees himself as the bereaved parent at a son's funeral pyre (2.297–301). On the other hand, not so with marital relations, since he finds sex with his reunited wife *de trop:* better not to engage in such *union* when the Republic is under assault ("nec foedera prisci / sunt temptata tori," 2.378–379).[57] Note the language here: marriage relations are *foedera*, compacts, and Cato refuses (in one sense) to "try" these agreements or bonds.[58]

Serpents and snakes, on the other hand, in ancient mythology and modern psychology, are category confusers par excellence.[59] For one, they can consume an object whole, showing its shape inside theirs, and yet they can also penetrate into holes and bodies; they are thus both envelopers and the enveloped. They represent the strange and apparently spontaneous generation of life from dead organic matter; and they also feed off the very matter that created them, as in Clytemnestra's vision of a reptilian Orestes biting his mother's breast. One version of Pasiphaë's punishment of Minos for his infidelities, for example, has him temporarily ejaculating serpents, scorpions, and millipedes; his partners discover to their discomfort that these vermin from within his body will consume them from the inside out after sex (Slater 1968: 105).[60] Snakes are also category violators because their way of movement cuts across the main biological genera: like other reptiles and insects, they "swarm," and swarming things are neither fish, flesh, nor fowl (Douglas 1966: 56).[61] And they confuse the boundaries of life and death: as if immortal, they slough off their "old age" *(geras)*, but they are also associated (at least in Greek tomb portrayals) with death, the grave, and the entrance to the underworld (Slater 1968: 84–86, 95). In short,

> In mythology and literature, the serpent is associated not only with the waters of chaos—with disorder and nothingness . . . or with the unconscious . . . but also with narcissistic concern over self-maintenance and protection from ego-violation by others . . . The most common symbol of boundary-ambiguity[,] it appears in connection with the boundary between life and death, consciousness and unconsciousness, male and female, and so on. Devouring and being devoured are associated with it, dying and being born, and everything that has to do with the edges of the body or with changes in its shape.   (Slater 1968: 91)

Piero Camporesi (1988: 265) reminds us that Ra, the Egyptian king of the sun, was attacked by a worm that formed out of his own spittle and then bit him in the heel: "The poisonous attacker issues from the very body of the attacked, like an uncontrolled putrefaction." And suitably enough, Lucan's unusual aetiology for the Libyan snakes sets their origin in an act of severing and a subsequent emanation from the body of the attacked: they are born of the blood that drips from Medusa's decapitated head as Perseus flies over the desert with his booty (9.696 ff.).[62]

Snakes, then, are a universal symbol of anxiety about boundaries.[63] To be sure, other critics suggest quite different reasons for the existence of the snake passage. *Quellenforschung* aside, the most frequent suggestion has been the aforementioned idea that Cato's march through the desert is an allegory for the Stoic sage's *durum iter ad leges*.[64] By this reckoning, "the text represents the difficult path which is that of virtue," as S. Viarre (1982: 109) would have it. Another interpretation is to take the passage as an illustration of Cato's (and Lucan's?) *amor mortis,* so that "his expedition is a march towards death" (Due 1962: 115). And the two views can easily be combined, as with Morford (1967), who takes the passage as a vehicle for the facing of death and sees Cato's staunchness in the face of these deaths as an exemplum of Stoic *patientia* and *virtus*.[65] All these views share a careful avoidance of any mention of the comic, the ridiculous, the grotesque; to acknowledge the presence of this element would be to deflate the tragic and teleological goal of the doomed march toward righteousness, the Republic, and Stoic self-abnegation.[66]

On a different tack, Fantham (1992b: 109) eloquently argues that the Medusa episode and Cato's travels in travail reflect Rome's ethical collapse, so that "the evil of Medusa is matched by the evil of man: he kills face to face what he should not look upon or kill, he carries evil with him to pollute an innocent and unpopulated region." Quint (1993: 144–145) sees the bizarre and spectacular deaths as an acting-out of Stoic contempt for the body, noting that the greater his soldiers' suffering is, the more steadfast Cato's ascetic composure.[67] And Johnson (1987: 57), asking "What feeds the bitter levity that can set a cartoon Cato in a desert of cartoon snakes?" finds the answer in "the violence and the anger unleashed by a knowledge of lost freedom." For this critic, Lucan is fed by "a radical pessimism (which is not very far from pure cynicism) about humankind and the world it lives in" (p. 62), and the ludicrous promenade of snakes in book 9 acts as a bitter, mocking denunciation of the self-delusions of Stoicism—we feast on "the dark side of both the Stoic and the epic in a comic ballet, an ugly freakshow" (p. 56). As the reader will see, I will finally disagree with this conclusion, as with all pessimistic or fatalistic readings of the poem. For the nonce, however, it seems to me that there is an additional explanation for the "cartoon Cato in a desert of cartoon snakes" that has never been mentioned, and that is simply that what we have here is the confrontation par excellence of the principle of boundary violation and the principle of boundary maintenance, two obsessive concerns of the poet throughout this epic. Cato, as the human antithesis of civil war, faces the dissolution and death that is its product, as if Stoic self-control and the Stoic belief in mind over matter had come face to face with the most gruesome, most destructive possible manifestation of sheer materiality. Who wins the battle to decide what truly constitutes the human self? On the one hand, "Whatever a human is, the ghastly nature of this sickness showed" (9.779); on the other, it is Cato's unwavering gaze that induces his men to suppress their groans even as their material bodies fall to pieces; as he watched, he "overcame the misfortunes in another's body, and as spectator he taught that great pain can do nothing" (9.888–889). But perhaps the constraints applied by Stoicism are not, in the end, enough: such philosophy does nothing for poor Aulus, who slurps down his own blood to slake his thirst despite Cato's disapproving presence (9.747–748). And Cato finally marches his army away from the sight: no men should know that thirst can do so much. To drink your own blood, after all, is the final defeat of mind ("I can control my thirst") over matter ("my blood is liquid"): and matter has the last word.

I have already suggested that the *Civil War's* stress on the discontinuity of the self extends curiously across the border that separates text and reader, complicating the integrity of our own responses to

Lucan's epic. What the snake passage shows well is that Lucan is not content to present us merely with the tragic, if sickening, spectacle of human bodies torn apart, stripped of agency and animation. This would be to stay within in the realm of tragedy; we would read his account with the morbid fascination we bring to news stories about downed jets or other disasters entailing massive loss of human life, perhaps trying despite ourselves to relive in our minds the victims' last moments, perhaps deciding to switch off the television or put aside the newspaper because the story is making us sick. Tragedy allows this reaction as it allows sorrow and horror; what it does not allow is nervous laughter, for that is the realm of the grotesque. And the grotesque is, above all, a mixture of categories, a crossing of boundaries. I can discuss here only a small fraction of the work done on this genre, but enough, I hope, to show how perfectly the *Civil War* aligns itself under this rubric—not only in its subject matter but also in the responses it elicits from its readers.[68]

A fusion of incompatible elements: a mixture of horror and comedy, fantasy and reality, order and disorder; a loss of identity, a distortion of natural size and shape, a fragmentation of order: this is the grotesque.[69] Theorists of the genre stress that one of its salient features is the eerie confusion of the animate and the inanimate,[70] so that "the mechanical object is alienated by being brought to life, the human being by being deprived of it"; inanimate objects and isolated body parts are treated like living wholes (Kayser 1981: 183, 152). But the body's fate in this genre is worse than mere loss of life: the human torso is the object of acts of unusual cruelty, presented to the reader in detail that is both startlingly vivid and artificially artistic, that focuses on everything that is extravagant and exaggerated, abnormal and novel (Thomson 1972: 8). And as in Lucan, it is the body's boundaries and openings, its spillings over, that are of special interest:

> The grotesque body is not separated from the rest of the world. It is not a closed, completed unit; it is unfinished, outgrows itself, transgresses its own limits. The stress is laid on those parts of the body that are open to the outside world, that is, the parts through which the

world enters the body or emerges from it, or through which the body itself goes out to meet the world . . .

The grotesque image displays not only the outward but also the inner features of the body: blood, bowels, heart and other organs. The outward and inward features are often merged into one. (Bakhtin 1968: 26, 318)

The grotesque narrative, which is marked by "a self-conscious delight in spectacle and paradox" (McNeil 1990: 171), thus puts the body on display; even as it focuses on the ludic dimensions of talking about death, it uses bodily disintegration or violation to undermine (yet again) the category of the unitary self. But the fascination with boundaries extends beyond the body. Through its interest in everything that is deformed, that violates natural limits, the grotesque sees to it that *all* the categories we apply to our own world view are put under siege, so that some critics have thought it stands for "an attempt to invoke and [then] subdue the demonic aspects of the world" (Kayser 1981: 185, 187).[71] Finally, the grotesque is experienced in particular in the act of reception. Reading this kind of narrative "awakens openly contradictory perceptions—laughter over deformation, disgust over the gruesome, surprise over the boldness of the impossible creations" (C. M. Wieland, quoted in Barasch 1971: 148).

Such criteria reinforce the argument that Lucan's *Civil War* is fundamentally untragic, despite its subject matter and the high moral tone of its narrator. As more and more critics—with Ralph Johnson's (1987) interpretation in the vanguard—are coming to accept, it is too ridiculous, too absurd, to be tragedy. Its grotesqueries may provide us with a frisson of horror, but there is no emotion provoked: no Dido, no Euryalus, only the human body as a bundle of reactions.[72] Recall, for example, the Monty-Pythonesque fate of the Massilian who has one hand chopped off while grasping an enemy ship; when he grabs it with the remaining hand, that is lopped off too, but, nothing daunted, he flings his mutilated torso against the ship, one newly streamlined missile. Or the fate of one Catus, riding high on the poop of a Roman ship. Within seconds, he is pierced in chest and back alike, at the same time, at the same height, by two enemy spears that meet in his body, in *medio pectore*. Paradoxically, these two opposite wounds, each with spear protruding, effectively cancel each other out. In Lucan's strange anthropomorphism, the blood doesn't know where to go—out the front? out the back?—so it goes nowhere, until the pressure in the man has so built up that it drives both spears out simultaneously, thus dividing Catus' life in two and distributing death between his wounds (3.585–591). All these episodes are described without any hint at pain or suffering; the protagonists are simple machines for mutilation, comically pursuing their ends as various body parts fall off around them—again, another factor contributing to the reader's emotional distance from the events.[73] Lucan's treatment of the body, his style, his content perfectly match the defining characteristics of the grotesque: as we have already illustrated, he merges categories, destroys boundaries, blends animate with inanimate, reverses agency. Indeed, discussions of the *Civil War* as "mannered" or "baroque" have come close to saying the same thing,[74] and a few critics have specifically designated aspects of the narrative "grotesque." Martindale, for example, remarks on Lucan's fondness "for grotesque violence and horror, for 'rhetoric' and hyperbole and bombast, for lack of all Virgilian 'restraint' "—a *terribilità* that combines "wickedness and violence and horror and black humor and ostentatious verbal paradox" (1993, 66, 70);[75] and Johnson (1987: 56) points to the "comic-ugly" and identifies this oxymoron as "an essential aspect of Lucan's narrative style, of his art."

Other critics, however, while recognizing Lucan's dabbling with the absurd, seem to think that it is *malgré soi* and, as a favor to the author, hesitate to condemn him of an unmitigated nosedive into error. Discussing the naval battle at Massilia,[76] Narducci (1979: 83) warns that "the ridiculous is dangerously close;" for Hunink (1992), "the scene becomes almost absurd"; "the 'overkill' produces an almost comical effect" (at 3.588, 3.617); and Marti (1964: 179) complains that "the horrible is everywhere exaggerated, in passages that are sometimes closer to melodrama than to tragedy." Quint (1993: 143) nicely sums up the simultaneous fascination and alienation of the reader perusing Marius Gratidianus' grotesque death scene (2.177–193):

> Because it is unspeakable, the scene of horror elicits hyperbole and exaggeration, but these often slip over into poetic playfulness and virtuosity, into a kind of perverse wit. Lucan cannot resist the detail of the still-flapping tongue, the fractured epigram about sparing death, the double simile, or the sarcastic rhetorical question at the end. Here, too, the poem's brilliant rhetorical surface calls attention to itself, and thus creates distance from the very horrors it seeks to bring home.[77]

But Quint's comments, again, are couched in the language of authorial *slippage:* Lucan "cannot resist" this excess, slips into it, and so unwittingly alienates us. I am arguing here that such alienation is not a side effect of narratorial high jinks but a necessary and standard feature of the grotesque, which relies on the conflicting reactions it arouses in the reader for its uniquely disturbing effect.

Our alienation is supremely important for Lucan: it ensures that we will find it difficult to become emotionally embedded in his narrative, that we will feel a sense of detachment from the events at hand that makes it impossible for us to truly pity the fate of any character mowed down in war.[78] "The grotesque transforms the ugly into spectacle" (McNeil 1990: 43):[79] we are the viewers, but we observe the violence from a strange plane that leaves us numbed to it.[80] Like the Romans of the late first century themselves, we are at risk of falling into the tendency Barton (1993: 105) identifies as "a shocking voyeurism, a seeming emotional and moral paralysis, what [Tacitus] calls an 'inhumana securitas,' an 'unnatural' absence of care."[81] At the same time (and again, it is this double reaction that is the essence of the grotesque) we cannot help but react viscerally to the sheer violence done to the human body. We are thus divided between distance and detachment, embeddedness and alienation. We are riven down the middle. Only later will we see that Lucan's whole epic, to some degree, is such an enactment itself of distance and involvement, cynicism and hope, all in relation to history and the chances for human participation in it.

To draw together the themes of this chapter and cast some final light on Lucan's literary response to the upheavals that ended the Roman Republic, I want to speculate further on why a writer reflecting back on the civil wars would home in so narrowly on the particular themes of fragmentation, boundary violation, subject-object confusion, disruptions of agency. I have already suggested that one answer lies in the nature of civil war itself. Another might lie in the author's understanding—perhaps even the understanding of the dying culture of the Republic—that boundaries, paradoxically enough, are synonymous with freedom. As Hannah Arendt was to point out almost two millennia later, "To abolish the fences of laws between men—as tyranny does—means to take away man's liberties and destroy freedom as a living political reality; for the space between men as it is hedged in by laws, is the living space of freedom" (1958: 466). Arendt, of course, was writing in the wake of another war, but in many ways her response to National Socialism's grip over Germany in the mid-to-late 1930s and early 1940s is curiously evocative of Lucan's vision of Rome under Caesar; for him, too, a flagstone in the road to tyranny is the disappearance of law. Pompey and the other strongmen of the falling Republic were praised by Cicero for observing the laws even when they did not have to;[82] and eventually, Lucan claims, they stopped altogether and so too the magistrates (1.175–177). Indeed, the *Civil War* is *about* the massive failure of the laws any longer to restrain men, about *ius datum sceleri;* as Lucan's Cato recognizes, he is the last guardian, and a powerless one, of the limits of justice and law (2.316). The laws of the Republic were the laws he strove to uphold; their abuse was constitutive not of freedom but, finally, of subservience; and when Pompey lost at Pharsalus it showed that the gods refused in the end to sanction any longer the "Romanas . . . leges" (7.350–351).

The fate of the laws is particularly important because the integrity of societal boundaries and restrictions is related to the ease with which we maintain a continuous hold on our own identities, just as the problem of the self seems to share a symbiotic relationship with the malaises of the state—and, as I have suggested, something seems to be wrong with the integrity of the *Civil War's* subjects, both human and otherwise, as if Lucan were providing an aetiology of the subjects whom he felt to be under siege in his own time. Mary Douglas (1966 and 1970) has argued that a society with firm rules, taboos, and traditions facilitates the maintenance of a strong sense of order;[83] to create boundaries is to create a system, and even—ultimately—to create the distinctions that let us know and name the world. Again, "the drawing of symbolic lines and boundaries is a way of bringing order into experience . . . Symbolic boundaries are necessary even for the private organizing of experience" (Douglas 1970: 50–51). And closer to home, Martha Nussbaum's wide-ranging work on Greek tragedy and philosophy has suggested that in fifth-century Athens, too, the experience of the ravages of war expresses itself through the conviction that such laws and conventions are prerequisites for the quality we call being "human": "*Nomos,* though human and contingent, is stable and . . . through *nomos* humans can make themselves stable . . . The annihilation of convention by another's acts can destroy the stable character who receives it. It can, quite simply, produce bestiality, the utter loss of human relatedness and human language . . . The death of *nomos* leaves behind nothing like it for human life" (1986: 417).[84]

But at Rome these boundaries were becoming increasingly fragile. Lucan's own times, the tyranny which he projects back upon the figure of Julius Caesar and which the civil wars precipitated by ushering the Julio-Claudians into power, was a time when the privacy and rights of the individual itself were under siege. The exaggerated social mobility of the era, the sense among the Roman upper classes that even the very walls of their houses were porous and their secrets unsafe,[85] were phenomena that went hand in hand with the slow death of the subject's legal and moral identity and the attack upon the political and social efficacy of these same upper classes; stripped of their former powers as senators and magistrates, they complained all too often of the hypocrisy the maintenance of these roles entailed. Lucan, as always, puts it more strongly still (7.641–643, 645–646):

> Every future age was conquered and enslaved by those swords. What did the children and grandchildren do to deserve to be born into empire? ... Fortune, if you planned to impose a master on those born after the battle, you should have granted them a battle too.

He and his contemporaries are slaves, the ultimate example of humans without civic rights and the power to change their own situation. Such is the result of a state without laws, of a Pompey and a Caesar who were both (in Cato's assessment of the former) "far inferior to our ancestors in recognizing the limit of the law" ("multum maioribus inpar / nosse modum iuris," 9.190–191).

Legal and juridical boundaries, of course, were not the only objects of violation; there was the attack upon the rights of the physical body to be reckoned with. Emperors could punish men at will, and sometimes did. The gruesome sites where bodies were ripped apart to the cheers of audiences—the gladiatorial games, the *venationes*, the *spectacula*—all thrived.[86] Glenn Most and others point to circus spectacles and other organized carnage as a stimulus for a new disrespect for the body, for a new sense of its vulnerability and permeability.[87] Indeed, the body becomes a plaything, and death the ultimate game—for the spectator, of course.[88] As Seneca famously attested, "Men seek pleasure everywhere ... Man, a sacred thing in the eyes of man, is now killed for fun, as a lark; and he for whom it used to be a sin to learn to inflict and accept wounds, now is led out exposed and unarmed; and a man's death is a satisfying sight" (*Ep.* 95.33).[89] Oddly enough, Stoicism's palliative effect was complicit in this disregard for physical integrity. Its attempt to lend to men a feeling of control over the self and a sense that their integrity as human beings was inviolable (given the right mindset toward suffering and death) came at the cost of jettisoning the body.[90]

Indeed, it is tempting to link the new precariousness of the status of the individual to concerns either addressed or exacerbated by the emphases of Stoic philosophy at Rome. Quint (1993: 144–145) and others[91] have already suggested that the disregard for the human body that seems to lurk behind Lucan's mutilated corpses has its basis in the Stoic deemphasis of the importance of our physical frame, the pathetic bodily covering that Epictetus calls "a corpse," "a paltry piece of flesh," "a pint of blood."[92] But as I have argued, what the *Civil War* seems to suggest is not a reiteration of this contempt but rather concern about its ramifications for personhood and the way it seems to go hand in hand with other problems with the integrity of the self. A similar problem arises from the Stoic treatment of the issue of agency, or rather the surrender of agency. In its Roman incarnation as a kind of map for a *modus vivendi,* a somewhat ill-defined "dominant system of thought,"[93] Stoicism was generally positive toward withdrawal from active agency in matters of state: indeed, this quietism is a feature of Stoicism that recurs in the philosophical *and* the political thought.[94] Studies of Roman Stoicism acknowledge the presence of tension between the duty to state and the value of withdrawal and meditation, a tension well exemplified in Lucan's Cato (on this, see Chapter 4); however, P. A. Brunt (1975), laying out the literary support for the Stoic endorsement of political withdrawal, concludes "that their teaching tended to promote not active resistance to government but entire withdrawal from political activity" (p. 10): the aim of Stoic thinkers was to help men conform their will to what happened (p. 23). This is a stance bitterly rejected by the narrator's cry in book 7: "Since you gave us a master, Fortune, you should also have given us the chance to fight!" (7.646). Even the traditional moral vocabulary began a transformation under the pressure of this philosophy; "*virtus,* while remaining the active principle par excellence, began to be used to describe passivity, endurance, resistance" (Barton: 1993: 65); Seneca aspires to be a Stoic stone[95] and notes with bemusement the frantic need of his fellows to be *doing* something—attending a trial, traipsing down to the forum, going to the theater (*De tranq.* 12.1–7). Under the empire, apathy and autonomy come to be redefined as virtue, and once-despised *otium* can bring the former statesman rewards.[96] For these reasons, and others that will become clear in Chapters 4 and 5, I would suggest Lucan felt that Stoicism was *not* the answer to crises of his time; in its disregard for the body, renunciation of agency, and emphasis on interior retreat as a way of maintaining sense of integrity of the person, it was too complicit with attacks on the integrity of the self that were already in place.

The issue of integrity, of course, concerned state as well as self. The relationship of bodily wholeness and identity was actually a Stoic *zētēma;* and if Stoics like Chrysippus asked how far material continuity was necessary for individual identity,[97] then surely the same question could be asked of the state, especially after the fall of the Roman Republic. Does true *Romanitas* live on under the emperors? Or, as Lucan puts it, did the battle at Pharsalus have the power to decide "what Rome was" (7.132)? Rome after Pharsalus (at least in Lucan's claim) was a different city: once Pharsalus' rivers had flowed with Roman blood, once the destiny of mankind had been decided, it became a strange capital indeed, a city teeming with the dregs of the world, a place where civil war was now impossible: there were not enough citizens left to give meaning to the term "civil" (7.404–407).[98] It is as if we find exaggerated in the fate of Pharsalus all the Roman anxieties about the growing power of outsiders, about the diminishing differences between Rome and not-Rome, about the rising social mobility of ex-slaves and the lower classes. Indeed, at 7.430 ff. Lucan actually bemoans the loss of the political subject (here in the literal sense of the *subjectus,* or subordinate): the Indians and Sarmatians and Germans now no longer fear Rome's sovereignty.

The dissolution of the self is a process accelerated by war, particularly a war in which there can be no sense of a just cause and no ideology to give meaning to the slaughter. Jonathan Shay's suggestive comparisons of Achilles' portrayal in the *Iliad* and the effects of Vietnam upon its disillusioned and nightmare-ravaged veterans are in fact much better suited to the violent and graphic text of Lucan's epic than to Homer's: in both cases, a shocking exposure to the brutalization of human flesh, the sense of the betrayal of "what's right," the overturning of the moral world of the soldier by the goals and comportment of his leaders, the lack of a good cause to fight for, and inevitably "the ruin of character."[99] Human language is similarly ravaged: terms like "victory" and "defeat" meld into each other in a meaningless blur of propaganda, and the survivors doubt their ability to express any "truths" in this too-pliant medium.[100] And the unified person under such circumstances is put under siege and split into two: horror seems to shiver the human participant into a detached observer figure and a suffering victim. As Freud would surmise (in 1915, well into the ravages of the Great War), "Our own death is indeed, unimaginable, and whenever we make the attempt to imagine it we can perceive that we really survive as spectators."[101] We might remember here the *Civil War's* strange detachment from its own scenes of dismemberment and death; or Tyrrhenus calling to his comrades to use his body; and read the curious echoes in other ironic accounts of the effects of war.[102]

Such is the period on which Lucan turns his reflective gaze, and his recreation of its stupid, senseless gore cunningly recreates for us the very issues that leave their brand on the participants in such war: the constitution of the self, the inversion of normal ethics, the inadequacy of prewar language media, the weakness of all definitions, boundaries, rules, laws. Responding to some of these factors, Barton (1995: 49, 53), herself a sensitive reader of Lucan, has suggested that boundaries at the end of the Republic "became a matter of will and desire . . . Morality, and adhesion to particular traditions and limits, require a powerful act of will. Preserving a sense of being, of identity, thus becomes a continuous—and ultimately exhausting—attack on the animus."[103] This seems exactly right: the subject was under siege, and this is what Lucan has to show us; and I mean subject in all the senses of the word, from the individual subject of any political regime, to the (usually active) grammatical subject of a sentence, to the Latin meaning of *subjectus* as an item "placed under a category or head"—that is, ordered according to a coherent system. *All* these subjects are depicted in collapse in the *Civil War*, fatally disrupted by the mess of human and linguistic boundaries, agency, and otherness. Whether he was driven by a desire to discredit the regime under which he lived or whether he truly felt life had fallen into an abyss brought into being after Caesar's victory at Pharsalus—and the question remains an open one—Lucan's description of the civil war, right down to the level of his syntax, renders the human being a thing, an unfeeling lump of matter that comes apart as its boundaries are violated, robbed of agency and animation, linked to the undermining of the sense of self; all as a graphic illustration of how civil war and the tyranny that followed could strip humans of their humanity.[104]

In any case, Lucan's perspective on the problems of his era was not an isolated one; a shared sense of the absurdity of life and the absence of God, a disillusion about the worth of rationality and morality, and a consciousness of the pervasiveness of human evil pervade the writings of his compatriots in the first century, albeit sometimes in the form of a stout denial of any such perspectives.[105] The opiate of Stoicism could provide a useful shield for some, a descent into cynicism a defense for others. It should not be surprising to find Lucan in good company. Noel Carroll (1990: 209–214) suggests that a fascination with horror and the grotesque is a side effect of convulsive social change and is most often seen in the aftermath of war, in times of cynicism about the government and fascination with countercultures.[106] It accompanies nostalgia, an instability of classificatory and moral norms, a sense of helplessness and paralysis, and an awareness of the human body's status as mere flesh, even "meat." Similarly, Barton (1993: 46) sees the Roman fascination with gladiatorial games even among the upper classes as "a response to an intense and excruciating feeling of humiliation and insecurity and an attempt to find compensation, even exaltation, within this feeling of inescapable degradation."[107] But Lucan's expression of the *Zeitgeist* is unique in the complexity and pervasiveness of his insistence on the precariousness of the idea of the person, its boundaries, its life, its agency.

This, then, is the grim project of the *Civil War*. By focusing on the violence done to the body and by reenacting problems of human agency and animation in his syntax, Lucan's poem refuses to keep in place the encroachment of the category violator, the boundary dissolver, the abject, but thrusts it instead upon our sensibilities. He refuses to define the Roman subject under civil war by excluding the abject, by keeping in place the laws, by preserving the integrity of the body. If keeping the subject contained and undamaged means keeping at bay the things that threaten it, the *Civil War* enacts a colossal failure of this task; for once the boundaries of state and body are shown to be changing and permeable, once the abject contaminates the subject (as when bodily contents become external), and once the idea of the person is made to straddle the categories of subject and object, the line that separates these two mutually exclusive categories can no longer do its symbolic work.[108] The poem acknowledges that the very idea of the subject is an invention, an effect of desire. "Abjection is the body's acknowledgment that the boundaries and limits imposed on it are really social projections—effects of desire, not nature. It testifies to the precarious grasp of the subject upon its own identity; an assertion that the subject may slide back into the impure chaos out of which it was formed" (Grosz 1990: 90). Without this act of exclusion, the grotesque otherness of our intestines has to be acknowledged as us. Subjectivity is reduced to the integrity of our insides, and thus to sheer matter, and finally (and paradoxically) to *lack* of subjectivity. We could even suggest that Lucan's poem asks of us, with Kristeva (1982: 4), "How can 'I' be without border?"[109] The answer, of course, is "I" cannot. No conceptual categories can. Hence a world without boundaries as the perfect image for a man obsessed with showing the destruction of the independence and integrity of an entire people. This is Lucan's *Civil War:* or at least, one very powerful side of it.

TWO

Paradox, Doubling, and Despair

The categorizing practices of pointing and naming indicate how shared knowledge is obtained through various forms of distantiation. Language is by nature a separation.
—*Gunnar Olsson*

IF WE WERE to look for a verbal form that inflicts on language what Lucan does to his bodies, it would be paradox. Paradoxes, like parasites, destroy the system that gives them life. They rely upon a vocabulary and a conceptual framework that are familiar and meaningful to us their audience, but they then destroy the integrity of this system by equating the familiar and the meaningful with the terms that were opposed to them in the original system.[1] They thus create a situation in which we have to keep two ways of signifying in place at the same time: the one old and familiar—in which, for example, "mercy" is a favor shown to those in your power; the other diametrically opposed to it yet dependent on its vocabulary, like Caesar's *venia* to Domitius after the assault on Corfinium (*BC* 2.511–525). Caesar forgives his enemy and spares his life; the result is that Domitius *flees* Caesar's gift in horror as the narrator comments, "Alas, much better could Fortune have spared Roman honor, even if it were by Domitius' death!" (2.517–518). "Mercy," which now punishes those who receive it, functions effectively in the opposite way to mercy as we knew it, but it is still, inconveniently, called mercy.

Here, as always, it is not so much the specter of a new system that throws us into confusion: it is the unholy mixing of the old and the new, confronted with each other in a language that their boundary-defying equation works to render obsolete. As G. Moretti (1984: 41–42) points out, "This process of terminological redefinition creates, from a linguistic point of view, the possibility of emphasizing the logical conflict between the old and the new semantic system, creating a friction between the term subjected to redefinition and the term employed in the old sense, when these two are used side by side." Thus our attempt to explain the new meaning of mercy harks back once again to the old framework: it is really "punishment." But even as we speak our statement slips into ambiguity, for what does "punishment" mean *now*? This somewhat simplistic example operates on the level of individual words, but the underlying contradiction that lays the foundation for any paradoxical idea always relies on system confusion, a jangling of frameworks: and in this sense, paradoxes, too, are about boundary violations. Since their juxtaposition of frameworks pairs ideas that belong apart, paradoxes bring into proximity and synonymy the opposed notions on which systems of meaning rely. If language—at least starting from Saussure—is thought to rely on the existence of distinctions between signs for the integrity of its ability to name, then paradox takes one step toward collapsing or confusing those distinctions.

When Lucan adopts and nurtures paradox, then, it is a gesture toward the collapse of the lexical and semantic system within which he works, as surely as his treatment of the body enacts the same step toward boundary collapse on the level of biological matter. The linguistic medium in which his epic is couched is one that threatens to self-destruct by destroying the differences on which it relies for meaning; as we work to make sense of what we are reading, we are kept in constant awareness of the fragility of this language under abuse. It is only the effort of our will to understand that keeps us shifting back and forth between ways of understanding, making sense of the contradictions, paradoxes, and collapses of opposites by supplying exegetical supplements to explain what the narrator really means. In the end, the imminence of this threat of the dissolution of the whole linguistic system is played out in as broad an arena as the one that featured the violated body. It turns up in Lucan's obsession not only with paradox in a multiplicity of forms but also with all manner of pairings and reductions of opposites, in his focus on the collapse of differences into the hegemony of the One, and in the concomitant sense of helplessness and paralysis in the dark mire of what history is turning out to be: in the suggestion, in other words, that no amount of human striving can make (recreate) a difference in the senseless mess that civil war has made of Rome. Here, then, we are traversing from rending the body to rending language; the discussion and overview of these themes provides a view, again, of *one* of the Lucans unearthed by critics: Lucan the cynic, the disengaged, the despairing; a Lucan who engages in "the effervescence of passion and language we call style, where any ideology, thesis, interpretation, mania, collectivity, threat or hope becomes drowned" (Kristeva 1982: 206); a Lucan who contemplates a catastrophe beyond meaning and beyond describing, with no remaining tools to take on an already impossible task.

Let us begin with the well-known idea of the civil war within the text, the signifiers pitted against each other, the equation of opposites such as *ius* and *crimen*, *virtus* and *scelus*, *clementia* and *supplicium*, the twisted plays of paradox and oxymoron that make Lucan's epic an enactment of the aporia of civil war. These are the *Grunddominante* of Lucan's work in that they effectively demonstrate the dangerous pliability of language that renders it an unstable tool for the maintenance of ethical or political norms.[2] The greater part of Lucan's paradoxical rephrasings of the events of the *Civil War* are addressed precisely to the overturning of these norms, so that morally laden terms such as justice, piety, and patriotism are equated with crime, evil, and treachery in a relentless series of paradoxes that begin with the epic's first verses and continue to its bitter end. These are the kinds of linguistic plays that have generated readings of the poem as endorsing a sense that language as well as bodies are collapsing, so that Lucan's paradoxes reinforce the destructive effects we have already seen in the preceding chapter.

The epistemological crisis they give rise to is, most generally speaking, the product of the manner in which these verbal operations wreak havoc on *same and other*. For example, modifications to a normative phrase or idea will replace one element by another that signifies its opposite; when the reader instinctively supplies the normative element through force of habit, the confrontation between mind and page creates a strange meeting of opposites. The oft-quoted line "they all flee to war" ("in bellum fugitur," 1.404),[3] for example, relies on the missing norm of *advancing* to war or invading—*bellum inferre* or the like—so that fleeing and attacking are equated: the result of both movements here is warfare. Or we could say that "fugitur" evokes the idea of movement toward shelter or refuge—in any case away from war—so that war and safety too are evoked as strange bedfellows. The frequent idea of death as a desirable is similar: "placuit mori" even though the norm is to be loath to die, so that pleasure and displeasure are uncomfortably linked as the emotions appropriate to the moribund. Elsewhere the dead will *stand* instead of lying; only the senators who are *exiles* are those who gather at Rome; the most loyal soldiers produce acts that are *monstrous* rather than praiseworthy; and so forth throughout the epic.[4]

The paradoxes work in other ways as well. When their focus is more directly nominal, antonyms are directly equated in a way that lets the narrator or other characters openly point to the catachrestic effect of civil war. "The name for unspeakable evil will be virtue" ("scelerique nefando / nomen erit virtus," 1.667–668) prophesies Figulus, for example, and thus echoes the first lines of the epic: *ius datum sceleri*. The equation here and elsewhere of *ius* and *scelus, virtus* and *nefas,* is akin to oxymoron: its effect is to produce a temporary situation in which different signifiers can point to an identical signified. They do so within an interpretive community that (1) must perish some future day when even the *passing* application of "crime" to an act such as kin murder cannot be understood, and (2) must for the present apply old signifiers to new states of affairs, relying on the double vision of the reader who understands how and why it could be both *ius* and *scelus* to murder one's family members. Paradox is generated because the new system must rely parasitically on the old: the new value of the *crimen* is assessed in terminology taken from the old vocabulary, and so lexical indices of meaning collapse upon themselves as old words are put to use for a different reality.

In another procedure that distorts the relationship between sign and signifier, an identical term will remain on both sides of the equation, while its meaning is forced into radical difference in one of its two appearances. When Cornelia learns of Pompey's death she vows to punish herself for remaining alive by—remaining alive ("poenas animae vivacis ab ipsa / ante feram," 9.103–104). Life, *anima*, is thus the undeserved good for which she must receive the punishment of *anima*. The paradox here is the result of the juxtaposition of two different systems of thought, systems distinguishable normally—life before the death of the Republic, or Pompey, is worth living, life after is not—but now juxtaposed in a jarring combination.[5] Similarly with Domitius, who refuses the punishment *(poena)* of forgiveness by Caesar (2.519–521). The result is an ethical framework for living that creates its own victims, who live according to one set of values without realizing that they are liable to judgment by another. Caesar's soldier Scaeva is one such throwback (6.140 ff.).[6] The embodiment of martial *virtus*, he fights as one man against many until reinforcements arrive, heedless of the gravity of his impossible wounds.[7] But, poor fool, he does not realize that civil war has overturned the value system within which he thinks he fights: his patriotic valor is the same thing as the basest evil (he did not know "in armis / quam magnum virtus crimen civilibus esset," 6.147–148), and once again we find ourselves caught in the paradox of describing the new system with the old[8]—and in "the strange Hegelian world where truths are decomposed (synthesized) into their opposite" (Johnson 1987: 55).

Even Lucan's much-bemoaned tendency to be repetitive in his

choice of vocabulary has this effect. It has not been properly remarked that his repetitions are often significant, bringing into play
contradictory notions by using a noun in divergent senses in such
proximity that the clash cannot but be noticed. We should not be
surprised, therefore, when Cato criticizes participation in civil war as
furor only to call abstention from the selfsame war *furor* three lines
later (compare 2.292, 295),[9] even though his repetition of the word
has boggled the minds of editors and several important editions opt
for the emendation "pudorem" at 2.295.[10] We will not complain, with
Mayer (1981 ad loc.), that the repetition of *duces* at 8.423 and 8.423—
once to refer apparently to living generals, once to dead ones—is
"vexing."[11] Nor will we observe with Fantham (1992a at 2.216–217)
that "it is a strong argument against the authenticity of 212 that *prae-
ceps* is again contrasted with *haerentes* after only three lines." And yet
she herself points out why this is so: what we have here is "a deliberate
inversion of the logic: in 212 the waterlogged bodies caused the ob-
struction, here the action is reversed as bloodshed pours from the
bank to dislodge them and release the waters."[12] Lucan's doubled
terms can forcibly draw attention to their own flexibility as nouns,
or to the reversibility of the ideas and events they describe.

All these paradoxes, of course, work as a suitable vehicle for the
representation of a world turned upside down, for the enactment of
"a rupture of logical order" (Moretti 1984: 49), and for the narrative
of a war that screams out its nature as "a perversion of civilized
values" (Martindale 1976: 51).[13] What I would like to emphasize here
is the force of *equation* as the operation that destroys the old linguistic
and semantic world of the Republic as it produces the paradoxes that
try to accommodate these changes. Lucan so often relies on this
operation because his epic tries to drive home to us that this kind of
collapse of all differences and boundaries is one of the causes (and,
paradoxically, effects) of the collapse of the Republic.[14] As we have
seen, this focus on merging is reminiscent of the grotesque itself,
which merges contradictory forms and concepts to produce an un-
classifiable hybrid. It is not surprising, then, to find paradox listed as

one of the elements that contribute to the grotesque mingling of opposites that characterize this genre: when Lucan pictures Scaeva so full of spears that he needs no more armor but becomes a kind of steel hedgehog inured to further attack, a ridiculous transformation of wounds into a shield, this paradox puts into play all the grotesque elements of horror and comedy, fantasy and reality, and the body as the recipient of acts of unusual cruelty.[15]

In Lucanian linguistics, in short, *opposition is a meaningless concept.* When not relying explicitly on the paradoxical, the poet still manages to merge difference into sameness, or to double unity into duplication, so that already in the first lines of the poem, we find two sets of *pila,* two sets of *signa,* and an *acies* that is *cognata;*[16] "the Words are already split and doubled, the signifiers are at War" (Henderson 1987: 147), and, as we have seen, the poem proceeds systematically to collapse the distinctions between inside and outside, friend and foe, Roman and foreigner, as the civil war sets up *civis* against *civis* on all fronts.[17] In the naval battle at Massilia, for example, the instability of authorial point of view renders the Romans hard to distinguish from the Massilians throughout.[18] Even the two sides of the war are originally set up as equals in evil, with little except age and ability to distinguish Pompey from Caesar.[19] The idea of the matched pair, *par,* emerges as a poetic shibboleth,[20] most of all in its application to these two, refigured as gladiators in the vast arena of the Roman Empire. Even the discriminating Cato thinks they are *pares:* he acknowledges that both sides are equally corrupt and that Pompey, like Caesar, plans to take over the world, "sibi ius promittere mundi" (2.321).[21] When the two sides finally clash in book 7, the poet introduces them with a doubling of the word *pars* that is unusual in its application to two sides of battle ("volnera pars optat, pars terrae figere tela / ac puras servare manus," 7.486–487).[22] Indeed, Lucan himself endorses the sense that even to *try* to justify one of the two when both are participants in the ultimate evil of civil war is a crime: "quis iustius induit arma, / scire nefas"[23] (1.126–127; in making this claim, of course, the narrator enacts his own entrapment in the inherited ethical terminology he condemns throughout: *nefas* has become sense-less, but he cannot but use it, paradoxical and self-undermining though his position might be).[24] Finally, and as the civil war contin-ues, the very offices and institutions of the Republic are doubled: two senates exist simultaneously, one in Rome and one in Epirus (5.17 ff.), two *imperatores* stand at the head of two Roman armies.[25] Even the phenomenon of the civil war itself, the struggle between Pompey and Caesar that is the subject of Lucan's poem, is not allowed to be unique, but is figured as the double or repetition of the earlier war of Sulla and Marius. As Caesar marches on the city, an old Roman laments that it's *déjà vu* all over again—the fates had exactly the same thing in mind in 88 B.C., when Marius was hiding from Sulla's min-ions but would soon take over Rome (2.67–70).[26]

This doubling of civil war itself takes an interesting twist when the narrator apostrophizes Julius Caesar in book 9 to tell him that he, too, along with the poet, will live on through the generations of read-ers to come (9.982–886): "Caesar, feel no ill will toward sacred fame. If it is right for Latin Muses to promise anything, then as long as Homer's honors endure, future generations will read me and you: our Pharsalia [*Pharsalia nostra*] will live, and no age will condemn us to darkness." *Our* Pharsalia? Even Lucan's rendition of the civil war, it seems, will not be allowed to stand as an original, but merely one of two. The second, of course, is Caesar's own *Civil War*[27]—in style and bias the very opposite of Lucan's, but here present as one of a pair. Most commentators on these lines cannot believe that Lu-can would so undermine his own "take" on the civil war as to set up parallel to it in time and fame the earlier version of Julius Caesar, and so read "me teque" as "the *Civil War* which I wrote and you fought," or alternately "the *Civil War* which I wrote and you star in."[28] Yet it seems appropriate enough that, like everything else that has to do with civil war, the *Civil War* itself is confronted with and equated to its opposite. Here in fact is "one of the most disturbing of Lucan's insights: that writing about Caesar makes him somehow complicit with and analogous to Caesar ... Caesar and his bard, together for ever, for better or for worse as they contemplate the ruins of Troy" (Malamud 1995: 182).

This reluctance on the narrator's part to stick to *any* one-sided endorsement might well explain the apparent switches in allegiance that have so troubled critics of the poem. At certain points in the narrative—for example, during the fraternization at Ilerda in book 4; the suicide of Vulteius and his men at 4.465 ff.; and maybe the glorification of Domitius Ahenobarbus in books 3 and 7—the Caesarian forces or individuals emerge as morally superior, or at least worthy of genuine admiration. The usual way of resolving the problem—that is, to suggest that Lucan was doing the best he could with the historical material he had to work with—is unsatisfactory: the narrator has no difficulty eliminating or distorting history in other places. Ahl (1976: 192), for example, argues that the favorable depiction of Caesar at Ilerda is "the by-product of dealing with an irrefutable case of Caesarian *clementia*." I much prefer the recent hypothesis of Jamie Masters (1992: 90) that the poet's voice here and elsewhere effects a mimicry of civil war in the splitting of the "authorial, dominating, legitimizing persona" of the narrator. This idea of a *fractured voice* well captures our inability to pin Lucan down to a consistent position for any period. (As will become clear, however, my own explanation differs from Masters'.)

Just as the corrupt language of Rome's citizens and leaders has made it difficult to distinguish verbally between original opposites, or to give voice to a political stance that does not undermine itself, or make any good ideological choice, so too what we have here is merely the last step in the author's systematic denial of the possibility of picking one side of a pair, of halting the collapse of pairs into ones, and, most of all, of giving voice to *any* coherent ideological stance in the weakened, empty terms of post-Republican Latin. And among these ideological stances, of course, belongs the anti-imperial bias of his own poem; Lucan does not exempt himself from the process he describes.[29]

Why this emphasis on sameness and doubling, with the former

closely linked to the latter? Why does the poet engage in this emptying-out of the very language in which he writes? Elaine Scarry (1985: 133–134) has suggested that war is always accompanied by a surge of inauthenticity in language:

> Within war itself, the indisputably physical reality of the mounting wounds has as its verbal counterpart the mounting unreality of language. The two—authentic physical content and inauthentic verbal content—are such inevitable counterparts of one another that they have often been understood as near synonyms [scil. as in Machiavelli's usage of "force and fraud"].[30]

Scarry is referring not only to the inauthenticity of official language in times of war, in which chauvinistic concerns produce ethical twistings of the kind we have seen above and, invariably, distort the truth about military casualties and successes; she is including the language of the victims, whose own subjugation (most so in cases of torture) forces them to use the terminology of their victors ("with God on our side, we triumphed") and thus "makes a mockery of the victim's subjectivity" (Richter 1992: 135). And so, "if the victim speaks, it is a discourse intimately bound up with both the pain of his or her body and the dominant discourse of the victimizing subject. In other words, the victim's discourse is based on transgression" (ibid.).

But there is more. Like the violence against human bodies, this operation on language destroys the *boundaries* necessary for coherence. Where abjection confuses I and other, inside and outside, identity, system, and order, the result of paradox in all its forms is to confuse dichotomous categories in language, so that the narrator tears at the Saussurean fabric of language as relations just as he has torn the fabric of human social relations and the flesh of human bodies. The result can be seen in the existence of two indistinguishable sides;[31] where the ideology of civil war is concerned, this means that any attempt to exert voice or choice, to make a difference by picking an option, is rendered meaningless. Not only the question of which side Cato should choose but broader issues too are contami-

nated by what crosses the once-stable borders of all ethical terminology; sin and virtue, patriotism and treason, life and death—which
of these can now be surely evaluated? The language of civil war has
rendered them all the same.[32]

Fittingly, a collapse has been taking place all along on the level of
history as well, as the multiplicity of the Roman Senate and magistrates is reduced first to the power of the first triumvirate and then,
after Crassus' death, to the hegemony of just two men, the pair Caesar
and Pompey. The end of the civil war will enact the final collapse,
the result of any successful attempt at dictatorship: Caesar alone is
left, all in one, completing the movement from multiplicity to the
unitary for which civil war is the enabling condition.[33] Here is the
quintessential version of the "transition, at the moment of the entry
into war, from the condition of multiplicity to the condition of the
binary; a second attribute is the transition, at the moment of ending
the war, from the condition of the binary to the condition of the
unitary" (Scarry 1985: 87).[34] And other writers have compared this
process precisely to the collapse of the canonical and the normative
in literary style, the rejection of Vergil and the embrace of syntactic
violence, so that the unusual movement toward the unitary within
the text itself is seen as a warlike process enacted against the literary
past:

> From the perspective of the collapse of canonical forms, war and all
> forms of horror represent the return to power of the "same." But this
> is not a "same" based on the notion of alterity, which in some way
> would restore the principle of identity and a semblance of cohesion; it
> is a "same" which suspends all difference. In this regard war is the
> theme that engenders the greatest *equivalence,* especially by the regres-
> sion of the human to the animal. This equivalence is particularly per-
> ceptible in the stereotypical metaphor of the slaughter-house.[35]

This collapse into the same and the unitary is a reversal of accounts
of Creation, which (as Martindale 1993: 52–53 notes), "whether in
Genesis or Ovid or elsewhere, often contain the notion of *separation,*
of making ordering distinctions ... Most art helps to conceal the

possibility of the abyss from us: Lucan unusually takes us some way towards it."[36] Lucan is writing about an un-doing of the world, and for him the "abyss" is the empire itself, the rule of One to which Rome is abjectly heading.[37] This rule, after all, not only emanates from one person but (at least in Lucan's ideology) takes away freedom of choice from all his subjects, makes history and its narratives meaningless.[38] No wonder Lucan himself abjures narration of the battle of Pharsalus and prefers a (short-lived) silence at 7.556. There is by this point, from the vantage of his own lapsarian situation in time, nothing to say, just as there are no choices left to him and his fellows, for whom all was decided so long ago in this day of battle.[39] And this paralysis, this lack of choice and voice, *is* civil war. As Henderson (1987: 124) concludes, "Lucan offers no 'call.' No glimpsed remedy, alternate promise." There is nowhere for the reader to turn, no place for him to direct his hopes; passivity is the only option, it seems.[40]

Here, then, is *stasis* in every sense of the word: both civil conflict and stillness, both aggressive action and lack of movement.[41] Like the Latin *seditio,* stasis is a noun that stands for violent political strife even as its etymology lies in the apparently contradictory meaning of standing or stillness (in Latin, *seditio* comes from *sedeo,* to sit).[42] Loraux (1987: 108) traces the double sense of this noun in its Greek context: "Stasis: verbal noun derived from the verb *histēmi.* Synonym: kinesis, movement, or, more exactly, agitation . . . But, for the philosophers, there is also evidence of stasis as a noun for being-stopped, for standing upright in immobility. Here everything becomes complicated, caught between agitation and immobility." But her comments are suggestive for Lucan's own interpretation of what civil war means; for him, too, civil war is a stasis, an equilibrium effected by the equal confrontation of the two halves of the city (Loraux 1987: 109).[43] The locking of the two sides, the balance maintained by their match, once again returns us to the idea of identity and paralysis; stasis-conflict is also stasis-stillness, and in such a situation there is no sense in picking one side over the other. As Martha Malamud

(1995: 187) puts it, "Lucan's poetic accomplishment is a text in stasis representing a world in crisis. Civil war blocks any resolution . . . Lucan piles up paradoxes and arrives at an impasse." Lucan's manipulation of his linguistic medium in this epic has this realization as its message: for the victims of such a war, distinguishing between the two sides demands an effort that the slippery, empty terms of their corrupted language cannot sustain. So is it that the victims of the war simply cannot decide which side to pick: the cities of Italy, like Rome herself, are *ancipites urbes* (1.266, 2.448), while the citizens of Rome know full well that freedom lasts only as long as no such choice is made (2.40–42). The Massilians abjure an alliance with either Pompey or Caesar (3.307–355), and Brutus passionately recommends neutrality as the best course (2.234–284; "What of Cato and his choice?" my reader may ask. What of Cato, indeed. That issue drives the second half of this book). Even the narrator steps in to express his approval of those who do not fight at all, who can simply escape from the unholy conundrum of civil war into a peaceful (at least for the nonce) neutrality. Pompey's soldiers at Ilerda, who first fraternize with Caesar's troops and then slaughter them at the order of their commander Petreius, are forgiven by Caesar and allowed to retire from the fighting;[44] and Lucan observes almost enviously (4.382–385, 398–401):

> Alas for the wretches who fight on still! These soldiers, safe now and harmless without their armor, yield their weapons to the victor and scatter to their cities, free of their cares . . . And of this burden too Fortune relieves the carefree men: that anxious partisanship is absent from their minds. Caesar was the cause of their safety, Pompey their leader. Thus they alone can watch the civil war happy and with no prayers for either side.

Suitably, Caesar, that whirlwind of action, despises neutrality: for him, civil slaughter is a glorious thing; and, as he tells would-be deserters who don't plan to go over to Pompey, it is better to be a traitor than a peacenik (3.348 ff.).[45] But in every other way and every other direction, stasis/paralysis seems to emerge as the hopeless partner of stasis/conflict. Hopeless characters, a hopeless narrator, and the sense that there is no halting the downward spiral of Rome's history.

The *Civil War*, then, seems to be a poem that offers no way out. For its narrator, for its characters, for its readers, Rome's history—looking forward from the point of view of the citizens under civil war, or backward from the point of the narrator himself—was headed and did head toward imperial darkness; ideology became and *is* a mere game with words. The conditions that brought on the civil war that ended the Republic have also brought on a new mode of human existence: one in which the citizens of Rome—the few that are left—have been stripped of their ethics, their agency, their language. They reside amid the rubble of their categories for thought and amid the detritus of their city. They have no political voice any more, but then they do not need one, because everything is the same, one man rules everything, and choices are no longer a possibility. Choices are in fact meaningless: while the Republic was crumbling in the throes of war, what need was there to pick between sides that were equally corrupt, or between moral standards that could be reversed with a mere twitch of a noun? What need, when even grasping at the knowledge of which side had the greater justification in going to war is a criminal attempt, *quis iustius induit arma, scire nefas?* Stasis has even taken over the possibility of *knowing* which side to back, if only in one's mind, if only as a secret belief or a last flourish of ideology.

The apparent pro-Neronian stance of the proem can offer no counter to this position; its exaggerated praise of Nero as an emperor whose advent justifies the horrors of the preceding century notoriously self-destructs in the reader's hands. Indeed, this reading of the poem itself as a paralyzed clash of opposites does much to solve the "problem" of the proem's panegyric, which has been variously interpreted to be eulogy, satire, a bow to convention, or (correctly, I think, but for other reasons) as a text that will not and cannot let its status be fixed. I would suggest that the proem, exactly like the figure of paradox, relies on the reader's choice of a temporal vantage point from which to understand its "meaning," even as the selection of any single such vantage point renders its meaning incorrect. This is true of both our position *in* the poem (the further we read, the clearer the anti-imperial bias becomes; and in any case a negative interpretation is guaranteed if we privilege the narrator's own warning about "all the words with which, for so long now, we have been lying to our masters"; 5.385–386); and our position *outside* the poem, depending on which period in Lucan's life we believe generated these flattering/ironic lines. The early 60s A.D., soon after his praise of Nero at the Neronia of 60? Later, after the reputed ban on his recitations? At the end of his life, before he dashed off to join the conspiracy?[46] In which framework shall we place ourselves? Our choice determines our answer, unless we step out of any single framework and view the proem, like the paradoxes, as a text that conflates systems.[47] The proem both relies upon imperial ideology and pushes it to the point of discomfort; it announces its status as sincere and as fake; it generates in its readers an inability to choose.[48]

For this Lucan, the collapse of the old life was not the product of a choice on anyone's part, not even Caesar or Pompey; it was inevitable, part of the fabric of a history doomed to destruction.[49] Indeed, Caesar himself emerges more as the expression of some force behind history than as a mere human, an idea that has echoes in the political theory of other times; Hannah Arendt (1958: 466) has observed that all leaders of totalitarian government are imbued by their own propaganda with a sense of being larger than life, the earthly representative of a vast force in history that hurtles events along in the way it has chosen and that is abetted by the acts of mindless terror the dictator presses upon his people:

> Total terror, the essence of totalitarian government, exists neither for nor against men. It is supposed to provide the forces of nature or history with an incomparable instrument to accelerate their movement . . . Terror . . . as the obedient servant of natural or historical movement has to eliminate from the process not only freedom in any specific

sense, but the very source of freedom which is given with the fact of the birth of man and resides in his capacity to make a new beginning. In the iron band of terror, which destroys the plurality of men and makes out of many the One who unfailingly will act as though he himself were part of the course of history or nature, a device has been found not only to liberate the historical and natural forces, but to accelerate them to a speed they never would reach if left to themselves.

Like these madmen, Caesar sees himself not so much as a holder of arbitrary power but as the tool of the vast laws that rule the universe,[50] and so too does our narrator see him. As Ralph Johnson (1987: 103) puts it: "Lucan's Caesar is less a representation of a historical figure than a symbol for certain inscrutable forces that operate behind and beneath what is called history. He is an evocation of a mysterious process out of which certain events in Roman history (and in other histories as well) gather their energies and burst forth into the world."

In this process larger than man or men, in which the figure of Julius Caesar emerges as a personification of the unpredictable power that seems to stand behind Rome's downward spiral, intervention in the affairs of men can make little difference.[51] And since nothing can be done about any of the calamities driving Rome to destruction, Lucan's universe as we have seen it so far is neither understandable nor curable. If anything, the ways in which we normally understand human history, such as (scientifically) the positing of cause-and-effect relationships, or (religiously) a belief in the plans of God or providence, or (ideologically) the triumph of a people or a way of thinking, or (teleologically) the idea that things undergo a meaningful process, that there *is* a final cause—none of these seem to offer any explanatory escape for Lucan. Indeed, the gods withdraw from any kind of intervention in this epic, and even their existence is repeatedly questioned; the benign providence of the Stoics disappears, to be replaced by the "invida fatorum series" (1.70)—or, better, what Johnson calls the broken machine, the fiction of history;[52] and chaos may well rule the entire random machine of the universe: "The phantom of entropy is loose in the cosmos" (Johnson 1987: 125). So much for teleology. Ideology, too, is impossible when no clear boundary separates the two sides. And the idea of causality, so important in Stoic philosophy, is relentlessly undermined.[53] For one, individual scenes in the epic are notoriously episodic in nature, leading to a sense of narrative fragmentation that many readers have criticized as a lack of skill or condoned as the necessary side effect of Lucan's "historical" epic, but which Quint (1993: 131–157) has more sensitively analyzed as a strike against the teleological structure of Vergilian narrative.[54] The destruction of canonical form goes hand in hand with the refusal to make sense of history; interpretation is impossible for the narrator and the narrated alike.[55] More direct still is the narrator's own expression of confusion where cause and effect are concerned. On occasion he is happy to set up causal links, as in the exploration of the causes of civil war with which the epic begins; yet elsewhere he wonders if chance rules everything and "nothing is destined" (2.12); and so what happens to the Republic is portrayed as beyond understanding. The most famous of the poem's epigrams rely for their effect on precisely this reversal of normative causality; Caesar's repeated pledges that "this war will make the loser guilty," for example, neatly inverts the issue of responsibility by replacing it with the power of propaganda.[56] Nor can foreknowledge, for Lucan, be equated with understanding. Prophecy plays a striking role in the poem, but the foreknowledge thus gained helps no one: from the seers of book 1 to the Sibyl in book 5 and Erictho's sickening procedures at the center of the poem, the content of the future is always the same, death.[57] For Sextus Pompey, for Appius Claudius, this knowledge is futile. The rest of the time it is *lack* of knowledge that marks the struggling efforts of the characters (Henderson 1987: 159 n. 102).[58]

Under the same rubric of causality demolished must fall the uncertainty about whether civil war is the punishment or the crime. As the epic opens, we find the narrator denouncing the *nefas*, the *scelera* of his countrymen who raised their hands against each other (1.6, 1.37); and yet those same citizens are said to spout "*just* complaints against the savage gods" as they leave for war (2.44), and Lucan himself, immediately after denying the existence of these selfsame gods, consoles himself with the thought that vengeance for their cruelty is still possible (7.454–459). Similarly, when Cato debates with Brutus whether or not to participate in the *furor* of his fellow citizens, he first calls the civil war a crime against the gods ("nefas," 2.286) and then a crime *of* the gods (2.288). And this confusion, of course, renders expiation impossible. In Lucan's diseased world, the expiation and the crime come all too close to being the same thing—the civil war itself, which is at times figured as punishment for Roman sins, at times the sin itself. "The disease and its cure are identical; the expiation is an aspect of the crime; it is the crime from another viewpoint" (Barton 1984: 233).[59] All this plays itself out in a poem that declares itself to be both the vehicle that announces the death of the Republic and the result of this death; the epic's own linguistic medium decries the effect of the imperial One on language and simultaneously shows itself the victim of that effect. History with meaning? Far from it.[60]

This is the Lucan of most recent readings of the *Civil War:* the Lucan whose writing subverts his own epic's place in generic tradition as it proclaims the invalidity of all claims to cohesion and indeed, to a coherent belief system per se. And yet this is only one Lucan, the deconstructionist whose presence in the poem has been ably illustrated by scholars such as Ralph Johnson, John Henderson, and Jamie Masters, and to whom the past two chapters have been dedicated. The existence of this narrator cannot be doubted—and yet to concentrate on him alone is to submerge the other Lucan: the partisan, the hoper, the vivid presence in the poem that manages to believe in the possibility of a different future despite itself. Diametrically opposed to the cynical figure who depicts the sundering of bodies and words and puts his own poem under the sign of the Same, this Lucan is wildly partisan even as the content of the *Civil War* alerts us to the faults of his position. He is a figure better known to us from older studies of the poem, where the focus on the biographical context of his work has given us a Lucan who writes and dies as a protest against the empire he lived under. In the end, what will give this poem its meaning, and solder together two major critical schools of thought, is precisely the simultaneous presence of the naysayer and the partisan.

The previous two chapters have presented the grounds for a grippingly negative interpretation of the *Civil War*. This reading has had a powerful pull for recent readers of the epic; indeed, the present critical climate has rendered it one of the most compelling positions on the poem. The collapse of the autonomous individual amid the wreck of linguistic systems and subject-object relations, the hopelessness of meaningful narrative in a meaningless world, the impossibility of representing the trauma of Romans killing Romans— "Shun this part of the war, O mind, and leave it in darkness, and let no time learn of such evils from my poetry, that so great is the license granted to civil war" (7.552–554)—all these are undeniable aspects of Lucan's epic world, and for readers of our times I think they are more than undeniable: they ring true with an evocation of the particular horrors of the twentieth century. Lucan's attempt to convey what he would represent as the unspeakable physical and psychological brutalities of the civil wars of the first century B.C. fastens, uncannily enough, upon the actual truths of what happens to the human subject *in extremis* and on the realities of the societal and psychic results of the totalitarian agenda, and so he produces a picture that has curious resonances in the history of our own century. Certainly Nazi Germany and Stalinist Russia have rendered unhappily familiar such regimes' assault on moral standards, the surveillance of citizens, the spread of fear, the paradoxes that arise from the overturning of norms of law and human behavior. We know well that terror is the tool of all such regimes—"the essence of totalitarian government," in Hannah Arendt's words (1958: 466). And Arendt, along with Czeslaw Milosz, Alexander Solzhenitsyn, and other voices from the past, all attest to totalitarianism's focus on "the destruction of a man's rights, the killing of the juridical person in him . . . the murder of the moral person in man" (ibid., p. 451). Suddenly the darkest visions of the human imagination become alive in history, and, with them,

> it becomes evident that things which for thousands of years the human imagination had banished to a realm beyond human competence can be manufactured right here on earth . . . The totalitarian hell proves only that the power of man is greater than [one] ever dared to think, and that man can realize hellish fantasies without making the sky fall or the earth open. (Ibid., p. 446)

I bring up this analogy here because it is difficult for readers of Lucan not to be struck by parallel after parallel between the visions of his imagination and our own history. As I have noted, even the figure of the restless, madly self-confident Julius Caesar, that demonic and charismatic force "who felt he had accomplished nothing while anything still remained to be done" (2.657), seems tailor-made to evoke, for us, a crucial feature of such regimes—the charisma invested in the figure of the leader and the exaggeration of his powers of agency. Henderson (1987: 138) remarks that Caesar himself seems to represent the very principle of "subjectivity as active agency" in this poem in which other subjectivities are faring less well; similarly with Hitler, who himself and whose regime was associated with energy and agency: Arendt (1958: 306) notes the "perpetual motion mania of totalitarian movements which can remain in power only so long as they keep moving and set everything around them in motion." Moreover, Hitler's regime identified itself with the forces of nature and history: its rise to power was supposedly inevitable and inexorable, its present existence temporally eternal, as evidence by the well-known Nazi projection of the "Thousand Year Reich" and "revolutionary immortality," and the National Socialists' belief that they were children of the gods (Lifton 1986: 14, 449)—like Lucan's Julio-Claudians, claimers of spurious divinity. Finally, Arendt (1958: 307, 387) notes the moral cynicism of the leaders: "would-be totalitarian rulers usually start their careers by boasting of the past crimes and carefully outlining their future ones . . . The propaganda value of evil deeds and general contempt for moral standards is independent of mere self-interest, supposedly the most powerful psychological factor in politics." These men believe everything is permitted to them: Lucan's Caesar, anyone? The Third Reich meets the Pax Romana.[61]

Our knowledge of Stalinist and fascist regimes aside, I think we read Lucan's epic with another, still darker piece of recent history as our lens. I am referring here to the Holocaust: not only to its unnarratability,[62] but to the scattered testimony of its survivors and the deliberate and crushing destruction of the very idea of the human that was so successfully carried out by its Nazi perpetrators. Here, too, Lucan's grim visions may become for us more than the fancy of a long-dead poet striving for the expression of evil, precisely because the inexorable disintegration of subjectivity, the sense of the futility of language, the complete loss of agency, are not themes alien to our times: we know that these developments are possible as the goals of those who would destroy millions of their fellow beings. The topic is a difficult one, and far beyond my powers: here I would just like to remind my readers of how some scholars and writers have *tried* to talk about the Holocaust, and to suggest that Lucan's view of a world gone mad may mean more than he could have guessed to his readers.

As is well known, the Nazi program was not simply that of mass extermination; it was to eliminate identities as well as bodies, to erase the humanity of its victims. The chosen site for this operation was the concentration camp (Disch 1994: 118). But the aim of the camp was not to kill its victims—"at any rate not quickly"—but instead to manipulate them "in such a way as to make it destroy the human person as inexorably as do certain mental diseases of organic origin" (Arendt 1958: 453); in other words, to render the human being inhuman, a thing without spontaneity, agency, sensation. Innumerable sources and witnesses attest to the Nazi treatment of human beings as objects, not living beings, not only physically in the camps (where the process continued after death, so that humans were evaluated in terms of their capacity to be turned into soap, felt, lampshades),[63] but also in their ideology, their philosophy, their medicine. Götz Aly, in his annotation of the Posen diaries of the Nazi anatomist Herman Voss, points to a number of passages in which the human subjects of his analysis emerge as machines or tools:

> The upper extremity is connected to the torso through an intermediate piece, the shoulder strap. On the torso, the shoulder strap forms a mobile socket for the free upper extremity, the arm, like the bed of a traveling crane . . . At the elbow joint, this stem is interrupted by a joint, so that the interior of the moving shank is also accessible. Thus the arm is divided into two sections, an upper and lower arm. The lower arm is attached to pliers that are movable at the wrist—the hand.[64]

Aly (1994: 147) comments: "These various mechanical comparisons are reductions of complex human functions—as if the hand were a pliers or the mouth simply a chewing tool that Voss' view of human beings—which he formulated with the use of Polish and Jewish bodies available to him in the camps—was that of mechanical instrument"; for Voss, his subjects were "not people, but apparatuses, motors; they had not been killed, their functions had been 'interrupted.'" Here and throughout the Nazi redescription of ideologically "undesirable" human life, animate beings become inanimate objects, and living humans are things without will or agency—in Arendt's famous term, a "bundle of reactions" that merely responds to stimuli. "Pavlov's dog, the human specimen reduced to the most elementary reactions, the bundle of reactions that can always be liquidated and replaced by other bundles of reactions that behave in exactly the same way, is the model "citizen" of a totalitarian state" (Arendt 1958: 451).

This program—the Nazi will to destroy individual human identities, to turn their victims into tools of labor fading slowly into obsolescence—was all too effective, according to the testimony of survivors. The result of the Nazi program of cumulative psychological and physical agony was that death-camp prisoners became object-like in their own eyes, stripped of will and agency and curiously detached from their own bodies and selves. Bruno Bettelheim wrote of his own experience in the camps that his persona had split into "one who observed and one to whom things happened" (1952: 52). The author, as he refers to himself in a striking distantiation from his role as narrator, became "convinced that these horrible and degrading experiences somehow were not happening to 'him' as a subject, but only to 'him' as an object . . . It was as if he watched things happening in which he was only vaguely involved. Later he learned that many prisoners had developed this same feeling of detachment, as if what happened did not really matter to oneself" (ibid., p. 62)—as if we can here find Voss's own view curiously internalized in its victims. Self-estrangement, doubling, a lost sense of the unity of the self are the pervasive themes of the testimony of Holocaust survivors.[65] Like the Bettelheim of the camp, prisoners became objects even to themselves; their sense of identity was destroyed; they underwent a kind of doubling that left them the curiously detached spectators of their own suffering.[66]

At the same time, the Nazi program carried out a pervasive attack on moral and legal boundaries, both within and outside the camps. The Nazis managed to make even the victims guilty, by forcing them to participate in the running of the camps and in the deaths of their fellows. Guilt and innocence, terms that had to be kept distinct for the moral coherence of the victims to stand uncontaminated by any official language, became instead confused, as did, grotesquely, victim and executioner:

> The SS implicated concentration-camp inmates—criminals, politicals, Jews—in their crimes by making them responsible for a large part of the administration, thus confronting them with the hopeless dilemma whether to send their friends to their death, or to help murder other men who happened to be strangers, and forcing them, in any event, to behave like murderers. The point is not only that hatred is diverted from those who are guilty . . . but that the distinguishing line between persecutor and persecuted, between the murderer and his victim, is constantly blurred. (Arendt 1958: 453)[67]

Under such conditions, questions of conscience became meaningless, and moral choices contaminated. What could it mean to be a good citizen under the Nazis? Or, less obviously, what are we to think of those who collaborated in the hope that they could make more of a positive difference thus than by resisting?

Even the language of the victim is not exempt from this grotesque merging; instead, it becomes the language of the tormentors, as the torture victim adopts the language of his or her torturer. This is a phenomenon attested in all torture, one of its goals even: "The question and answer ... objectify the fact that while the prisoner has almost no voice—his confession is a halfway point in the disintegration of language, an audible objectification of the proximity of silence—the torturer and the regime have doubled their voice, since the prisoner is now speaking their words," as Scarry (1985: 36) notes in her important study.[68] Indeed, Scarry can point to the dissolution of boundary between inside and outside as one result of prolonged physical agony: the victim feels confusion about source of the pain and his body itself is felt, paradoxically, as being its cause rather than its subject. Truly, "the lesson of the camps is the brotherhood of abjection" (Arendt 1958: 453 n. 156). The tormentors' ideal is that in the end nothing should be left of the person the victim once was; his language and body are equally violated; his self, his world have dissolved: we are left with the helpless, gibbering Winston Smith of George Orwell's *1984*, willing to scratch down "Freedom is Slavery."[69]

The horror was efficiently redoubled by paradox. Outside the camps, the Nazis' destruction of the guideposts of moral life was partially enabled by the manipulation of linguistic terms and the use of language rules that "kept Nazi functionaries from equating the crimes made legal under the regime with their old, 'normal,' knowledge of murder and lies."[70] In the death camps, even a crazier twisting of language took place. Lifton (1986) chillingly analyses the role of paradox in Nazi ideology here, pointing out that the Nazi program of exterminating the Jews was accompanied by propaganda about "healing" the fatherland, so that (for example) it was the so-called Hygienic Institute that distributed the fatal gas Zyklon-B. As Stein (1993: 490) puts it, "It was the fantasied organic body of Germany that was being 'disinfected' of Jews in the gas chambers."[71] Killing and healing merge in the incomprehensible horror of the death camps, a boundary destroyed on the way to death. Indeed, Lifton would even argue that this "medicalization of killing—the imagery of killing in the name of healing"—was a crucial element of the step to systematic genocide: for at the heart of the Nazi enterprise lay "the destruction of the boundary between healing and killing" (1986: 14). And the camps destroyed other boundaries: not only between healing and killing, with the hearses painted to look like Red Cross vans and camp physicians carrying out sadistic experiments upon their "patients," but also between life and death. Indeed, the camps were full of the living dead, humans on the verge of extinction from starvation or disease who were dubbed *Muselmänner*—"camp jargon for the living corpses" whose inability to support their own frames made them look at a distance like Muslims in prayer (ibid., p. 138).[72] In the end, "the insane mass manufacture of corpses is preceded by the historically and politically intelligible preparation of living corpses" (Arendt 1958: 447).

For those of us at all familiar with these grim details, Lucan's representation of horror rings uncannily true. His linguistic and narrative tactics are linked to the undermining of the sense of self. It is as if the poet, for his own purposes, was groping for a way to create a discourse about the shape of absolute evil, the physical and spiritual openings at which it invades its human subjects, and how one could put into narrative form the appearance of this kind of evil in history. But for us his readers, this discourse has already become the shape of history almost two thousand years later. If the bodily and linguistic violence of his epic does in some way represent the subject under siege, as I have argued in these past two chapters, it is tempting to conclude that there exists, both in the human imagination and in human practice, a tragic awareness of the common denominators of what breaks the human spirit, makes objects out of human subjects, and passes beyond the power of description. And it is tempting for us to read the exploitation of *this* vision as the project of the Lucan we know.

THREE

Pompey as Pivot

Our passional nature not only lawfully may, but must, decide an option between propositions, whenever it is a genuine option that cannot by its nature be decided on intellectual grounds; for to say, under such circumstances, "Do not decide, but leave the question open," is itself a passional decision . . . and is attended with the same risk of losing the truth.

—*William James*

There are cases where a fact cannot come at all unless a preliminary faith exists in its coming . . . Believe that life *is* worth living, and your belief will help create the fact.
                                                        —*William James*

I N A F A M O U S episode of book 2 of the *Civil War,* a hesitant Brutus approaches Cato to ask whether he intends to participate in the coming conflict between Pompey and Caesar. Brutus himself will urge Cato not to, for he considers participation madness. Better to stay above the fray in Epicurean tranquillity, better *not* to choose, better stasis as inaction rather than stasis as war. And indeed, Brutus' address here is characterized by all the paradox and self-negation of this epic's mode of expression: as I have already noted, he first suggests that Cato's participation would acquit the civil war of guilt ("an placuit . . . inmixtum civile absolvere bellum?" 2.249–250) and then soon afterward reverses the direction of contamination, worrying that Cato alone will be *made* guilty by participation ("accipient alios, facient te bella nocentem," 2.259). Here it is the *idea* of guilt, not an actual noun, that literally alternates between one front (Cato) and the other (civil war); but Brutus then goes on to equate *virtus* in such a war with *scelus* (2.263, 266) and to proclaim such paradoxes as his intention to be the victor's enemy only when the war is over (2.284). Antonyms become synonyms, Cato will absolve the war even as it will make him guilty, and no choice of side is justifiable: this is the *Civil War* we know well, a place where nothing remains uncontaminated by its own opposite and where all efforts at ideological justification must consequently fall apart.

And yet Cato—while he fully participates in the idiom of the epic, criticizing participation in civil war as *furor* only to call abstention from the selfsame war *furor* three lines later (2.292, 295), and acknowledging that both sides are equally corrupt and that Pompey, like Caesar, plans to take over the world, "totius sibi ius promittere mundi" (2.321)—joins Pompey's party nonetheless, an act of will and agency that is strangely jarring precisely because Cato has endorsed, by his language, the Lucanic sense that acts of political partisanship make no sense in civil war. He has no illusions about Pompey's corruptness and megalomania, yet he feels he can make a difference in a world that is busy collapsing every difference, and he joins one of the two parties in the hope that his presence will stand as a reminder to the victor that there were other stakes in the battle besides personal power and glory ("ideo me milite vincat, ne sibi se vicisse putet," 2.322–323). In short, Cato bursts out of stasis and inaction and intervenes in the corrupted action of the epic out of a refusal to be a mere spectator to the fall of the Republic, to which he has a responsibility as *civis* even as he acknowledges that civil war is *nefas*. Unlike Brutus, who hears his words and is roused to excessive passion for civil war (2.325)—because any passion for civil war is too much passion by definition—Cato acts not out of desire but out of responsibility. He knows well that his support is for nothing but an *inanis umbra*, the empty ghost of liberty (2.303); he knows the outcome is damned either way; but despair of the goal is not reason enough for passivity.

As if mimicking Cato, as if fighting against the linguistic fabric of his own epic, a Lucan entirely other than the one we have been studying breaks forth in due time from the negating, equalizing force of the *Civil War*. This is the Lucan of "furious partiality,"[1] the narrator who bursts into the poem to praise one leader and condemn the other, and who exhorts us to share his horror at the death of freedom; here, one might think, must be the Roman senator who in the end died trying to depose the hated emperor Nero. He is a figure well known to us from over a century of modern criticism: for many, it has been tempting—and why not?—to apply the poet's biography to the interpretation of his poem, summoning up the *Vitae* and what we know of his life and death to read the *Civil War* in ideological as well as literary terms. The Lucan that emerges from this interpretive process—and he has as real an existence in the poem as his *Doppelgänger*—bears little resemblance to the poet foundering in a meaningless world: paralysis and resignation are not his responses to the self-destructive lingustic fabric of civil war and the *Civil War*. *Signa* and *signa* may be carrying out their impossible battle within the paradoxes of the text, choice may be impossible and knowledge *nefas*, but the poet nonetheless carves out a parabolic trajectory that leaves him, at the end, clearly, even rabidly, in favor of one of the two leaders, whose goodness he proclaims even as the text of the poem must leave us skeptical. In the persona of narrator, he enacts a choice and professes a stance whose very *unjustifiability* will turn out to be the clue to its meaning. For if he does not bring us, his readers, along with him in this movement toward ideology and belief, that is, perhaps, just part of the point.

Pompey is the pivot in this process. More: unlocking the mystery of his changing representation in the poem is the key to the double readings of the *Civil War*. For years, scholars have puzzled over the inconsistencies of this representation, which at first seems to present Pompey on a level with the hated Caesar, and then to modulate into explicit sympathy and even adoration as the voice of the narrator continues to break into his own poem. One tactic has been to deny any changes in the narratorial voice in the first place, a solution I shall more or less ignore once I have repeated the salient points of Pompey's transformation below. Another, currently out of favor, has been to claim for Pompey the status of a Stoic *proficiens,* a man on the way to wisdom; his representation is said to change because the character himself does.[2] Alternatively, some scholars have suggested that the figure of Pompey is inconsistent throughout the poem, with no particular trend to be detected in one direction or another: Pompey is simply a human, with his own strengths and weaknesses; the poem's picture of him is thus "true to life," a refusal to idolize the flawed being who, in the end, could not save the Republic. There is also the school that blames the poet's incompetence for the character's strange vicissitudes: given the facts with which he had to work, given the episodic nature of his writing and his indifference to narrative continuity, Lucan could not provide us with a properly epic hero. Thus several clashing Pompeys cohabit the text together, depending on the goal the poet had most immediately in mind. And a fifth solution is to revert to biography, suggesting that the change in Lucan's attitude is due to the deterioration of his relationship with Nero and perhaps his new inclination toward revolution.[3] To my mind, none of these explanations makes satisfactory use of the evidence.[4] The narrator's enactment of a change of stance toward Pompey is real enough—but paradoxically, it is also not convincing, despite the explicit addresses to the reader that seem intended to win us over to his position. The Pompey he shows us offers us surprisingly little ground for such a favorable reevaluation, a situation that could have been easily rectified by further manipulations of history and narrative had Lucan so wished. And the attention that this discrepancy draws to itself does more to tell us about the narrator than about his flawed figurehead Gnaeus Pompeius, known as Magnus.

First the evidence. When we are introduced to Pompey in book 1, his inferiority to Caesar in age and ability is hardly offset by any moral superiority, while the text carefully matches the two in the balanced double simile at 1.129–157.[5] Cato, considering their merits, concedes that both sides are equally mad for power (2.321); the narrator endorses the sense that any attempt to justify either side is criminal ("quis iustius induit arma, / scire nefas," 1.126–127);[6] and the citizens waiting apprehensively in Rome feel that either man's victory would be an evil (2.40–42), even comparing the coming conflict to the grisly years of civil war between the morally decrepit Sulla and his equal in virtue, Marius.[7] Indeed, if Caesar cannot tolerate the presence of a superior in the capital, Pompey cannot even tolerate an equal (1.125–126; interestingly, and as if he could not accept so negative a view of the ill-fated Pompey, Dio Cassius, when he borrows this idea, has Caesar rather than Pompey be the man who could not abide even an equal).[8] In fact, as book 2 ends and Pompey continues his southward progress to Brundisium while Caesar overruns Italy, his braggadocio renders him actually foolish to our eyes: he boasts to his troops that it is not Caesar from whom all things flee, but Pompey whom all things follow (2.575); but when we next see him he has yielded Italy to his rival without a battle and is *fleeing* ("profugusque per Apula rura") headlong through Apulia to Brundisium (2.607–609). His heavily rhetorical claims of moral superiority (see 2.531 ff. in the same address to his troops) have already been undermined by his characterization in the text. And to make matters worse, he blusters that Caesar is headed for defeat as surely as Carbo, now moldering in a Sicilian grave, was beheaded by Pompey's orders— "Carbo felt the edge of our ax" (2.546–547). As is well enough known, the sources roundly criticize Pompey's inhumane treatment of Cn. Papirius Carbo, whose head he sent to Sulla—and here he ironically boasts of the same fate he will endure at his own enemy's hands.[9] The rest of the speech consists of obvious lies about Caesar's career (a coward, a military flop) and a round of praise for his own: "I'm more *felix* than Sulla himself," he cries at 2.582—another unfortunate allusion.[10] No wonder his soldiers refuse to clap once the rodomontade ends.[11] Given the rubbish that Pompey mouths, Kirk Ormand

(1994) seems quite justified in dubbing him unreliable, an *auctor vix fidelis*, both here and at the moment of his defeat (8.14–18): what he says just cannot be trusted.

And yet something strange is already afoot. While Pompey is making a poor show of things in southern Italy, Lucan stops for an exclamation about Caesar's pardon of Domitius: shocking that a man should have to be forgiven for following the army of his country, the Senate, and *Magnus* (2.519–521). At the end of book 2, he enters the narrative to editorialize again, this time fervently praying that Roman soil might remain unstained by the man so dear to her—"sui Magni" (2.736). So far, there are only small touches of narratorial favor among the general gloom, but as the epic progresses their frequency and intensity increase. Although the portrayal of *events* gives us little reason to share the poet's growing enchantment with his hero—Pompey's commanders orchestrate treachery and butchery at Ilerda in book 4; the general himself does not follow up his victory at Brundisium in 6, turns tail at Pharsalus after botching the battle in 7, and wants to petition the Parthians for help in 8—the narrator's *voice*, most noticeably in his apostrophic interventions, seems oblivious to the meritless cavortings of his hero. Ilerda, of course, is a notorious sticking point. Why does Lucan let Caesar emerge so favorably from this episode, granting clemency as he does "voltuque serenus" (4.363) even after the Pompeian troops under Afranius and Petreius butcher the soldiers they had embraced as brothers? As Jamie Masters (1992: 74) points out, we are left here with "a Petreius loyal to the Pompeian cause, but denigrated as a perpetrator of civil *nefas*, an Afranius who betrays the cause but is showered with authorial approval, and an apparently benevolent Caesar." But when the narrator steps in to comment, he again enacts his pro-Pompeian stance, precisely by *lamenting* that Caesar's goodness has let him be the better cause.[12] The fact that his response to Petreius' brutality is one of sorrow for its temporary effect on the moral superiority of Pompey's side shows neither a *lack* of partiality in the Ilerda episode nor favoritism to Caesar, but the opposite.[13] Caesar, he cries, never were you more fortunate than now, "since thanks to this one crime of civil war, you will be the leader of the better cause!" (4.358–359).

And this sets in motion a trend of events which cast Pompey in a bad light and to which the narrator responds nonetheless with pro-Pompeian apostrophes. When Pompey botches the follow-up to his victory at Brundisium in book 6, readers modern and ancient might roll their eyes, but the narrator enters the text to apostrophize Caesar and inform him that this good luck should be put down to the moral fiber of his opponent: "It pains me and will always pain me, Caesar, that your worst crime has been an aid to you: namely, that you fought with a pious son-in-law" (6.303–305). Indeed, Pompey is allowed to shore up this interpretation of his actions with a noble speech about his desire to avoid warfare in Italy; should we take our cue from the narrator and believe him here, although we could not in book 2? By book 7, on the eve of battle, the narrator actually imagines Roman citizens mourning his defeat as if it were the funeral of Brutus (7.39); this is in fact the moving climax to a long apostrophe in which the poet again expresses his and Rome's love for the doomed general in the most sentimental of terms (7.29–32):

> O happy man, if your Rome could have seen you even in a dream! Would that the gods had given one last day to your fatherland and to you, Magnus, on which, though both of you knew well your doom, you might both enjoy the last fruit of so great a love.

And yet Pompey's performance is less than stellar during the all-important battle at Pharsalus. Most strikingly, while he is about to flee the battlefield while the fighting is still in progress, Pompey is allowed to suggest that his departure is in fact a kind of *devotio;* that in order to save the men still fighting from unnecessary death on the battlefield he will offer himself in their place (7.659–664):

> "Desist, o gods," he said, "from destroying every nation. Magnus can be wretched while the world yet stands and Rome survives. If you desire

more suffering on my part, I have a wife, I have children: so many hostages did I give to fate. Is civil war unsatisfied, if it extirpates me and mine? Are we too small a slaughter, if the world is not included?"

And he asks the troops not to lose their lives on his behalf: he is not worth it (7.669). But now the *devotio* is set on its head: instead of rushing at the enemy in the hope that his death will end or expiate the conflict, Magnus (the narrator tells us) fears that should he die the fighting will never stop (a fear explicitly countermanded by the events of book 9, where his soldiers no longer want to continue the war now that their leader is dead)—and so he skedaddles from the battlefield and leaves the troops busy with mutual slaughter.[14] A strange *devotio* that saves the sacrifice and offers up the beneficiaries, but this noble flight instills not the least bit of discomfort in our narrator, who now addresses Pompey in rapturous terms and for some fifty lines.[15] "There was no weeping or groaning from you, Magnus, only a venerable sorrow" he cries; "you are still superior to fortune's vicissitudes; you proved by your departure that the senators of Rome were not fighting for you—they were fighting for freedom and they died for it" (7.680–697).[16]

The trend continues. It is worth noting that by book 8, the adjective *sacer* in its positive meaning of "holy, sacred" has become one of the most common adjectives applied to the man; his appearance is holy in death (664), as are his face (669) and his decapitated head (777); his very ashes are holy in the loyal Cordus' view (769); the name scratched on his modest gravestone is twice holy, the second time in yet another apostrophe by the poet (792, 806); and in this same apostrophe we find the narrator wishing aloud that he himself could take Pompey's charred bones to Rome and telling us that future visitors to Egypt will stop to worship at Pompey's shrine (8.855 ff.). By the beginning of book 9, our unlikely figurehead is treated to a full-fledged catasterism, soaring to the stars and smiling down at the ridiculous world below, as his spirit takes up occupancy in the hearts of the unsuspecting Brutus and Cato.[17] But lest we still doubt that something strange has happened to the narrator's voice, a startling deviation from the epic norm leaves us no choice but to believe: the narrator himself reenters the text before the grim happenings at Pharsalus to exhort *us* to side with Pompey too—in other words, to carry out the same move toward a political choice that *he* as narrator has carried out. In perhaps the most famous passage in the epic, while our author is contemplating the future responses—our responses—to his *Bellum Civile*, he *tells* us how we, the readers he imagines poring over his epic some day far from then, will respond to his text: we will favor Pompey. Perhaps, he says, I too, by writing this epic, will be able to offer assistance to great names, "magnis nominibus" (the echo of *Magne* at 212 is not fortuitous), and as future generations read my work, they will still favor you, Pompey (7.207–213):

> Among later peoples too and generations to come, these events (whether their own fame will carry them into the future, or whether my vigilant work too can help great names), when they read of these wars, will provoke both hope and fear, and prayers unheard; and all will peruse your fate breathlessly, as if it were still to come, not past; and still they will side with you, Magnus.

The narrator thus boldly attests to our support for the man whom his very own text depicts in a highly problematic way. He claims to speak for our response, a moment unique in all of classical epic: we *will* favor Pompey as we read with bated breath of the tragic events of the *Civil War*.[18] Yet Pompey is not easy to like as he emerges from the fabric of this epic, and we are tempted *not* to favor him, whatever Lucan says. The poet seems to dictate our response at the same time that he problematizes our ability to provide it by not making Pompey more admirable, a strange state of affairs indeed. And it has left many a critic most uncomfortable: Désiré Nisard was already complaining in the last century that Pompey is ridiculous but Lucan seems not to have noticed; he concludes that the poet has been duped by his hero![19] More recently, Donato Gagliardi (1970) has tried to explain that our agreement with Lucan's projection is based not on the figure of Pompey himself, presumably too unlovable for anyone, but on the abstract idea of the leader of a just cause. But this is not what the narrator says. On the other hand, Ormand (1994: 41–43) focuses on the term *attoniti*, suggesting that we are stunned because Pompey does *not* turn out to be heroic; Lucan, in other words, anticipates our difficulty with the epic's presentation of its protagonist. If this reading is right (although it seems more intuitive to me to read *attoniti* as indicating we are glued in fascination to Lucan's page), it points once again to the sharp contrast between two Pompeys, one apparently our projection as much as the narrator's, the other the figure in the text.

The contrast between the narrator's present attitude toward Pompey and the reservations that were apparent at the beginning of the epic is sharpened by the verbal echoes in this and other late passages that evoke less happy moments. When the poet informs Pompey that the future readers of the *Civil War* will all favor him and take his side over Caesar's ("omnes . . . adhuc tibi, Magne, favebunt," 7.212–213), his choice of terminology brings to mind the very different reaction of Cato in book 2, "nor does it escape me that Pompey too, if fortune favors him [*si fortuna favebit*] promises himself mastery over the whole world" (2.320–322). Earlier, it took fortune's favor to make Pompey lord of the world; now, we are told to lend ours to the process so that Pompey can live on at least as the literary favorite in the world after the Republic. And as Frederick Ahl (1976: 172) has noted, Pompey's very words as he prepares to sign on the Parthians in his desperate attempt to regain Rome chillingly repeat Caesar's as he crossed the Rubicon in 1.200: "Roma, fave coeptis" (8.322).[20] Is Pompey still grubbing about at the level of Caesar's moral sludge, despite the narrator's enthusiasm? Postgate (1913 at 8.209) certainly thinks so:

> Though this message to Parthia is an invention of the poet's, as a disclosure of what its inventor thought in keeping with his hero's character, it is highly instructive. The selfishness, the callousness and the prodigious vanity which we can descry in [Pompey's] arguments . . . are only too true to life. In all Pompey's career there was little more discreditable than his relations with Parthia.

The infamous Parthian episode—which Lucan did not have to include, far less invent—does nothing for the narrator's new hero on the eve of his murder. Pompey, thinking of his reputation as always, claims the Parthians always venerated him, and in any case their defeat on Pompey's side would still be a victory for Rome; if this seems dubious, it is all the more so when Lentulus, who opposes the scheme, emerges as exceeding all in *virtus* and *nobilitas*.[21] Indeed, the narrator, for once, has nothing to say; no apostrophe praising the sullied Magnus.[22]

There remain further stains on Pompey's character that seem to suggest that Lucan is letting us see the fragility of his support for the man despite himself.[23] Is his death, over which the narrator apostrophizes in the most tragic of terms, indeed so tragic? Proponents of the "Stoic improvement" school should be put off by Pompey's defiant dying claim to be *felix* whether or not the gods try to take this away from him (8.630–631): certainly not a Stoic response to death, and at any rate another reminder, at the moment of Pompey's greatest pathos, of his early mentor and civil-war monger, Sulla Felix. His resolution to hold his breath to avoid crying out and marring his reputation is reminiscent of his enduring fixation on public opinion: the baldness of "nunc consule famae" (8.624) may cause unease. It has led one critic to draw a contrast between the exterior that Pompey presents to the world, Stoic and enduring, and the internal Pompey, machinating to the last: as Ormand (1994: 49) has suggested, this in turn undermines the reliability of all Pompey's representations of events, so that "by allowing us access to the full text of Pompey's death, Lucan defeats the apparent purpose of that text: Pompey dies, as he lived, an *auctor vix fidelis*."[24]

At any rate, it seems that the poem's other characters and especially the relatively uncompromised Cato are left cold by the narrator's metamorphosis; more exactly, they are not made to share his sentimentality and favoritism toward the ever inadequate leader. Their presence in the poem and their responses to the Pompey of the later books seem to function as a kind of anchor to help us keep our moorings, to ensure the stability of our reading of Pompey despite the narrator's wild enthusiasm. The most salient examples of this reservation on the part of the epic's characters come from Cato. To begin with, there is his heavily guarded funeral speech for the dead man. While we are told he favors the Pompeian cause "pectore toto" after Pompey's death (9.23), his attitude toward Pompey himself remains highly ambivalent, a self-canceling blend of praise and blame.[25] Pompey may not have snatched power when the people were willing to be slaves, but he also preferred war to peace (9.199), and (most damning) the *libertas* he presided over was merely *ficta,* the Senate a screen for power (9.204–207).[26] Later in the same book, Cato will wax particularly ferocious against the fallen leader when Pompey's own troops want to put down their weapons and return home, and here the terms *regna, rex,* and *dominus* are brandished with startling ease. In fewer than twenty lines, Cato labels the dead Pompey as a potential *dominus* no less than three times (257, 266, where he is equated with Caesar and Crassus; and 274), as *rex* once (262), and once as striving for *regna* (258); and, to add insult to injury, he informs the soldiers that their old general's decapitation at the hands of an Egyptian minion should be considered Ptolemy's *gift* to them ("Ptolemaei munus," 9.268)! Harsh words indeed, coming as they do after his "eulogy" of the murdered man—and a short space after the narrator has apostrophized Fortuna to call this same death a stain upon the gods (8.604–606). More strikingly still, this criticism of Pompey clearly echoes Lucan's own criticism at the beginning of the epic. "Fortune has spared one of three tyrants," scolds Cato (9.265–266), and repeats Lucan's assessment of the triumvirate as precisely three tyrants, *tres domini,* at 1.85. The Parthian murder of Crassus is recalled as a favor. And Cato also reminds these troops that Pompey too sought to rule Rome in the event of his victory: this is the Pompey Lucan knew in book 1, before he was to claim with partisan fervor (and error) at Dyracchium that had Pompey followed up on his victory—had he had the ruthlessness of a Sulla—Rome would have been *free* of kings, master of herself (6.301–303). The poet of the poem's opening, and Cato throughout, know Pompey for a man who wants power; yet the narrator's increasingly partisan voice says otherwise.[27]

That the narrator has taken up Pompey's banner seems beyond doubt. The question we ask ourselves is why, and especially why in this fashion. Lucan has proved himself perfectly capable of historical distortion; why not produce a Pompey whose banner we too could take up? Why invent the Parthian episode, why not alter the slant at Ilerda, why make Pompey so unadmirable and yet resolutely refuse to acknowledge the character's weaknesses? As Masters (1994: 159–160) well points out,

> There is a difference between recognizing passionate commitment to a political ideal, and being persuaded oneself of that ideal . . . Lucan runs a very real risk of alienating his reader, either by apparently being swept off in a frenzy of fanaticism to which the reader may not necessarily assent, or by alerting the reader to the fact that she or he is being so obviously manipulated—so explicitly appealed to as if by an author who has an axe to grind and a case to plead.

On the other hand, most of the critical responses to this change in the narrator's stance, such as Nisard's, manage to stay clear of the unease that Lucan's endorsement must arouse in the reader by choosing to read the poem instead as simply an erratic and badly executed apologia for Pompey[28] or by taking an ambiguous stance toward the change in the first place. Charles Martindale (1984: 69–70) fudges nicely:

> There is . . . no fundamental change in the treatment of the three main characters . . . There is a stronger case to be made for a change in the conception of the character of Pompey, who is certainly more sympathetically presented later in the poem. But in fact throughout Pompey displays a mixture of good qualities and weaknesses (even in book 8 he thinks of enlisting the support of the Parthians).

What exactly does this mean? The critic seems to want to have it both ways: there is no change, there is change, there is no change. Others are more forthright in declaring the narrator's stance as simply ambivalent throughout the poem, with no detectable change in one direction or another.[29] Robert Schröter (1975: 101) has gone so far as to suggest that Pompey as we have him is actually a composite, a figure who carries out four different poetic functions, not particularly well integrated by Lucan: he is Caesar's rival for absolute power, the leader of the republican party, a sympathetic and tragic figure, and a traditional epic hero. But once again, this view does not account for the clear change in the author's bias; instead of being a jumble of functions (unless one function comes to predominate) or a continuous mixture of good and bad, *something* is happening to the figure of Pompey in this epic.

On the other hand, we cannot accept the view, originated by Berthe Marti (1945), that Pompey represents a man making steady progess on the road to wisdom and self-knowledge (Stoic, as per Marti, or otherwise), and finally attains this pinnacle at the moment of his death.[30] Thus at the beginning of the poem he is the Pompey we have limned above (p. 368):

> In books one and two, blinded by excess of ambition, Pompey joins the wicked compact which will deprive Rome of freedom (1.87) and aims at increasing his power. He dreads the prospect of an equal (1.126), and his jealous resentment of Caesar's exploits urges him, in spite of his declining years, to enter the conflict. Filled with a vanity which knows no bounds, he courts reputation, is lavish to the common people, and is swayed by popularity (1.132) . . . Moreover, because he has always been fortunate, he lacks determination and vigor in time of danger and flees Rome at the approach of Caesar (1.522).

But soon enough he is making giant steps toward (specifically Stoic) improvement, struggling to rid his mind of the fear of death and acquiring "dignity and a measure of humility" (there is no evidence of this in the text Marti [p. 389] cites, namely 5.44 ff.). The faults we have seen above are reduced to mere "traces of his former guilt," his *devotio* is taken at face value, and by the time he dies he is resolute in the face of destiny: "Though fully aware of the fact that Heaven is now against him, he feels no rebellion." The problem is that this reading ignores all the problems in the text: Magnus' ambition is alive and strong when he proposes enrolling the Parthians on his side, he *is* scared of death as he flees through Thessaly at the beginning of book 8, his dying words *are* a defiant response to fate ("sum tamen, o superi felix, nullique potestas / hoc auferre deo," 8.630–631), and Cato considers him a would-be tyrant even after his death. Marti ignores most of these details; those she does account for are labeled temporary "relapses." Nor is it at all clear that the poem's underlying structure is informed by Lucan's Stoicism, as Marti has to assume to make sense of Pompey's own progress;[31] but here, too, she has elided the problems, so that when Lucan seems to "lose sight" of fate's ultimate providence, these lines are not characteristic of the poet's real thought, but merely "rhetorical" outbursts representative of "passing moods" (pp. 356–357). We find a similar approach in the other proponents of the *proficiens* theory.[32] E. Narducci (1979: 129), for example, dismisses the debate over appealing to the Parthians as evidence of *Lucan's* weakness for including declamatory topics, and argues that Pompey's concern with future fame at the moment of his death reflects a "different kind of *fama*" (p. 128);[33] M. Rambaud (1955), G. Conte (1968), and R. Lounsbury (1976) see all of book 7 as a huge exoneration of Pompey's responsibility for losing the war but don't ask why this attempt at exoneration is abandoned in later episodes (and, as Brisset [1964, 120] points out, the claim that Pompey *had* to yield to Cicero's urgings that the battle begin is false);[34] and no one asks why Lucan, that master tailor of history's fabric, includes so much negative information about his apparent hero.[35]

Other proponents of a change in Lucan's attitude toward Pompey avoid the question of Stoic progress as the motivational force behind Pompey's "improvement," and thus open up the possibility that the change is not so much in the *character* Pompey as in the narrator's stance toward him. With these readings I have more sympathy, though not with their explanations of the sources of the change. Most notably, Vivian Holliday (1969)[36] has actually suggested that Lucan's inconsistencies can be attributed to his reliance on Cicero's correspondence of 54–49 B.C.; as Cicero fluctuated, so too did Lucan. The neutral correspondence from 54 to 51, then, accounts for his non-partisan attitude in the first three books,[37] while the favorable tone of the letters of 51–49, in which Cicero declares allegiance to Pompey as the leader of the Senate, have influenced the more positive portrayal of the later books of the *Civil War* (pp. 51–52).[38] But there are several problems here. For one, Holliday's argument would mean that Lucan was blindly copying the fluctuations of Cicero's own opinion of Pompey over a period of several years—so that for both the *Bellum Civile* and Cicero's correspondence, "the attitudes toward Pompey and Caesar progress from an almost non-partisan point of view to a Pompeian bias" (p. 52; because both see Pompey more and more as identifiable with the cause of the Senate). Second, why would Lucan pick 54 B.C. as the date for the beginning of his borrowings? As early as 59, Cicero was calling Pompey "nostri amores" (*Att.* 2.19.2); are we to think that Lucan chose to start his reading at a more cynical point in the two men's relationship, hence the (randomly) nonpartisan nature of the first books?[39] And finally, Cicero's stance on Pompey does not show the kind of development Holliday suggests. Cicero reverts to his criticism of Pompey's faults early in the correspondence of 49 (see *Att.* 7.21, dated to February of that year). Soon enough he moves from complaining about Pompey's tactics and personality (Pompey has betrayed his allies and abandoned his country, *Att.* 8.7) to questioning his very aims: Pompey too is a would-be tyrant, chasing after Sulla's kind of power ("genus illud Sullani regni iam pridem appetitur"):[40] as much as Caesar, he wants to be king. *Att.* 9.14 and 10.4 are equally open-eyed to Pompey's ambitions and his cruelty. And to clinch the Sullan comparison,[41] we read in *Att.* 10.7.1 that Pompey will use his victory as Sulla did, that is, as brutally as possible—with a proscription ("Sullano more exemploque vincet").[42]

Significantly, the Sullan comparison recurs throughout the *Civil War*: on Curio and Caesar's lips, to be sure, but also in the laments of the citizens of Rome, in Cato's eulogy, and in Pompey's *estimation of himself* as "luckier than Sulla."[43] And when he flees through Thessaly, we are told he curses the "Sullan acts of his youth" (8.25). But not so for the partisan narrator, who apostrophizes Rome in book 6 to *deny* the analogy (if Sulla instead of Pompey had been at Dyracchium, his brutality against his own countrymen would have ensured a quick end to civil war, 6.303). We can explain this situation better with an emphasis other than Holliday's: Lucan repeated in his poem the anti-Pompeian criticism of his predecessors, but chose to reject them only in his voice as partisan narrator, thus reminding us of their existence and dissociating himself from them as narrator simultaneously. *We are not allowed to forget the Pompey of the early books.* (Nor could some of Lucan's contemporaries: as Seneca put it, Pompey's and Caesar's troops were fighting, "non an servirent, sed utri," *De ben.* 2.20.2).[44]

Finally, the biographical solution. The remaining subscribers to a change in Lucan's attitude toward Pompey generally turn to Lucan's life for an answer, and here the conventional wisdom is that a quarrel between Lucan and Nero soured the former on the latter and spurred him to adopt an increasingly pro-Pompeian and anti-Julio-Claudian point of view.[45] This is not the place for an exhaustive critique of the scholarship on Lucan's life, a pointless attempt in any case given the unreliability of the ancient *Lives* and our uncertainty over even the simplest problems of dating (when were Lucan's magistracies, a sign of continued good favor? When did the quarrel take place? When were the different books of the *Bellum Civile* recited and/or published?). But insofar as the life has been said to inform the book, an approximate consensus of critical opinions supplies us with the following scenario.[46] Sometime after his flattering performance at the Neronia of 60 A.D., and probably soon after his quaestorship (his assumption of which is tentatively dated to December 62), the young M. Annaeus Lucanus fell out of the imperial favor. He may have caused offense through one or another of his literary productions, possibly even through the early part of the *Civil War*. In any case his response to Nero's punitive ban on further publications (according to this solution) was to change the tenor of the epic, which was already complete up to three books and possibly up to 6, by showering favor upon Pompey and ranting about the oppressive regime whose head he had praised in book 1. At the end, almost as if convinced by his own partisan rhetoric, and despite the fact that Nero, once toppled, would merely be replaced by another emperor, he signed up with the Pisonian conspiracy late in 64 A.D. and was eventually exposed and forced to commit suicide with his co-conspirators in 65.[47]

From this makeshift life different readers have drawn what they pleased, usually assigning the change in Lucan's political stance to the moment of his quarrel with Nero, dated in turn to after the publication of the first three books and the ban on further poeticizing and/or legal practice.[48] Hence the metamorphosis in Pompey's fortunes, as the poet embraces him out of pique with his erstwhile friend and patron. It is of course a highly speculative conclusion; but even if we accept it, the same problems remain to plague us. Why such a clumsily executed transfiguration? Why hints of favor to Pompey beginning in book 2, and an episode that makes Caesar look good in book 4? Worse still, why does Cato dub Pompey's decapitation a gift in book 9? And why is the narrator's partisanship consistently *de trop*, so that his catasterized hero makes us snicker even when we've been told we will react quite otherwise? The truly informative details to emerge from the attempts at biography are, to my mind, only two: first, the fact of Lucan's participation in the conspiracy, *for whatever reason*, which is attested to by every single historical source on the poet; and second, the apparently puzzling information that restoration of the Republic was never the driving force behind the conspiracy in the first place, suggested by Tacitus' comment that one M. Julius Vestinius Atticus was excluded from its ranks precisely because he suffered from delusions of *libertas*.[49] For here return the two most striking features of the *Bellum Civile* itself: its furious partiality in favor of the old Republic (this is no poem in favor of *any domini*, Stoic *rex* or not) and the impossibility of justifying that very partiality.[50]

All these readings alike elide two crucial and simultaneously present facts: (1) Pompey *is* presented in an improving light, and we *are* told to favor him; and (2) the poet makes it almost impossible for us the readers (and, loosely speaking, for Cato the character) to accede to this new view.[51] And not only us. The poet's opinion was shared by at least some of his contemporaries and other writers on the civil war, whose view of Pompey in no way attributed to him a nobler motivation as the war continued. None of these treatments of the "problem" of Pompey have taken the step of attributing the narrator's transformation to a deliberate tactic of the writing, thinking poet, who has set *himself* up as a character in the poem as well—the impassioned voice that intervenes to praise Pompey and condemn his foes, the voice that wants to carry his remains back to Italy, the voice that wishes it were still possible to fight. The only way to explain the transformation in the narrator's attitude toward Pompey, surrounded as it is by further signs of Pompey's nonheroic status, is to understand this transformation as an enactment of a change in the one character readers have the greatest difficulty separating from the poet himself, and that is the figure of the teller of the story, the narrator of civil war. These are our two Lucans: the despairing cynic, the man whose text destructs bodies and language and seems to preach a philosophy of meaninglessness, nihilism, detachment, and refusal-to-choose; and the narrator who comes to enact a wild partisanship, frothing in gushy pathos over the figure of Pompey even as he leaves behind his doubting audience whom he all but orders to follow in his path. Understanding this poem necessitates grasping the internal rift that has made the epic *so difficult to reconcile to itself*—the rift that has given rise to ideological readings of the poem as an impassioned defense of the Republic's last hero *and* to deconstructionist readings of the poem as a self-destroying artifact.

Jamie Masters' recent essay in *Reflections of Nero,* coming on the heels of his suggestion of the poet's "fractured voice" in the 1992 study *Poetry and Civil War in Lucan's Bellum Civile,* is the only account I have seen that acknowledges this crux of Lucanian interpretation, the fault line that runs down the center of this poem and forces the elision of one or another of the two main interpretations. It does so by coming squarely to grips with the problem of Pompey, with our inability to side with the narrator's voice only. For Masters, "explicit authorial approval of Pompey is not hard to find ... but this is so often qualified, undercut by irony, or simply contradicted, that it is hard to come away from the poem without having felt its deep ambivalence about Caesar's great rival" (1992: 152). His comments on the striking prediction at 7.205–213 are to the point (p. 162):

> We cannot fail to recognize here the white heat of pro-Pompeian ardor; but in recognizing, precisely in recognizing, we cannot fail to disbelieve. It is all too much; it is all too blatant; and it all too obviously runs itself aground. And so what we are left with is a choice: either Lucan, as a propagandist, is extraordinarily inept, and has a monumentally unrealistic conception of just how much a reader's intelligence can be insulted; or he never intended that his "case" should convince anyone.

But while Masters endorses the latter view, he suggests as the answer to the puzzle that Lucan's stance is a pose he adopts but does not endorse. Lucan's poem is to be taken as "a *reductio ad absurdum* of politically committed writing," an illustration of the malleability of history, and possibly a showcase for imperial tolerance (pp. 168 ff.). In the new atmosphere of literary freedom under Nero, in other words, Lucan's purpose was to show that "even full-blooded anti-Caesarian hysteria" would not draw the emperor's censure.

Masters' thesis hovers close to the truth, but I think it falls short in the end. For one, it cannot throw illumination on Lucan's final (and fatal) act of partisanship, his participation in the conspiracy against Nero. Second, it reduces the whole poem, the years of effort that went into it, to the level of an educated prank: "The response of the 'intelligent reader' to Lucan's political tub-thumping is to be amused by it" (1994: 168). More, it does not explore the distinction between the narrator's own voice and the other, more critical, voices of the poem. And most of all, I would suggest that Masters goes too far in privileging one voice—the Lucan of "furious partiality"—and too far in eliding the other—the nihilist deconstructor of systems.[52] Instead of following him all the way to his conclusions, then, I want to continue to search for a different explanation of the strange facts of the *Civil War* even as I acknowledge the validity and importance of his main point. The strangest fact of all, that the narrator chooses to believe in and to justify one of the two protagonists in a context in which belief and justification have both been rendered futile, is the striking development that makes the *Bellum Civile* more than it seems to be—more than a clumsy justification of a tarnished figure-head, more than a hopeless wail into the oppressive darkness of the Empire, and more than a long and elaborate joke about political rhetoric. Why Lucan chose to juxtapose these two very different attitudes toward the potential for meaningful involvement in politics—or at least, the potential for meaning even to exist in ideological issues—within the confines of one poem, is the question that remains to be answered.

Before we advance any further along this line of thought, however, there is some fine-tuning to be done. In the course of this chapter I have referred many times to the figure of the narrator, distinguishing him from the Lucan who wrote the poem but (so far) not spelling out the terms upon which this distinction can be made. It relies in fact upon a striking innovation in epic narrative: the development of the narrator into the semblance of a character himself. This is the effect of Lucan's unparalleled use of apostrophe throughout the poem, which repeatedly brings the narrator's own concerns and reactions before the reader's eyes—and this to a degree that has (as usual) brought down upon his head accusations of un-Vergilian excess and empty glee in all things exclamatory;[53] as Martindale (1993: 67) puts it, "Lucan's 'bad taste' is frequently illustrated by his 'over-use,' or 'abuse,' of the apostrophe . . . which becomes a sort of master-trope within the *Pharsalia,* and which can arouse considerable embarrassment in his modern interpreters."[54] Consequently, few critics have delved into why the narrator might figure so largely in his own poem, aside from his purportedly hamstrung sense of self-control or the presence of a stylistic tic picked up from declamatory practice; at best, apostrophe is seen as a way of generating pathos, a call to the reader's emotions.[55] Thus its purpose is "both to move and to teach, and to do so by shifting the attention of the audience, establishing a diversion through which the speaker guides the response of the listener. The speaker pretends to feel, for example, anger, fear, or sympathy, in order that through himself his audience may confront ... these same emotions."[56] And yet it seems clear that in Lucan's case at least, the narrator's frequent interventions in the text of his poem, his expressions of horror and hope, even the furious quality of his falls into cynicism, function to provide a readerly handle on the character he constructs, and in a way that is unmediated by the filter of epic events: if the narrative seems sometimes dispassionate and critical, a mirror on the empty war of words and bodies, and sometimes less detached, as during Pompey's death scene and Cornelia's reaction to the grisly sight, the narrator's apostrophic outcries at least can leave no doubt about their author's perspective upon the events he is describing for us.

The poet addresses everything: men, gods, Fortune and the Fates, but also cities and countries, rivers and mountains.[57] The extensiveness of this tendency to apostrophize has led some critics to suppose that the motivating force behind his reliance on apostrophe in general is merely metrical: a convenient short foot here and there to keep the hexameters on schedule. It is true enough that not all the apostrophes are clearly motivated, although there is no reason to argue that metrical exigencies cannot go hand in hand with a desire to sustain the illusion of narratorial participation at metrically convenient moments. But in any case the argument from meter has been analyzed and overturned by J. Endt's careful study of Lucan's prosody (especially the poet's choice and placement of vocative forms, often with no metrical convenience).[58] Indeed it is clearly inadequate in the face of the barrage of narratorial apostrophizing in this poem: Lucan's apostrophes can extend over five lines and, intermittently, over entire scenes of particular import; and, as we have seen, he often relies on such addresses to counteract the impression provided by the text. Such is the effect of the strange juxtaposition of the end of book 7 and the beginning of 8, for example: after the narrator first addresses his defeated hero and praises his courage and equanimity as he leaves the battlefield (7.681–691), we see a terrified Pompey jumping at the sound of the wind in the trees (8.1 ff.).[59]

Nor does the argument from meter do anything to explain those interventions in which the narrator simply steps in to comment on events in his own person, reporting on the future consequences of the disastrous developments that led to Pharsalus or staunchly claiming that the battle between Caesar and *libertas* will go on forever. Here, too, he emerges from the fabric of his epic as an impassioned, angry, and not always despondent member of the Roman aristocracy, lamenting the destruction of the old order and its values and denouncing the abuses of power that led to civil war.[60] Even his skepticism about the existence of the gods in so awful a world does not stop him from reviling them for their faults; so strong is his *indignatio* when he turns to them or to Fortuna that once again no precedents can be found for the harshness of his language,[61] and indeed all attempts to claim Lucan himself for the Stoic school of thought are hard pressed to explain his far from complacent attitude about divine benevolence.[62] Our overwhelming impression of the narrator as active participator and impassioned character[63] is further strengthened by the device Berthe Marti (1975: 86–87) singles out as unique in Latin epic: "the interruption of the narrative by an anonymous *persona* whose voice expresses sentiments identical with those of the author but who, unlike him, is totally ignorant of the future"—as if the narrator were so swept up in past events that they become for him virtually real, reversing the irrevocability of what has already come to pass.[64] The narrator is here like his readers, who he believes will produce *peritura vota* as they peruse his text;[65] in the words of John Henderson (1987: 135–136):

The narrator attacks his (traditionally omniscient) epic Muse author-ity, putting you, his readers, into the frame with incessant apostrophe, persistently figuring as the Neronian Lucan who rages at his heritage of Caesarian subjection but also inventing a(n anonymously limited-consciousness) voice which *lives* the drama of the narrative, in igno-rance of its eventualities . . . the *perverse* narrator forces you toward intervention.

Lucan's reliance on apostrophe, then, innovates in three areas: the unprecedented frequency of these interventions of the narratorial voice; the violence of the emotions to which the narrator gives ex-pression, often encompassing hatred and disgust;[66] and his apparent mixture of blindness and foreknowledge where the epic's future events—and indeed its future reception—are concerned. I shall have more to say on the importance of these innovations at the close of this chapter. Here, however, I will be concerned almost entirely with what the narrator has to say to Caesar and Pompey, and what he says about them when addressing other characters in his poem;[67] as we might have guessed by now, the figure of the narrator never ex-changes his hate for the one with his love of the other, even when (as we have seen) the events that unravel before us provide little support for his views.[68] He first speaks of them in the same breath, when he ascribes to each the reasons for their ambition (1.121–124); but from here on, the addresses to Pompey increase in number in a tragic crescendo to the battle at Pharsalus and maintain their fevered pitch to the end of the epic, while Caesar comes into focus more intermittently, and eventually as the object of the narrator's bilious denunciations.[69] Already in book 4, the narrator steps in to lament the fact that Caesar's conduct at Ilerda has rendered him morally superior to his rival—"what a stroke of good luck for you," he notes dryly (not "what genuinely good behavior"; 4.254–259). By the time of the mutiny in book 5 the narrator has become harsher still, asking Caesar why he never sickens of bloodshed, why he rushes on through right and wrong alike (5.310–316). But the nastiest attacks come with Pharsalus, when Caesar is scourged for treading on corpses and refusing a pyre to the decaying dead (7.721–723, 7.803–824), and with the present of Pompey's head to a Caesar shedding crocodile tears in book 9 (1046–63). And then there are the references to Caesar's longed-for assassination: at Pharsalus, the narrator turns to Brutus and gloats over the prospect of Caesar's death at his hands (7.586–596); in Egypt, he pleads with fate not to let Caesar's head leave his shoulders without Brutus' intervention (10.341–342).

Pompey, however, emerges in glowing colors; such glowing colors that it becomes difficult for readers to quite swallow his canonization. As he flees Italy and takes to the open sea, the narrator laments his undeserved fall: indeed, the gods specifically granted his death abroad, that terrible *nefas,* out of mercy to Italy (2.725–734). He loved Caesar; nothing is said about the reverse (5.472–475). As for his failure to follow up his success at Dyrrachium, the narrator intervenes to put it down to Pompey's *pietas,* not to his ineptitude: "It pains me and will always pain me," he complains to Caesar, "that your worst crime has been an aid to you: namely, that you fought with a pious son-in-law" (6.303–305). And the climax to these addresses comes, of course, with the famous lines I cited earlier in which the narrator turns to *us* in his anxiety that we, as future readers, should favor his hero Pompey. The lines are unique (7.207–213):

> Among later peoples too and generations to come, these events (whether their own fame will carry them into the future, or whether my vigilant work too can help great names), when they read of these wars, will provoke both hope and fear, and prayers unheard; and all will peruse your fate breathlessly, as if it were still to come, not past; and still they will side with you, Magnus.

Now Vergil too steps in as narrator to assure poetic fame to his characters Nisus and Euryalus at *Aeneid* 9.446–449, the closest passage to Lucan's above.[70] But even this address, the famous *fortunati ambo,* fails as parallel: Vergil's narrator gives no mandate to his readers, he makes no performative attempt to *tell* them whom they will favor—even as we cannot fail to be affected by the supremely moving text. But the narrator of the *Civil War* is eager to push us to a choice we may not care to make. And from here on he remains at the highest pitch of pro-Pompeian emotion.[71] After his rendition of the brave flight from Pharsalus and Pompey's tragic death, he wishes Rome would bid him unearth Pompey's bones from their humble grave and carry them to Italy (8.842 ff.), and he has the harshest of words for Ptolemy and the "sacrilegious hands" (8.551–552) that dared to probe Pompey's guts—"*our* guts," he says—with the sword. Our narrator even moves toward the deification of his hero as some kind of demigod, suggesting to Magnus that his grave will take precedence over a local shrine of Jupiter (8.846–872; the catasterism follows at the beginning of the next book),[72] describing Achillas' death as "an offering to your shade, Magnus" (10.524–526).

Such is the narrator's stance toward the two rivals. Nowhere here do we find the ambiguities that step in to close the gap between their moral standing in the text: Pompey, next to godliness, is driven not by lust for the throne of Rome but by love of his country and his wife; demonic Caesar cackles over the carnage on the battlefield and has the sickening temerity to weep over his enemy's head. The narrator has no reservations; only we, and Cato, do.

Where, then, does this chapter leave us? For the present, with a conundrum. In a poem in which the selection of any side in civil war is regularly presented as *nefas,* the narrator sides with Pompey, and does so with a vengeance. In a text that draws great attention to its capacity to self-deconstruct, knit as it is in language that is obsessed with the reduction of meaning to senselessness, bold ethical judgments are made that show no anxiety about their own vulnerability to moral relativism and inversion. Pompey is *pius,* his character embodies *virtus,* his murder is a *scelus*—precisely the terms that Lucan's epic has taken such pains to empty out, to bitterly overturn. And in a world in which prophecy sees only death, the future is known slavery, and the gods are long since gone, the narrator still hopes to render his hero divine, foresees worship at his shrine, and proclaims the eternal struggle between tyranny and freedom (7.695).[73]

All these contradictions are crystallized in the figure of Pompey, the catalyst for the narrator's rejection of paralysis and his movement toward choice. If we focus on his treatment in the text, we find that civil war is not here the kind of stasis that produces paralysis but the enabling background to impassioned ideological belief and the near-worship of a Roman who is, historically, as tarnished as his peers.[74] Lucan the narrator goes against the dark vision of his own poem— a poem that emerges from recent criticism as a black hole sucking in all hope and meaning—and deliberately picks a belief, a hero, a vision *untouched by the poem's pervasive cynicism* even though he bungles, loses his head, and the war. And yet this is not simple hero worship: the body of the poem makes sure of that. The narrator's rendition of a Pompey to believe in is not so easy for us too to endorse, and in defending this vision he presents us with an apparently skewed point of view that is more likely to alienate readers than carry them along on the tide of belief. Lucan, in other words, presents us with an interpretive challenge, with work to be done in synthesizing the narrator's perspective and the conflicting conclusions we might draw from his text. We are simply not allowed to remain comfortable with either view for long; neither predominates; we do not know what to make of this protean Pompey. Why?

More: in defending Pompey, and in his impassioned interventions in general, the narrator gives body to himself. Instead of remaining quietly in the background, and as if rebelling against the very dissolution of the subject voice we examined in Chapter 1, the narrator steps in to enact an outraged Roman reacting to the collapse of his Republic and the indignities that this collapse has meant for him and his kind. As Gordon Williams (1978: 291) would have it, "Lucan's personality intrudes more and more as he realizes less and less escapably the logical impossibility of compromise with any aspect of Caesarism." I have been arguing that Lucan is in fact hostile to Caesar and his line from the beginning; but his personality does seem to loom increasingly large as his addresses to his favorite increase in number and intensity. His "I" comes to pervade the poem, refusing to be quiet under a regime that *he* claims has rendered him a slave (7.640–645) and forced him to take refuge in false words of praise; that age may have invented "all the terms with which for so long now we have been lying to our masters" (5.385–386), but Julius Caesar seems to benefit little from this polite circumspection when the narrator has cause to address him. Lucan judges the world of the civil war as if the old ethical terminology had never done service for the imperial propaganda machine; certainly, *his* juridical and moral identity does not seem to feel the strain of his times, nor do his scenes of gruesome dismemberment ever give him cause to question the nature of his own personhood. The malaises of state and body in the *Civil War*, far from muddying the subject ego of the narrator himself, merely establish a backdrop against which his voice emerges strident and unwavering. So while we might agree that the vivid quality of this poem's apostrophic intermissions invites a conspiracy of the readers' own feelings, heightens their involvement and their sympathy, we would have to argue that apostrophe in the *Civil War* does far more than that: the narrator's unusually invasive presence is perforce a creating of a powerful and uncompromised subject, an ego that will *not* go quietly into the dark night.

Jonathan Culler has remarked (1981: 149) that "nothing need happen in an apostrophic poem ... Nothing need happen because the poem itself is to be the happening." I suggest that here it is the narrator that is the happening, the product of his own voice.[75] In this poem whose subject matter and style seem to assault the integrity of the human subject and question the possibility of its existence under conditions of civil war and the subsequent tyranny, the shape of the narrator's personality strongly emerges to give the lie to the collapse of individuality. How this is connected to Pompey's transformation and the meeting of ideology and cynicism will be for the next two chapters to elucidate.

FOUR

❀

The Will to Believe

To realize the relative validity of one's convictions and yet stand for them unflinchingly, is what separates a civilized man from a barbarian.

—*Joseph Schumpeter*

THE PHILOSOPHER Richard Rorty provides us with a term we can put to good use as we try to understand the conflicting ideological stances—the cynical detachment and the intense involvement—of Lucan's *Civil War*. Among Rorty's concerns has been to examine the experience of believing in an ideal while accepting the contingency of that ideal, its nature as pure construct, as a fabrication to fit our needs. Much of his argument in his recent work *Contingency, Irony, Solidarity* grapples with the particular problem faced by members of our own postmodern society who have come to terms *intellectually* with the nonexistence of God, the historicity of supposedly transcendent value systems, and the absence of moral absolutes to live by; who believe these lacks truly define the human condition; and yet who simultaneously believe in the worth of a life ruled by the very values they accept as the productions of a particular time, place, and people, and continue to live their own lives accordingly. Religious and moral truths are dead truths for such people, but they choose not to live (or cannot live) according to their own knowledge of this condition; life is not livable without the ethical edifices of which we acknowledge man as the architect. Rorty (1989: x) calls such people—

among whom he evidently numbers himself—"moral ironists": for him, an ironist is "the sort of person who faces up to the contingency of his or her own most central beliefs and desires—someone sufficiently historicist and nominalist to have abandoned the idea that those central beliefs and desires refer back to something beyond the reach of time and chance"; *moral* ironists are those of us who apply this knowledge to our moral beliefs and desires in particular.[1] We recognize that "anything can be made to look good or bad by being redescribed," we renounce "all attempts to formulate criteria of choice between final vocabularies," or the vocabularies with which we justify our beliefs and our lives; and, most important, we simultaneously have a vocabulary with which we justify our actions and beliefs, have doubts about the worth of that final vocabulary, and realize that any argument phrased in this vocabulary cannot resolve these doubts (p. 73).[2]

A good way of describing Lucan, at least as the author of the *Civil War*, is as a *political* ironist. His narrator lays claims to beliefs that the body of the epic exposes as constructs, and yet these two perspectives live on side by side. He devotes his immense skill as writer to composing an epic that painstakingly dismantles the linguistic media upon which it relies, applying to this task all his arsenal of paradox, oxymoron, and syntactic inversion, and yet he unselfconsciously uses the very terminology he has deconstructed as he praises what is ethical and condemns what is evil.[3] Most strikingly, he flaunts his ideological engagement and investment in the figure of Pompey, whom he has resurrected as the pious protector of the dying Republic, even as he continues to write an epic in which Pompey fares ill indeed as material for a hero.[4] Where Rorty suggests the coexistence of ethical commitment and ethical ironism as the unlikely bedmates of the modern intellectual, Lucan instead seems to enact the coexistence of political cynicism and despair with political commitment and fervor even in the face of the deadlock of upper-class myths of power lost. His startling juxtaposition of these two perspectives in one text necessarily wreaks havoc with critical attempts to make sense of the poem. And the solution to this startling clash is to find the poem's meaning not in the one message or the other, but in our ability to grasp the coexistence of the two as an illustration, for their writer, of the paradox intrinsic to giving meaning to human existence (at least for a few) in the first century A.D.

The poet's two versions of himself, then, equated as they are in one textual mirror with the events of his prehistory, set up a paradox not so dissimilar to the other juxtaposed opposites that make up the poem's fabric: just as the narrator can take sides when no sides can be taken, just as he can pray for a different outcome when the outcome has long since come and gone, so too he can urge us to continue a struggle that he elsewhere seems to regard as over and done—and in any case hopeless. But I want to be careful to distinguish this analysis from the suggestion that Lucan's *Civil War* consciously puts on display a fractured narratorial self, a voice with which Lucan's persona imitates the schizophrenic split in authority that is characteristic of civil war. Once again, this is the position of Jamie Masters, whose argument is that "the inexplicable disparity of authorial 'point of view' " effects a fracturing of the narrating voice that is the result of the narrator's "mimicry of civil war, of divided unity, *concordia discors*" (1992: 87–90). As one of the only accounts that acknowledges, rather than erases or excuses, the undeniable rift down the center of the poem, Masters' valuable discussion well demonstrates the interpretive payback of accepting the poem in its full complexity.[5] But I nonetheless disagree with his interesting conclusion, precisely because it cannot account for the uneven emphasis that the text accords the narrator's wish to believe in a Pompeian ideal over and against the ways in which Masters sees him siding with Caesar and his deadly efficacy; and because it must elide, in the end, the real Lucan's final choice of anti-Caesarian action through his participation in the Pisonian conspiracy.[6]

Combine the two Lucans, the cynic and the idealist, and you get the composite figure who stands behind the contradictions of the *Civil War*: a man who seems to believe that the criteria for making political decisions have become irrevocably tarnished, just like the political vocabulary in which they are couched, but who *chooses* to believe in them and to act nevertheless. The author of the *Civil War,* like an atheist who prays despite himself for forgiveness for his views, lives in a universe in which such paradoxes are possible, even necessary, if its inhabitants want to derive any meaning from the dark possibilities voiced by Lucan's poem. Better to pick a side, write its defense, choose an ideology, create your beliefs, than to disappear into the still maw of dissolving identities and self-consuming language. Carlin Barton is not far from making the same point in her strikingly original exploration of the different "universes" of the *Civil War's* author; for her, too, there are two Lucans, one living in a "curable" world in which hope and expiation are possible, the other damned to the black, incurable world of despair with which critics like Ralph Johnson have made us so familiar.[7] For Barton, too, Lucan's epic is the expression of "the existence of simultaneously functioning distinct and irreconcilable thought patterns, all of which are equally 'true' and/or 'untrue' " (1984: 120).[8] And in the end,

> for Lucan, like Orwell, confrontation had more of hope in it than compromise. And by not holding back, not restraining himself Lucan objectifies, concretizes "the other" both for good and for bad. When one does not restrain oneself opposition is sensed as a reality. Thus Lucan, in the course of his poem and his life, increasingly identifies an external source of evil . . . Lucan settles his loyalties in the course of writing; he becomes a partisan in the course of writing . . . *Lucan may have . . . an unassailably detached appreciation of the weaknesses and "guilt" of both Pompey and Caesar but this did not prevent him . . . from "taking sides."* (1984: 276; my emphasis)

It is the poet's willful identification of an external (and containable) source of evil that shapes his narrator's character into Pompey's defender; it is his "unassailably detached appreciation" of the two men's mutual guilt that maintains a certain distance from the two up to the end. Since neither view can survive on its own—one is a counsel of self-delusion, the other a counsel of despair—they live in their own *concordia discors.*

Now, in using *Contingency, Irony, Solidarity* as a springboard for discussing the contradictions that emerge from the *Civil War,* and in terming Lucan's paradox that of a "political ironist," I certainly do not mean to draw parallels between the position of modern liberals in the academy (for we should not mistake the particular milieu of Rorty's ironists) and a disillusioned member of the Roman aristocracy almost two thousand years ago.[9] The coexistence of mutually exclusive perspectives, the enactment of a political "will to believe"— if I may make yet another analogy—is unique neither to our century nor to Lucan's.[10] Even as a layperson of philosophy it seems to me worth remarking that similar perspectives are well known to previous centuries—at the very least, in William James's famous essays in *The Will to Believe* and Blaise Pascal's "wager" on the existence of God; and, more recently, in Richard Rorty's work and, in a political rather than a religious context, in the writings of Slavoj Zizek. James's two essays "The Will to Believe" and "Is Life Worth Living?" essentially provide an apologia for religious belief that defends the choice of belief in the face of inadequate evidence. His view shares with Pascal's wager the paradox that it would have us make a deliberate choice in favor of transcendent values although such values are normally based on blind faith rather than on deliberate choice; choice implies the ability *not* to believe, the working of a kind of rationality, and justifications for the decision that are not religious themselves. It is only once the decision, based on factors such as utility or emotional reward, has been made, that this same decision is itself proved "true" retroactively—from the standpoint of him who does have faith. As Gerald Myers (1986: 391) explains,

> It is by a decision, which then gathers reasons around itself, that we are motivated to choose one belief instead of another. When we understand that competing reasons are at a standoff, we realize that no reason activates a choice; our decision must be hoisted under its own strength.

And James himself readily acknowledged the "benefits" of such a decision: "By being faithful in my poor measure to this over-belief, I seem to myself to keep more sane and true."[11]

The paradox of a belief that proves itself true only after one has made the decision to adopt it repeats itself in the ethical as well as the religious arena; like religion, a system of ethics requires in the end a choice accompanied by commitment, and the enactment of these two actions by the individual predates the perspective they then make possible. "If, as James believed, such questions as 'why be moral?' and 'why go on living?' must be confronted before an ethical standpoint can be developed, then the whole structure of ethics depends upon resolution or commitment. The decision to be moral is better described as a decision that makes morality possible than as one that is itself moral" (Myers 1986: 389). So, too, Lucan's political ironist, for whom the move to ideological belief could not be justified on the basis of political facts—at least, not the ones with which his epic supplies us. To be sure, my analogy is checkered in not a few ways. While both writers seem to me to be aware of the compelling importance of man's *need* to believe—whether the object is religious or political—James easily avoids the intense contradiction generated in actually believing. He does so for several reasons: most importantly, because James's "will to belief" was not, according to Myers (p. 453), "the creation of a belief or the decision to believe; it was rather the deliberate choice to endorse a religious belief *already in place.*" For James, the nonexistence of God is no more likely than his existence; and subjectivity, or the subjective need to believe, is already "a blurry apprehension of objective realities" (p. 455). Thus Lucan, unlike James, could not move from the premise of the need-to-believe to the conclusion that faith is rational (ibid.).[12] But both thinkers enact to their own degrees the phenomenon I am calling "ideology in cold blood"; meaning must be *given* to human life by a conscious decision that, if necessary, is willing to shut its eyes to rational appearances. Myers (pp. 389–390) compares this stance to that of Sartre and other existentialists, for whom, too, "One must *give* life the required meaning; what is mandated is not the discovery of a missing reason but the decision to treat one's want as being satisfiable."[13]

Pascal's famous wager (fr. 418) is also worth considering here.[14] This difficult text argues not only that one *must* bet on the existence of God (for a choice has to be made, and this one has by far the greatest rewards) but also that the *enactment* of belief is crucial to the eventual formation of belief:

> You want to find faith and you do not know the road. You want to be cured of unbelief and you ask for the remedy: learn from those who were once bound like you and who now wager all they have. These are people who know the road you wish to follow, who have been cured of the affliction of which you wish to be cured: follow the way by which they began. They behaved just as if they did believe, taking holy water, having masses said, and so on. That will make you believe quite naturally, and will make you more docile [*vous abêtira*].

Here, too, belief has to be reached by nonreligious considerations, and can justify itself only in retrospect: go to church regularly because you know it will eventually make you believe (and once you do you will know you are doing the right thing—as Pascal evidently believes of himself). But Pascal, unlike Lucan, is enjoining this paradox upon others, not urging himself to follow its dictates; for him, the evidence for Christianity "is such as to exceed, or at least equal, the evidence to the contrary" (fr. 835). For Lucan as for Pascal, "man is a paradoxical creature who is both great and small, strong and weak. He is great and strong because he never gives up the demand for pure goodness and truth unmixed with baser matters; he is small and weak because he can never even draw near these values, to say nothing of attaining them" (Goldmann 1964: 196). But whereas Pascal posits the existence of these values, Lucan is willing to create them. What these two examples should set in relief is the uniqueness of Lucan's willingness to say: "There are no transcendent values; there is no hope for man and his ideals" even as he shows his own belief in human ideals.

These texts are all concerned with belief in its religious manifestations; more recent work on this kind of ironism focuses instead on political belief, the possibility of any wholehearted faith in ideological solutions to societal problems. Often harking back to Pascal, such writers suggest that here, too, the road to belief is behavior, although as Zizek (1989: 34–36, 40) cautions,

> Belief . . . is radically exterior, embodied in the practical, effective procedure of people . . . The lesson to be drawn from this concerning the social field is above all that belief, far from being an "intimate," purely mental state, is always *materialized* in our effective social activity . . . What distinguishes this Pascalian "custom" from insipid behaviorist wisdom ("the content of your belief is conditioned by your factual behavior") is the paradoxical status of a *belief before belief*: by following a custom, the subject believes without knowing it, so that the final conversion is merely a formal act by means of which we recognize what we have already believed. In other words, what the behaviorist reading of Pascalian "custom" misses is the crucial fact that the external custom is always a material support for the subject's unconscious.[15]

A belief before belief: action and conviction are collapsed so far that they become impossible to tell apart, and to carry out the motions is, in a sense, to believe. Maybe Lucan, too, was willing to collapse the two, as if by his own performance of the motions in his poem he was numbing himself, and others, to the impossibility of human ideals and just doing what had to be done. *We all create our gods: the important thing is not to let knowledge of this stop us from doing so.*

If we return from these speculations to the poem proper, we find that Lucan's Pompey is not our only test case for this hypothesis. The divine itself—although it is the Olympic pantheon rather than the Judaeo-Christian God that is at issue—likewise emerges as the ground on which the ironist can lay out his contradictory stance, enacting cynicism and belief-despite-itself in a single text. We see the same two Lucanian faces clearly in the poet's addresses to the gods, who, like Pompey, are both tarnished and necessary: the poet does not believe in their existence, and yet he is ready to curse them for their indifference to mankind.[16] He tells us that the divine is an illusion, and then addresses this illusion in his own voice. He hates the gods for not existing, and never stops to deplore this paradox. And so it is with the idea of fate. I am not interested in exploring this epic's ambiguous relationship between the role of fate, fortune, and the gods,[17] but so much is clear: that at separate times Lucan both denies and invokes the fixed rule of fate, and both denies and invokes the existence of Jupiter and the rest of the Olympic pantheon.

As many scholars have noted, the *Bellum Civile* is not the "godless epic" it has sometimes been hailed as; the gods may fail to intervene, but they are often treated as if they exist, and they are regularly the object of the prayers and laments issued by narrator and characters.[18] At the epic's opening, they loom conspicuous in their absence: The poet's question "Quis furor, o cives, quae tanta licentia ferri?" (1.8) lacks the normal invocation of a Muse for the answer and the traditional answer of divine wrath *as* that answer. For the nonce, the anger of the gods, fuel of Homer and Vergil's epics, is missing; it is the wrath of the citizens, not of any divine powers, that spurs on the poem. Yet the gods are there, creeping back into the fabric of book 1 in the guise of *superi*. Lucan tells them (37) that he has nothing to complain of, if civil war was necessary to bring us a Nero; he comments that the ocean's tides are mysterious because the gods have wished them to be so (417–419); the same gods fill the sky with portents of civil war (524–525); and the haruspex Arruns reads Jupiter's warning in the flabby liver and bloody entrails of his victim (631 ff.). And the very first line of book 2 restores us to tradition and to divinity: "And now the anger of the gods was clear to see.") The vexing issue of divine presence and absence is further complicated by a nice touch pointed out by D. C. Feeney (1991: 275): while Lucan as *vates* denies in book 1 that he needs the inspiration of Bacchus or Apollo to tell his story (63–66)—Nero is enough for his vatic efforts, for the answer to the question "quis furor, o cives, quae tanta licentia ferri" (1 ff.)—the matron later in book 1 who predicts the terrible future to come is not only compared to someone possessed by Bacchus; she is also explicitly driven into her prophetic frenzy by Apollo; and what is *her* request but "Apollo, tell me the nature of this madness that makes Romans fight Romans" (681–682). It is the same question as Lucan's, only this time the gods have returned to give the answer, as Lucan will confirm at the beginning of book 2.

The gods are often in evidence in the rest of the epic as well, both in the stories told by its characters and in episodes the poet describes for us directly. The guilty Marius is protected by their anger in book 2; when an assassin raises a sword against him, he sees "the terrible gods that punish crime" (80) and falters (a worse fate awaits the felon). The unappetizing witches of Thessaly are able to force the gods to heed their wishes with spells and herbs, although the same gods ignore the beseeching of mere mortals (6.443–444); worse, they are able to bind to their will the "reluctant deity" (6.446). Most strikingly, the narrator himself repeatedly addresses the gods in his own voice, at times naming them and explicitly asking for their help in turning aside Rome's downward trajectory. The flooding in Spain is followed by an excited prayer to Jupiter and Neptune: please wipe out the war by a tide of floodwater, the narrator begs; the failure of his request brings back the more typical cynicism ("secundi . . . veniam meruere dei," 4.122–123).[19] So disturbed is he by the course of events that he sometimes has difficulty believing just what the gods, who must be behind it, are doing: as Pompey's forces clamor for him to join forces at Pharsalus, the narrator asks in horror, "Does this please you, ye gods, when you have already decided to overthrow the world, to add guilt to our errors?" (7.58–59). And of course, here as elsewhere, he places the responsibility for Rome's downfall squarely at the gods' feet (which does not prevent him from placing it at other feet as well). Addressing Apollo too, he wonders why his oracle remains silent: "Have the gods not yet decided on so great a crime, and are so many men's dooms held back because the stars still hesitated to condemn Pompey to death?" (5.203–205).[20] And finally, he steps in at Pompey's death to decry his tomb, the crime of the gods: "Away with those stones, full of the guilt of the gods!" (8.799–800). In other words, the narrator is willing to show us a face that believes in the gods even as he blames them. Indeed, even if the gods are not such as they have been fabled, the epic offers us still other alternatives to their nonexistence; Sextus Pompeius might be right in believing that the gods exist but know nothing (6.433–434); Erictho's power might mean they are mere subordinates to powers stronger and more sinister. Or are they? The poet is not sure, and steps in to wonder, "What mutual agreement keeps them bound to her will? Is it necessary to obey, or does it please them to do so?" (6.493–495).

And yet, the same narrator who addresses these gods so passionately is ready to intimate that they do not exist. He omits them at the epic's start; he allows for gullibility in those who believe in them (3.406); and he is particularly insistent as the moment of crisis nears in book 7. Here, as the twin armies hurtle toward each other, the narrator steps in again to proclaim the delusional nature of religious belief: "Truly we have no gods; although the ages are driven along by blind chance, we lie and say that Jupiter rules" (7.445–447).[21] But as he continues his lament, his reasoning must leave his readers puzzled. If there were a God, he would intervene to prevent the battle at Pharsalus; he did not, however, intervene; this means, again, there are no gods to watch over the affairs of men. Well, we will exact our revenge on them for their nonexistence by creating our own gods: we will foist the dead and deified Caesars on them and make them their peers. In other words, our best revenge for the nonexistence of the gods will be to punish them by deifying dead emperors; the narrator simultaneously believes and disbelieves in the existence of the gods, with this paradoxical resolution as the result.[22] Nothing daunted by his own reasoning, the narrator apparently forgets that he is addressing a nonexistent phenomenon and intervenes again at the end of the book, wondering how Thessaly so offended the gods and asking them to limit guilt to this one country (7.869–870). Just so, he had intervened at the beginning of the book, asking them why they have chosen to make men guilty of Pharsalus (58–59).

The role of fate is open to the same doubt: the narrator does not know if there *is* such a thing as a fixed fate for the world, or whether everything happens by chance.[23] Even Apollo's relationship to the future as it is revealed at Delphi—or not revealed, as the case may be—is in doubt: the poet cannot say whether he creates the future or merely predicts it. But the passage that best brings out the paradox of his stance is the one in which he addresses Jupiter, who may not exist, and asks him why he chooses to reveal the future to us poor humans by portents (2.4–15):

> Why, ruler of Olympus, did you decide to add this worry to care-worn humans, that they should know through fearsome omens the disasters to come? Whether the author of the world, when (as the fire yielded) he first took up shapeless realms and crude matter, fixed for eternity the causes by which he controls all things (himself abiding by this law), and divided up the world which bears the centuries ordained by the fixed path of the fates—or whether nothing is decided but uncertain chance wanders and time and again brings change, and hazard rules mortal things—let it be sudden, whatever you plan; let the mind of men be blind to future fate; may it be allowed to the fearful to hope.

Whether Jupiter shaped the world and fixed its destiny at the beginning of time, or whether Fortune rules everything, Lucan doesn't want to know what Jupiter is planning; instead, let it be sudden, so that man can have hope and be blind to the suffering that is to come: "Liceat sperare timenti." I hardly need to point out the ironies of this passage, which addresses a possibly nonexistent deity to ask him if he exists/controls the world, or if Fortune holds the reins, and then asks the deity to hide the future either way.[24] To be sure, the question the narrator is asking here seems to echo a debate common between the Epicurean and Stoic schools, the former backing *fors incerta* as the force behind things, the latter an omniscient deity, and as such we may not be dealing with the possibility of a nonexistent Jupiter, just an unknowing and uncaring one.[25] But there are two details that suggest our poet is open to the suggestion that Jupiter himself is a cipher. First, the declaration in book 7 that there are no gods ("sunt nobis nulla profecto / numina," 7.445–446) precedes the statement that "mortal matters are a concern to no god" ("mortalia nulli / sunt curata deo," 7.454–455); in other words, a statement that could be taken as addressing divine indifference *or* nonexistence crops up in a context that suggests the latter. Second, the terms of the debate have already been set out in Figulus' speech at 1.642–644, a passage from which Jupiter is elided in favor of chance and fate:[26] "Either, he says, this world wanders through eternity bound by no law . . . or, if the fates drive it, ripe destruction is being prepared for our city and the human race" ("aut hic errat, ait, nulla cum lege per aevum / mundus . . . / aut, si fata movent, urbi generique paratur / humano matura lues"). In any case, as Donato Gagliardi (1989 at 1.642–644) comments, "Figulus' doubts mirror the poet's perplexity too." And, paradoxically, his very doubt at the beginning of book 2 is framed by the act of apostrophe that implies the speaker's belief in the existence of his addressee.[27] Feeney (1991: 281, 282–283) observes of this confusion:

> The poet enmeshes himself in the same difficulties as his characters and . . . deliberately refus[es] to stand outside his creation to provide a focus . . . A divine apparatus is capable of sustaining many ambiguities, but not this fundamental inability to decide whether the action of the poem is design or happenstance . . . If a recurrent and prominent possibility in the poem is a despairing anarchism, the poet still cannot abandon altogether the compulsion to blame the guilty gods, nor can he deprive himself of the claustrophobic sense of trapped inevitability which is provided by the language of Fate.

But more than this: Once again, the narrator *enacts* belief even as he acknowledges the lack of any grounds on which to hold that belief.[28]

My point here is that the narrator's treatment of the gods is essentially the same as his treatment of Pompey. The narrator is not the victim of a "fractured voice": that implies one side is unaware of the other, a kind of narrative schizophrenia. Nor is he the victim of a struggle without resolution.[29] On the contrary, it is crucial for the narrator's final position that the left hand know well what the right is doing; it is from the conjunction of these two, the positive and the negative, that the epic lets us damn the present and believe in it, damn the loss of ideals (political or religious) and behave as if we still possessed them.[30] It is out of this conjunction that we choose to believe, or to take action, or to pick sides, even when we believe, too, that this effort is hopeless. Lucan has double vision: the result is that he engages in ideology in cold blood, does it as a decision that knows itself for what it is. In his view of what humanity is and needs, he has to: where Pascal wagered on God, where James acknowledged our need to believe, Lucan wagers on the worth of political involvement and political beliefs, and *enacts* our need to believe in the possibility of political ideals and ideological meaning.[31]

With all the emphasis I am placing on choice and commitment, it is perhaps worth taking another look at the figure of Cato, who has so startlingly laid bare in book 2 the essential paradox of the epic. "Well I know that Pompey, too, promises himself world dominion" (321), he tells Brutus—and then signs up under his banner. He does so not to defend freedom, for freedom is already dead and Rome herself is or soon will be a lifeless body ("exanimem," 302); law and justice, for which he fights in vain, are empty now and meaningless (316). Cato aims instead to defend freedom's *name* and *empty ghost,* which he will follow to the grave ("tuumque / nomen, Libertas, et inanem prosequar umbram," 2.302–303). Cato, in other words, is fighting for an ideal that he pronounces already dead in his world.[32] He is fighting for a shadow and a name, for the shadow of a name ("magni nominis umbra," 1.135), and for a Pompey who can *represent* to mankind that which he is not. All the more convenient here that Pompey's position had been ratified by the Senate: the trappings of authenticity are all there. Indeed, in the funeral "eulogy" for the fallen leader that Cato delivers after Pompey's murder off the coast of Egypt, it is precisely this ability to be put to ideological use that he praises in its sullied host (9.202–206): "He was a name famous and revered among nations, and one which helped our city much. Real belief in liberty perished long ago, when Sulla and Marius were let into Rome; with

Pompey lost to the world, now make-believe belief has perished too." Pompey was an easel holding up the pretty picture of liberty. It was only an illusion, but that is all men need. It is all they need even if they know their belief is a sham, a *fides ficta libertatis;* since they need to believe, the appearance of liberty is enough—the *frons senatus,* the *color imperii* (9.207). It lets them continue to deceive themselves, and this deception gives their life meaning.

In fact, and given his status as a symbol rather than a reality, it is more convenient to have a dead Pompey than a living one: as Cato goes on to say, Pompey was fortunate ("O felix," 9.208) that the Egyptians forced on him the death he should have voluntarily sought—otherwise he might have been happy to keep living under Caesar's rule (211), presumably an awkward situation for those trying to put his *nomen* to good use. Cato seems to be pointing here to Pompey's most valuable asset to the state, his ability to be turned into prop for ideological belief; Pompey the hero may be a fiction, but he is a fiction with value. Or perhaps we should say he *was* a fiction with value—after all, Cato uses the past tense, and the fiction is said to be dead—except that the poem itself reenacts this "make-believe belief" and resurrects the *nomen.* After all, what the poet hopes to do in the present is precisely to be of service to *magnis nominibus*—the perfect pun for Pompey. Such a reading is well supported by Feeney (1986a: 240), who sees in the poem a gradual transformation of "the values by which [Pompey] is to be assessed," revealing to us "a process by which Pompeius does live up to his name, becoming in fact 'magnus.' " But where Feeney sees a bona fide transformation of the man that begins after Pharsalus, when Pompey can shed his past and his confining role as *dux,* I suggest that the process Feeney has put his finger on is Pompey's transformation not into a real hero but into a real *nomen*—as the development of the narrator's own response to him would seem to illustrate.[33] Hence the poem's emphasis on names and shadows. As Feeney (p. 242) notes, "he and *Libertas* are both 'umbrae,' 'nomina.' "[34] Exactly; but that is all they are. The poem itself shows us that much: Pompey's status as ideological figurehead works for the narrator, but it cannot work for us, or the point would be lost.[35]

Let us turn back to Lucan's Cato, who has made the issues so clear. Here and elsewhere it is easy to contrast his emotional state with the narrator's; indeed, the latter's inability to accept with benign imperturbability the setbacks of the Roman past hardly mark him out as an ideal Stoic, whatever the philosophical underpinnings of the natural world represented in the *Bellum Civile*. This point has already been well defended by the scholarship, so I will not dwell on it; but it is worth pointing out the peculiarity of calling "Stoic" a narrator who cannot control his rage and grief, who decries the role of the gods and their cruelty, and whose view of history seems rooted in decline.[36] While some elements of the poem's representation of the world are certainly Stoic in derivation,[37] the narrator himself does not believe in a providential fate, in any manifestation of an eternal order whose ultimate end is good.[38] The option was there for him: he refused it. As J. Adatte (1965: 238) puts it, "Lucan himself, whether through inability or consummate art, does not raise himself, or *will* not raise himself, to the level of the Stoic vision of the universe." And so Lucan may claim that Pompey's death is ennobled by his bad treatment and tiny tomb, but his anger over this fate has little of the Stoic about it;[39] he may pronounce Cato inspired by a god within him, but he has little faith in this god; and he may praise Cato for not caring what the future may bring, but he himself cares about the pain of knowing the future. Whereas Cato boldly states that the oracle can tell him nothing he does not know, and "it is not an oracle that makes me sure, but the sureness of death" (9.582–583), the narrator seems to believe in the fearsome truth-telling capacity of oracles and omens, and wishes the information men gain thereby could be vitiated altogether (2.14–15). We should not confuse the narrator's perspective on these matters with his characters'; if Cato might believe (with Seneca) that "nothing bad can happen to a good man; opposites do not mix" (*De prov.* 2.1), the idea that our narrator would endorse this optimism is almost comic. After all, even what a *bonus vir is* has been terminally put into question by civil war.

Lucan's Cato is nonetheless an unusual figure for a Stoic, most notably in his behavior in book 2. There has been much discussion of the passage in which he rejects Brutus' advice of neutrality and declares his support for the flawed Pompey, and critical opinion on Lucan's portrayal of this scene seems more or less divided down the middle on two important issues: whether or not it is consonant with what we know of Cato's representation in other texts of this period, and whether or not his decision here and the justification he proffers are sentiments appropriate to an adherent of Roman Stoicism. The second question is more or less impossible to answer. True, we know that Roman Stoicism modified the Greek version to stress the worth of participation in public life. The question was whether this involvement continued to be appropriate when the structure of power had changed, when the beneficiary was no longer the state but a dictator or a monarch; and the answer could vary.[40] If the Roman Republic was "Zeno's ideal state in action, as Roman Stoics were quick to point out, [and] in such a state the wise man must participate" (George 1991: 242–243), the evolution toward the principate repositioned the focus of this question on the character of the *princeps* himself;[41] and even in the writings of a single man, Lucan's uncle Seneca,[42] the answer varied widely from prescriptions for tactful retirement to urgings to participate in whatever capacity possible:[43] "the work of a good citizen is never useless" (*De tranq.* 4.6).[44] As B. Shaw (1985: 53) well points out, the Roman appropriation of Stoic ideas is best represented by its ability to generate " 'maps' of various social orders that helped members of the ruling elites to transfer themselves from one set of political circumstances to another, while at the same time maintaining tradition"; we might expect, then, so charged an issue as political participation during the crucial decades that gave birth to the principate to be particularly rich in "maps," all with a Stoic tinge and not particularly consistent.

For one, whatever the philosophy behind the various Stoic stances on political involvement, it is significant that in practice the tenets of Stoicism did not spur men to open resistance in the political arena.[45] P. A. Brunt (1975: 10), for example, while acknowledging contradictions in this stance and indeed "a certain tension between the claims of public activity and those of study and meditation" in all Stoic writings on the wise man's role in the state, well lays out the literary support for the Stoic endorsement of political withdrawal[46] and concludes (p. 23) that much Stoic writing suggests that "their teaching tended to promote not active resistance to government but entire withdrawal from political activity":[47]

> At least after Zeno and Chrysippus . . . no Stoic thinker drew any such practical implications [about political reform] from the doctrines of the school: their aim was to amend the spiritual condition of individuals, not their material lot, nor the social structure. Epictetus held that it was man's task not to change the constitution of things—"for this is neither vouchsafed us nor is it better that it should be"—but to make his will conform with what happens.

Brunt continues (p. 28): "Epictetus merely insists that no commands of the tyrant can affect true freedom; a man can always choose to obey God rather than Caesar. Thus he only contemplates passive resistance."[48] And the potential for action and change in such resistance is low; although it might foster personal integrity, it has little impact on the political world. As Terry Eagleton (1991: 53) has remarked of such an ideology, it "may rationalize the wretched conditions of some social group, but it need not necessarily advance its interests, other than in the sense of supplying it with an opiate."

Nonetheless, Lucan's Cato comes down surprisingly strongly on the side of intervention; H. P. Syndikus (1958: 98) has remarked of him that "the Roman is stronger than the Stoic." Cato's parental feelings toward the state and his avowed determination to follow not it, but its ghost even, to the grave, put a strain even on the flexible framework of Stoic criteria for participation in public affairs.[49] As

Adatte (1965: 240) has noted, "Lucan would like to extract from Stoicism a little more than Stoicism can give, and he only attains his goal by a distortive association: by idealizing political liberty and bestowing on it the dignity of the wise man's internal liberty." And Cato certainly sets an odd figure against Horace's famous vision of the *iustus et tenax propositi vir* in *Odes* 3.3, a description of Stoic self-control that some critics believe to have been written with the historical Cato in mind.[50] Whereas Horace pictures a scene of world destruction that leaves his version of the just man completely unshaken—"If the shattered world should crash down, the ruins will strike him without causing fear" (*Odes* 3.3.7–8)—Lucan's Cato explicitly refuses such presence of mind under similar circumstances, and asks, "Who would want to watch the stars and the universe collapsing while feeling no fear himself?" ("sidera quis mundumque velit spectare cadentem / expers ipse metus?" 2.289–290).[51] Against the praise of the *impavidus vir,* a condemnation of the man *expers metus.*[52] Nor has Lucan's Cato read Seneca's *De ira* 2.6 telling us that anger is always incompatible with virtue; instead, he loses his temper at the well-meaning soldier who offers him water in the Libyan desert; "riled with anger" ("concitus ira," 9.509), he labels him a degenerate and throws away the offering.[53] And even his decision to fight in the civil war in the first place set him in opposition to the gods: famously, "the gods favored the winning side, but Cato favored the losers" ("victrix causa deis placuit, sed victa Catoni," 1.128). Contrast the more orthodox view of *EM* 74.20: "let whatever God favors win man's favor too"; and of *EM* 107.9: "It is best to endure what you cannot fix."

Cato's first lines in response to Brutus' query about his intentions adds to the subtle idiosyncrasies of his portrayal by Lucan.[54] When he imputes guilt to the gods for putting him in a position in which he too must be stained by civil war—because the nature of civil war is such that both participation and abstention are crimes against humanity—his ironic usage of ethical terminology aligns him with the epic's central concern with language's collapse into paradox, and puts on dramatic display his understanding of the impossibility of any meaningful justification of his participation. He rebukes Brutus gently (2.286–288): "Brutus, I acknowledge that civil war is the greatest sin; yet whither the fates drag virtue, it will follow unworried. It will be the gods' crime that they have made even me guilty." But what an odd rebuke. Cato first personifies himself as *virtus,* then calls himself *nocens.* In identifying himself as both simultaneously, he participates in the epic's ironic idiom, demonstrating the terrible pliancy of ethical terms in civil war even as he formulates an ethical judgment that relies on such vocabulary. He speaks of the gods as extant, and yet blasphemes against them by condemning them for condemning him, and thus effectively undoes their status as moral arbiters even as he grants them the power to render him "guilty." Even more important is his paradoxical turn of phrase in "whither the fates drag virtue, it will follow unworried." The contrast between being dragged and following willingly is usually the pivot on which a Stoic world view is distinguished from others; only the blind struggle against fate. And so Frederick Ahl (1976: 240) and others have cited Seneca's *EM* 107.11—"The fates lead the willing and drag the unwilling"—to point to Cato's Stoicism, whereas he is not in fact properly Stoic at all. Unlike the Stoic follower of fate's will, Cato here is *nolens* and *volens* at the same time; he is being dragged and follows simultaneously, and thus mingles the terminology for the Stoic with that for the layman.[55] What he presents us with in the end is a situation in which the one who is being dragged is able to preserve the illusion of choice by following willingly. Unlike Seneca's apothegm, Cato's self-description forces the paradox of willful self-deception in our face by making it clear that the dragging and the following are happening to the *same person.*[56]

We can gain further insight into Lucan's Cato by setting him directly against the Cato that emerges from Seneca's texts. Or rather the Catos, for Seneca's stance on Cato is more or less a double one: he produces two versions of the man, the one criticized, the other praised. Significantly, the Cato toward whom he has misgivings is censured precisely for his decision to participate in the civil war; this stance toward the republican hero is obviously different from Lucan's, who is at such pains to defend Cato's choice of Pompey's party. For Seneca in *Cons. ad Marc.* 20.6, it would have been better for Cato had he died at sea before the crisis ever came to pass; as it was, the addition of a few years of life "forced him to flee Caesar and side with Pompey"—apparently an outcome worse than a watery death in the Mediterranean! In *EM* 14, an imaginary interlocutor roundly criticizes Cato's participation in the civil war: he should have abstained, since he was fighting not for *libertas* but for a master (14.13):

> One might debate whether a wise man should have participated in matters of state at that time: "What are you thinking of, Marcus Cato? It is not liberty that is at stake now: she was ruined long ago. The question is whether Caesar or Pompey will own the Republic: what has this struggle got to do with you? Neither party is yours. An autocrat is being chosen: what do you care, which of the two wins? The better man might win; but the man who has won cannot but be the worse."[57]

In other words, Cato's participation might well have been a mistake. As Charles Martindale (1984: 74) points out, "The implied criticism does not necessarily represent Seneca's own view, but perhaps he has sympathy with it as no answer is given."[58] Martindale draws our attention to the expression of the same view in *EM* 22.8, this time in Seneca's own voice and in reference specifically to times of political upheaval: "When the wise man sees the crisis, the uncertainties, the predicaments in which he is involved, he will not flee, but he will gradually retreat into safety"; and elsewhere the philosopher waxes eloquent in favor of a discreet retirement from affairs of state when and where practicable.[59] As the interlocutor of *EM* 14 asks so directly, what is there in civil war that calls for a Cato? Certainly not liberty; only the choice of a master. And Lucan repeats the question in Brutus' comments and, indeed, in Cato's answer. And yet his Cato does participate, with the evident approval of the narrator.[60]

The other Cato in Seneca is also different from the Cato of the

Civil War. Indeed, the most striking divergence between Seneca's Cato and Lucan's occurs here and points us in the same direction we have been heading all along. More often than not, and despite the passages cited above, Seneca shows us a Cato uncompromised by his decision to fight on Pompey's side and take up arms in civil war. Now Cato is *praised* for his choice: but the nature of that choice looks completely different. Cato is said to be fighting for the "third" party, that of the Republic itself; he thus struggles against both Pompey *and* Caesar, and no mention is made of the manner in which he effected this resistance. And so we find him in *EM* 95.70:

> Certainly no one can advance with greater pride than a man who stood up to both Caesar and Pompey at the same time and, while some were supporting Caesar's power and others Pompey's, challenged both of them and showed that the Republic, too, had a party.

A similar premise underlies Seneca's approval in *EM* 104: here, too, Cato's participation in the *nefas* of civil war is refigured as the formation of a third party and thus as a choice unsullied by the dubious claims of Pompey's propaganda (104.29–31):

> And you could say of this man that, no less than Socrates, he allied himself with liberty[61] in the midst of slaves (unless you think perhaps that Pompey and Caesar and Crassus were the allies of freedom!). No one ever saw Cato changed during so many changes of the Republic ... And in the end, in that chaos of the state ... when some men were siding with Caesar, others with Pompey, Cato alone established a party for the Republic as well.[62]

This is not the Cato of book 2 of the *Civil War:* this is a Cato for whom a third party is possible. He crops up again in *De prov.* 3.14, fighting for his just cause all over a world caught up in civil war. This Cato does not believe the Republic is dead, as does Lucan's Cato. And here is the crucial difference. Seneca's Cato, whether he foolishly aligns himself with Pompey or nobly struggles against both enemies of the Republic, seems to believe the old Republic can be saved; he is actually criticized for this error of judgment in *EM* 14.14, and pre-

sumably this belief informs his formation of Seneca's "third party."[63]
Only with *his* death did *libertas* finally die: up to that last moment,
it lived not as a possibility but as a reality (compare *Const. sap.* 2.2–
3; *EM* 24.6; *Tranq.* 16.1). Lucan's Cato, on the other hand, believes
that liberty has been in the grave since the days of Sulla and Marius
(9.204–205)—and yet, when it makes the least sense, he participates
in civil war anyhow.[64] For although liberty is dead, its crucially important shadow lives on, and lets men act as if liberty still lived—
and the act, as both Pascal and Zizek would say, is not an inefficient
substitute for the belief. In other words, Lucan's Cato differs from
the closest contemporary representation of the historical figure on
which he is based by taking action *despite* his belief that the Republic
has long since ceased to be; he acts despite his lack of faith. And it
is precisely this small change that makes Lucan's Cato the model of
the man who chooses *fides ficta libertatis* rather than passivity and
despair. Cato practices ideology—not with Brutus' mistaken heat
("calorem," 2.324), but in cold blood.

To bring balance to our reading of the poem, we should remember
that much of the argument for the breakdown of systems and the
slide into despair came from the syntactic analysis of the *Civil War*'s
literary fabric. But I am not proposing one reading based on character analysis, narratorial intervention, and the events of the plot,
and another taken from Lucan's manipulation of his linguistic medium: both kinds of signifying (that is, syntactic and narrative) are
present simultaneously in the text, both play a role in the transmission of Lucan's complex view. To show this, however, entails a return
to syntax that will occupy most of this section—I hope not too joyless
a transition, but in any case one more suited to the classicists among
my readers.

What I am proposing is that one of Lucan's idiosyncrasies of style
can provide us with a final illustration of the way we automatically
strive to make sense of the world around us and do so even in the

face of the "hard facts"—the way we will always believe in the presence of meaning even when we have to create that presence. Little has been said about this particular idiosyncrasy: we tend to ignore it because the operation we carry out as readers to make sense of it is so simple and so obvious. And yet an operation *is* called for, and the meaning we extract contradicts the letter of the text. I am referring to Lucan's quirk of occasionally writing the opposite of what he means: more exactly, to his odd use of "and" where we would read "and not." To the surprise of anyone reading the text in the Latin original, it soon becomes clear that Lucan often employs positive conjunctions for negative conjunctions in sentences that follow an originally negative statement: he uses *ac, atque, et,* and *–que* where in each case we would need a *nec* to make the verses read as they must. It is common enough in Lucan that the commentators regularly label its occurrences as being "more Lucani";[65] it is rare enough elsewhere that the standard Latin grammars have nothing to say on it. Even Raphael Kühner's *Grammatik,* which treats the combination of *neque . . . et* at some length (vol. 2, § 158), has no examples of Lucan's unusual usage; the use of *neque . . . et* or *neque . . . –que* invariably means a positive statement in the second half, which, of course, is the normative practice, amply catalogued everywhere. Indeed, where Kühner does have a discussion of "single *neque* in the sense of *neque . . . neque*" (vol. 2, § 241.5 f.), he cites only examples in which the *neque* appears in the *second* of the two conjoined sentences.[66]

A few citations from Lucan should illustrate the peculiarity clearly enough. Immediately before Brutus' address to Cato in book 2, as the poet is stressing his courage and high spirit, we come across the odd statement, "But terror did not strike at the heart of courageous Brutus, *and* in all the fearfulness of dread disturbance, he was a member of the lamenting populace" ("At non magnanimi percussit pectora Bruti / terror, *et* in tanta pavidi formidine motus / pars populi lugentis erat," 2.234–236). Clearly for "and" we want to read "nor"; the passage as it stands paradoxically reduces Brutus to the level of those with whom it is contrasting him, and yet the point is surely that Brutus was not one of the lamenting populace (and so, here and at other such instances, in the scholia and the standard translations, with the exception observed in note 68). Why then this apparently sloppy writing on Lucan's part? Elaine Fantham (1992a at 2.234) ascribes it to metrical convenience: "The negative governing *percussit* is carried through to *et pars . . . erat*," a "replacement of the negative by metrically convenient *et/–que*." Here is the passage she adduces for comparison (2.354–359):

> Festal garlands do not hang at the wreathed doorway, *and* white ribbons traverse the twin posts, *and* also the marriage torches; *and* resting on ivory steps stands the couch and shows off coverings with painted gold, *and* the woman, wearing a towered crown on her head avoids touching the threshold when her foot crosses.

> Festa coronato non pendent limine serta,
> infula*que* in geminos discurrit candida postes,
> legitimae*que* faces, gradibus*que* adclinis eburnis
> stat torus *et* picto vestes discriminat auro,
> turrita*que* premens frontem matrona corona
> translata vitat contingere limina planta

This passage, supposed to stress the austerity of Cato's remarriage to Marcia, supplies us with a long list of the traditions from which the couple abstained; but again, a single introductory *non* is followed by a long series of *ets* and *–ques*.[67] So did Cato and Marcia secretly have a fancy wedding, with torches, covered couches, and a towered crown? Of course not; for the repeated *ets* and *–ques* we must read *necs*; but the letter of the text goes against this reading, and seems to indicate that Cato and Marcia, while tactfully pruning a few festive observances from the ceremony, went ahead and included the majority.[68]

Here and elsewhere, however, the argument from metrical convenience is unsatisfactory on two grounds. First, it does not explain why other poets did not engage in the same metrically convenient trick of using *et* or *–que* for *nec* or *neve*. Why is this characteristic *more Lucani* only? And why in this poem that makes it so easy for opposites to collapse into each other, and that has repeatedly illustrated the slipperiness of language under stress? Second, and perhaps more important, the argument from meter is deeply flawed in such cases in that it tacitly assumes that the verses in question (minus *et*s and *nec*s) were more or less already written when Lucan started scrabbling about for a conjunction that would fit the line he had: hence the convenience of one conjunction over another. In other words, take the line as it is, subtract the *et*, and, sure enough, a *nec* will not fit: ergo, Lucan used the *et* because he had to. But this is ridiculous. Not only does it suggest that there was no other way of composing the line in question, but as a proof it is strikingly circular, because few lines with *et* will allow the substitution of a *nec*, whatever the "reason" for the original use of that conjunction.

There is no point in citing exhaustively from every passage in which the poet engages in this play on positives and negatives; I provide a list in the notes.[69] Some such passages, however, are striking for their reversal of the poem's most basic plot elements and even the events of the world outside the poem, as if Lucan here, too, is playing with reversals of the impact of the *Civil War* on Rome's history. For example, if Pompey had been willing to follow up on his success at Dyrrachium, his death and those of Juba, Cato, and Metellus Scipio would never have taken place—or would they?

> Libya would not have wept for the slaughter at Utica, nor Spain for that at Munda, *and* the Nile, polluted with unholy blood, would have carried a corpse nobler than the Egyptian king; nor would naked Juba have lain on the African sands, *and* Scipio would have placated the Carthaginian shades by pouring out his blood, nor would life have lost holy Cato.

> Non Uticae Libye clades, Hispania Mundae
> flesset *et* infando pollutus sanguine Nilus
> nobilius Phario gestasset rege cadaver,

> nec Iuba marmaricas nudus pressisset harenas
> Poenorum*que* umbras placasset sanguine fuso
> Scipio, nec sancto caruisset vita Catone.   (6.306–311)

Of course, we carry out the necessary changes to make the passage make sense, especially given our knowledge of how history did turn out: it would be nonsense for Lucan to say that a conclusive victory at Dyrrachium and an end to civil war would have resulted (like its opposite) in Pompey's body floating down the Nile or in Metellus Scipio's death at Thapsus in 46 B.C. Or consider Pompey's unsuccessful exhortation to his army after the capture of Corfinium: "Will Caesar be victor over the Senate? Not with so blind a course do you drag all things, Fortune, *and* nothing shames you" ("Caesarne senatus / victor erit? Non tam caeco trahis omnia cursu / te*que* nihil, Fortuna, pudet," 2.566–568). Once again we have to transform –que into *nec,* since Pompey is trying to suggest that Fortune does feel shame over some extremes. (Ironically enough, as Due 1962: 119 notes, Fortuna did prove to be that shameless.)

Finally, let us take a look at Caesar's boundary-violating march into Italy (2.439–443):

> Caesar, mad for battle, is glad to have no paths except ones smeared with blood; he is happy to tread Italian land not emptied of the enemy, *and* to invade empty fields, *and* he does not waste the very march, *and* wages nonstop battles.

> Caesar in arma furens nullas nisi sanguine fuso
> gaudet habere vias, quod non terat hoste vacantes
> Hesperiae fines vacuosque inrumpat in agros
> atque ipsum non perdat iter consertaque bellis
> bella gerat.

This is a particularly good example of the way this stylistic oddity forces itself upon our attention. Lucan provides us with one series of *non* followed by *–que* that we will find ourselves translating as two negatives—Caesar is happy that he does *not* invade empty fields, for he likes killing his countrymen, as the preceding clause makes clear—and then a second series of *non* followed by *–que* that needs to be translated as a negative and a positive—Caesar does take pleasure in waging continuous battles, and that is why the march itself is not wasted.[70] Side by side, two different usages of the conjunction, daring us to make sense of them by violating the letter of the text, and not consistently at that.[71]

With these instances of syntactic looseness, then, Lucan's arbitrary manipulation of positive and negative conjunctions in the *Civil War* forces us to come to terms—if we stop at all to think about the way we are reading—with the fact that we ourselves are all too ready to step in and reread the text (that is, the hard linguistic facts in front of us) to make sense of what it says. The poet forces *us* to make the necessary adjustments in meaning, thus (a) playing with the reversibility of meaning and the identification of opposite terms that characterizes his antipolitical epic, and (b) making us show our complicity in picking one meaning over the other even when the two are confused, and thus one side over the other even when the two sides are confused. Can we read without intervening? We cannot. We are compelled to make sense of the contradictions in front of us. We care too much to let the "right" meaning vanish into the senselessness of the text we are given; we are prepared to "create" it if necessary, and most of us will argue that there is nothing really so peculiar about this at all. The meaning is "obvious," or Lucan's senseless conjunction is merely *metri causa*. In another Lucanian context, Masters (1992: 45) has remarked that "The norms of reading demand a partial non-reading; which is to say, any interpretation . . . involves the suppression of another (other) interpretation(s)."[72] That statement was never truer than here. But where Masters continues—"To be impartial, to be non-partisan, is impossible, or at least only possible if we stop reading the text (a Stoic withdrawal of the kind that Cato rejects?). To read is to be involved in the *nefas* of partisanship, or in the *nefas* of non-partisanship"—we might surely say that reading and choosing, for Lucan, is no *nefas* at all. It is necessary; and it is ironic in its knowledge of its own violence to the "facts," such as they are.[73] Such choice, such action, are the only forces that can give our existence meaning: and as Massimiliano Pavan (1970: 417–418) correctly concludes, "Lucan celebrates Cato because of his belief in an ideal, but also because of his active, not passive, participation in history and in historical reality."[74]

And so Cato sides with Pompey, and the narrator celebrates his tarnished hero even though he must leave us behind. Where Lucien Goldmann (1964: 60) remarked of Pascal's *Pensées* that "For tragic man, paradox is a constant source of scandal and concern: to accept paradox, to accept human weakness, the ambiguity and confusion of the world . . . means giving up any attempt to endow life with meaning," the *Civil War* lets us recognize the presence of the paradoxes and create meaning anyhow. For, along with William James, Lucan seems to have recognized that man has "a multifaceted need to believe, a need so strong that his belief made the difference between finding life worthwhile and not" (Myers 1986: 451). And perhaps this belief, *ficta* though it may be, is not always for nothing in the course of history: perhaps it can open up vistas impossible to predict before we take that ironic leap of faith. Although he could not have known or expected it to be possible, Lucan's Cato did make a difference in the end; he taught Pompey's army to fight for *libertas* rather than for a master; and this transformation turned the struggle, however briefly, into one between republicanism and Caesarism.[75] By participating, by acting in despite of his despair, Cato made the idealistic fight between liberty and tyranny possible; but there was no way for him to know this when he made his decision against withdrawal and in favor of struggle.

This is the nature of action and ideology as Lucan endorses it, and as he enacts it in his poem and his life, and as he urges us to enact it also. "Recognize," he seems to be saying, "that the world as it is is not built for belief, for religion or ideology. But recognize, too, that withdrawal based on this knowledge is not the answer. Make your own beliefs, create your own truths, and take a stance. You may save nothing from the wreckage around you: you will reap a reward nonetheless. Choose to make sense out of the world, and it will be yourself you save."

FIVE

History without Banisters

Symptoms are meaningless traces; their meaning is not discovered, excavated from the hidden depth of the past, but constructed retroactively—the analysis produces the truth . . . Every historical rupture, every advent of a new master-signifier, changes retroactively the meaning of all tradition, restructures the narration of the past, makes it readable in another, new way.

—*Slavoj Zizek*

Lucan's own Italy is a land of fragments, the residue of war. In its cities totter the walls of crumbling homes, and huge stones from fallen buildings lie scattered in disarray; rough scrub covers the ground, and the fields lie uncultivated (1.24–29). This is the poet's landscape of ruin, his fanciful vision of the material evidence of Rome's decline from its prewar might. It establishes for us the world in which he is writing his poem, forging meaning out of the fragments of history amid the chaos of its physical remains; in this environment he forces a confrontation between the specter of meaninglessness and the turn toward ideology and cohesion. The aftermath of the civil war has been the ruin of Roman integrity in more ways than one, but it is precisely amid these ruins that the poet seems to set up an alternative to accepting his own vision of fragmentation. For he selects the crumbling site of another once-great empire, another city sung of in epic, to present us with a view of just how the poet does make meaning out of rubble through a willful act of interpretation.

This city is Troy. It is surely no coincidence that Lucan's present Rome as described at the *Civil War's* start provides us with a striking parallel to the ancient ruins of Troy, visited by Caesar in book 9 on what becomes a nostalgic inspection of Rome's origins in the mythological and epic past (964–979):

> He tours burned Troy, a legendary name, looks for the huge remains of Apollo's wall. Dead forests now and trunks rotten to the core press on the palace of Assaracus, and hold with tired roots the temples of the gods, and all Pergamum is covered with scrub: the ruins too have perished. He sees Hesione's crag, Anchises' bedchamber once hidden in the wood, the cave where Paris sat as judge, the site of Ganymede snatched to the sky, the peak on which the Naiad Oenone mourned: no stone lacks a name. Unknowing, he crossed a stream winding through dry dust; it was the Xanthus. Carelessly he made his way through overgrown grass: the Phrygian local forbids him tread on Hector's ghost. Scattered stones were lying about without semblance of anything sacred: asks the guide, "Care you nothing for the altar of Zeus Herceos?"

In walking through what we can scarcely now call "Troy" Caesar is treading the scattered rubble of old walls, ruins taken over by underbrush, foundations held together by roots. And indeed, the earth he tramples would be meaningless were it not for the guide's intervention: through this man's eyes, through his interpretation of the overgrown grass and scattered stones, old Troy comes alive, the site of legend and history: through him, "no stone lacks a name." Otherwise Caesar is *inscius,* unknowing; without the Phrygian's ability to provide a narrative for the ruins, the fragments of history remain only that, a heap of traces *(vestigia)* with no internal cohesion and nothing to hold them together. No one asks about the nature of this native's authority; that is not the point. Certainly no witness to the fall of Troy, he nonetheless carves out a story from the little he has, and it is enough. For Caesar is happy with his version of history: inspired by the tale, he sees an ancient city where we could see only the ruins of ruins, and prays to its elusive gods.

The sad remains of Troy are witness to their own potential to go uninterpreted, to *not* be given meaning through narrative: without his guide, Caesar steps on ghosts and gods and knows it not. Is this an image of the risk that Lucan's Italy faces after Pharsalus, to fade into the oblivion of history? After all, the narrator stops the battle to inject just such a vision of ruin into his narrative: "Then all the Latin name will be a legend; the ruins, covered with dust, will barely show the site of Gabii, Veii and Cora, or the homes of Alba and Laurentum: an empty countryside" (7.391–395). Frederick Ahl, in his excellent comparison of these two passages, stresses the parallel between Troy, that *nomen memorabile,* and Rome, destined after Pharsalus to be a *fabula* too, to move from being the *Latinum nomen* of history (that is, the Latin League) to another kind of *nomen,* the kind attached to Troy's stones, a signifier pointing to something that no longer exists. Like freedom, Rome would be dead in all but its name; and Ahl comments, "Even the word *nomen* itself frequently has the connotation of 'name without substance,' or suggests an appellation that belies the true nature of the thing to which it is applied" (1976: 218). This is one reading of *nomen* the text itself presses upon us: Troy is a mere name precisely because it has no substance; the guide, as Kirk Ormand (1994: 52) notes, "is pointing out . . . to Caesar and to us what is *not there.* The text of ruin is essentially a contradiction, an expression only of what is not, or of what no longer is. No wonder that Troy is a *nomen*—the names of rocks have supplanted the rocks themselves, and given them what meaning they have."

But this is only one possible reading, and the word *nomen* has other reverberations in this text. For guide and poet alike, the existence of a *nomen* is the gateway to another version of history, the one created by the figure of the interpreter willing to work with stones and scrub, with only the fragments of the past. Lucan himself points this way: as the Phrygian guide finishes his tour, the narrator breaks into a strange apostrophe: "O great and sacred toil of poets! You snatch everything from fate and you grant mortal men eternity" ("O sacer et magnus vatum labor! omnia fato / eripis et populis donas mortalibus aevum," 9.980–981). Presumably the poet is talking of his own task in writing the *Civil War;* yet the use of the second person singular after the generalizing genitive plural *vatum* is jarring here, especially coming immediately after our guide has spoken his last words to Caesar. One way of explaining the singular is to read Lucan as apostrophizing *labor* itself, but other, more appropriate subjects for apostrophe remain: the nameless interpreter of the Trojan ruins, and Lucan himself as poet.[1] Are we to choose between these options? To some degree, I think, none of them can be eliminated: *labor,* the poet, the interpreter meld into one and accomplish the same goal. After all, as Ormand (1994: 50) sees, "the local guide does precisely what Lucan says a poet does, that is, preserves things from oblivion." And when the locals make history out of rubble and give *nomina* to the stones, their willful double vision, their ability to see ruin and create meaning, parallels that of the poet himself: Lucan, too, can see meaning and chaos simultaneously and, like the guide, chooses to impose a story of history, a belief in human possibilities and human heroes, onto the senselessness of his times and the fragments of *Roman* cities and bodies. The story that can be told is clearly a poet's story; the perished ruins that become the Trojan past for the *incola Phryx* are not any meaningful past but a literary one: when Caesar encounters Xanthus, Hector, the altar of Jupiter, famous sites from the *Iliad,* we almost wonder if the guide has his pocket Homer to hand.[2] The *Civil War* seems to be suggesting that to make sense out of rubble, to bestow meaning on empty *nomina,* is the quintessential responsibility of the poet, who can see both the ruins and what they can represent for humankind. It is true, as Ormand (1994: 53) remarks, that in reading the *Civil War* "we are reconstructing what is not there as surely as Caesar is reconstructing the lost tomb of Hector." But this does not mean that the text of ruin is unredeemable or designed to fail. It means, simply, that it is up to us to be poets for our empty *nomina.*[3]

Ahl (1976: 215) has well remarked that Troy is curiously reminiscent not only of Rome but also of Pompey himself. Commenting on

9.966–969 ("Dead forests now and trunks rotten to the core press on the palace of Assaracus, and hold with tired roots the temples of the gods, and all Pergamum is covered with scrub: the ruins too have perished"), he notes that these lines "recall the description of Pompey as the rotting oak in book 1, and the suggestion that Troy itself is now merely a *memorabile nomen* brings to mind the rendering of Pompey as *Magni nominis umbra.*" Indeed, both Pompey and Troy are *nomina,* and what the Phrygian does for Troy with Caesar as his audience our narrator does for Pompey with us as his audience: he takes the empty name and makes it into legend. The useless roots of Pompey-as-tree, the mere shadow of a name that is symbolized by that man's rotting trunk, have a function nonetheless, like the feeble roots at Troy holding together the fragments of the temples: they provide the enabling condition for Pompey-as-figurehead. At Troy, the ruins themselves have already been ruined; for Rome, Pompey's death stole away a belief in liberty that was already make-believe. No matter: we can make our own meaning out of the rubble.

And more: Pompey's defeat at Pharsalus meant that he was not only *like* Troy in resembling the fallen grandeur of a rotting trunk: in suffering this debilitating ruin he became a ruin himself. Lucan on several occasions uses this word to characterize the man after Pharsalus: a kind of *ruina,* unable to hold himself up. As Pothinus scornfully asks of Ptolemy, "Are you, Ptolemy, able to prop up the ruin of Pompey, under which Rome lies prostrate?" (8.528–529; see similarly 8.550, 2.731). The tree has fallen, the wall collapsed. The image of ruin is carried on to his death: the Roman Cordus, who gives his headless corpse its humble burial place, literally gives a name to fragments, to the "sparsis Pompei manibus" (8.751; an exaggeration, given that the body is only in two pieces and one is missing at that). "Hic situs est Magnus," he scratches on the gravestone; and the narrator steps in to look forward to the day when this *nomen* that Cordus has inscribed (8.792) will be a legend far greater than the humble remains that testify to its existence, and humans will no more believe in this sorry grave than we believe the Cretans' claim to Jupiter's birthplace (8.865 ff.).[4] Human hope and human belief rely upon this operation we willingly carry out on mere *nomina;* and our version of history may be both fictitious and necessary, perhaps our only choice in relation to the past.

Fingere is of course the task par excellence of the composing poet (see *OLD* s.v. 6a), and Lucan is well aware of the ambiguities built into this dual activity of telling and fabricating. Martha Malamud's excellent exploration of this theme in the *Civil War* drives home the poet's self-consciousness about the deceptive nature of his epic project and his willful rewriting of history; the funeral monument of Pompey in particular, she argues, raises "the general questions about the role of poetry in creating 'the truth' for future generations that Lucan poses in his avowedly false myth about the origins of the Libyan snakes.[5] The issues at stake involve Lucan's own narrative quite directly. What sort of a monument is Lucan creating in his text? Will . . . [his poem] obliterate the weak Pompey of flesh and blood and replace him with a divine but unreal hero?" (1995: 179).[6] In the end, despite these ambiguities, "Lucan writes anyway, ensuring that Pompey will have his mendacious moment, and that his poetic *fabula* rather than the unavailable *causa* will be handed down to posterity" (p. 187). Exactly: yet the project of poetry revels in, and does not apologize for, this endeavor.

Fingere is also the operation Lucan carries out on Pompey's *nomen,* as I argued in Chapter 4.[7] In this regard it is a potential means of fostering beliefs that are *ficta* in a double sense: expressed in poetry, for one, but also make-believe, in the latter case like the nature of *libertas*' continued existence until Pompey's death. I quote again from Cato's funeral speech for Pompey: "Real belief in liberty perished long ago, when Sulla and Marius were let into Rome; with Pompey lost to the world now make-believe [*ficta*] belief has perished too" (9.204–206). Pompey's death put an end to all the trappings of liberty: the independence of the Senate, the military commands granted to merit. But I have already suggested that these mere trappings provided those who lived with them with a crucial basis for belief, in much the same way as Pascalian "custom"; the fiction kept alive the possibility of action and belief.[8] And so, if *fingere* has worked as an aid to belief in the past, it can do so again in the future; what is needed is a story of history, a poetry (necessarily *fictum*) of ideology, to help men adopt yet again the *ficta fides libertatis*.[9]

Lucan therefore rejects "history" as such as any attempt at objective reconstruction of the facts, and in its place he adopts history as *story*, a biased and polemical account based on the subjective view of an individual making sense out of the past in the way he best can. Lucan's is history precisely from *the subject's point of view*. Opinionated and even wrong by the standards we call objective, it reasserts the individual's right to make sense out of his own past; it boldly rejects (even as it acknowledges and, indeed, uses) the paradoxes, inversions, and collapse of moral terminology that characterize language usage under the Empire and that suggest that attempts to create stories, especially ideological ones, must fall into meaninglessness. And so Lucan's is not a bias to be hidden or explained away: this kind of history proudly asserts its subjectivity as an inevitable condition for making meaning out of history. *Invidus qui vates ad vera vocat.*[10] Lucan creates a hero and composes a fervently ideological version of civil war and does so in cold blood, in full knowledge of everything that goes against the possibility of the story he is telling, a story for his readers, in his time, to his ends.[11] And he lets us share this knowledge: only if we understand the nature of this kind of belief as a belief-before-belief, see its impossibility and adopt it anyhow, can we understand what arises from his hopelessness and willfulness together.

Our poet spurns the perspective we think of as the historian's de facto pursuit, the imaginary Archimedean point from which the analyzing mind, looking down upon the events of this world, might with complete impartiality create truth rather than story. Unlike the other, prose versions of recent history available to first- and early second-century readers, Lucan's avoids the claim of "speaking from nowhere," the Tacitean *sine ira et studio,* the studied detachment and absence of a speaking "I" of Caesar's *Commentarii.* Lucan's rhetorical skill is expended in the opposite direction, toward the explosion of any myth of objectivity. For him, "history" in the sense he rejects is what strives to renders the past plausible, rational, comprehensible[12]—in other words, what the Julio-Claudians themselves might write as an aetiology of their rule, and what Augustus did write in the *Res gestae;* while to tell a "story," as he does, is "to break the usual 'rules of caution' and refrain from [those] rhetorical moves that would give one's position the appearance of unquestionability" (Disch 1994: 4). Indeed, to show up the claims of authoritative versions of history as being inevitably biased and based on special interests has often emerged as the particular goal of "marginal" narratives; and the *Bellum Civile,* given the conditions of its production, can surely claim this status for itself.[13]

> Marginal stories . . . show that the official claim to hold standards that are abstract, universal, and hence neutral with respect to power is false. The stories of marginal critics show the very pretense of an Archimedean vantage point to be false . . . Storytelling . . . makes visible the fact that experience never just *is,* but is always narrated, thereby directing attention to the discourses by which "experience" is produced, and to the processes of transcription by which it is constituted as evidence.   (Disch 1994: 6, 8)

The poet's stance toward Pompey radically exposes itself as just such a narration, and thus renders its own transcription questionable—as generations of critics will attest. Lucan did not choose to cover up this flagrant act of partisanship; indeed, he forces us to be aware of its weakness. His *Pharsalia* is *nostra* to the end.

In any case Lucan's topic was never one well suited to "objective" historiography. As a rendition of a crisis in history that encompassed the overturn of traditional morality, the collapse of political forms, and the gutting of linguistic boundaries, the unwieldy and self-destructive subject matter of this poem would have made a mockery of any pretense to objectivity or knowledge: its own cynical, empty medium would have consumed the attempts at "history," branded this attempt at rationality a lying farce. Instead, to counteract the pull of the black hole of which he writes, Lucan throws in another gravitational force, an irrational and passional adherence to a figure already fallen prey to the forces this man helped to unleash. And out of the clash of these two violent incompatibilities, an escape—perhaps—from the wreckage, the birth of a new understanding. So too would Hannah Arendt reject the idea of rational historiography when she, like Lucan, grappled with the problem of putting "the origins of totalitarianism" into words.[14] It could not be done in the terms of a history conceived as a disengaged science of representation; the recent horrors of the war had destroyed old categories for understanding and analysis; totalitarianism was beyond historiography and so, too, of course, was the Holocaust.[15]

Arendt's solution to these difficulties was to write another kind of history, to engage in "a fragmentary and discontinuous historiography whose aim is not to reestablish coherency but to collect mementos of past moments of resistance in the hope of inspiring continued struggle in the present."[16] For her, too, this kind of history would be a spur to new ways of imagining, a path around the dead end of the past. It was history as a story that knew itself as such; it was politics as storytelling, the production of a narrative specifically intended to inspire in its audience a potential for change and to reclaim some kind of goal for a people thrown into confusion by the traumas of the past. "Under these conditions one required a story that would once again reorient the mind in its aimless wanderings. For only such a reorientation could reclaim the past so as to build the future. The theorist of totalitarianism as the narrator of the story of totalitarianism was engaged in a moral and political task" (Benhabib 1990: 180).[17] So too Lucan seems to have grasped the inadequacy of rational and coherent narrative to evade the problems of his subject without trivializing or even erasing those problems; a transformation beyond understanding could not be expressed in the language of a traditional genre and the conventions of the culture that produced it. So too he seems to have set up a story whose function was reorientation and whose goals were deeply moral and political in despite of the medium in which they were necessarily couched. This too is the quality of a storyteller, on Arendt's view: an engagement with life rather than withdrawal from it, a kind of embeddedness in the material of history rather than a disinterested detachment from it; not only because the claim to Archimedean objectivity must always be a lie, but also because, as Lisa Jane Disch (1994: 80) well argues, "It is not impossible to adjudicate a conflict from an external vantage point, but to do so is to reframe that conflict in terms that are no longer public." Of course, such storytelling relinquishes history's claims to "getting things right." "To the objection that in the absence of absolute, superhuman standards there is no guarantee that we will get things right, Arendt assented: there *is* no such guarantee. There are no 'banisters' for us to hold on to. We simply are in the position of acting and judging without rules given to us from the outside" (Canovan 1992: 174).[18]

This kind of history is better conceived of as *effective* history rather than objective history; namely, a kind of history that is precisely oriented toward the production of a response. And Lucan refuses to dissimulate this orientation but announces it baldly, shorn of the rhetorical camouflage of objectivity (7.207–213):

> Among later peoples too and generations to come, these events (whether their own fame will carry them into the future, or whether my vigilant work too can help great names), when they read of these wars, will provoke both hope and fear, and prayers unheard; and all will peruse your fate breathlessly, as if it were still to come, not past; and still they will side with you, Magnus.

The *Bellum Civile* cannot therefore be seen as the work of a pure ironist, as recent critics have understood him. Lucan is more than a man composing "a dream of freedom which became and remained the nightmare of ruined Rome," to quote from Ralph Johnson's eloquent account (1987: 69). The epic is instead the quintessential product of the composite figure I have termed a political ironist: whereas the ironist pure and simple practices cultural criticism at a cynical distance from his subject, our author presents himself as both detached from *and* implicated in his project; the political Lucan and the ironist Lucan draw their doubled existence from the twin perspectives I have examined in this book. As an ironist critic interested in effecting change in those who read him, therefore, our author is no mere mirror to senselessness; amid the horror of collapse, he somehow preserves "a clearing in which [his] readers can reconnect to a project of political action" (Roth 1995: 149 on ironist critics in general), and this clearing, of course, is the possibility of ideological commitment despite the self-destruction of ideology; it is home to belief before belief.

The narrator's explicit engagement in the world of which he writes also points to an enactment of the possibility of a new beginning. Apostrophes, exclamations, hope and anguish, hope-against-hope, and a deliberate ignorance of future developments all suggest an emphasis on the here and now that strives to cancel out, if only by dint of a literary posture, the finality of all these events.[19] This is especially true of Lucan's "blind" addresses and prayers, the times at which, in Berthe Marti's analysis, "the poet imaginatively participates in a past seen as still unfolding and not irrevocably lapsed, where some options are felt to be still available" (1975: 88);[20] as David Quint (1993: 338 n. 33) has already argued, "this vicarious experience of a history still open to change is meant to be carried over into the present of Lucan's contemporary readers."[21] Indeed, present-tense usage in general has something of this effect, let alone the directness of apostrophe.[22] C. P. Casparis' careful study of such usages argues for the way historical presents not only signal the narrator's subjective attitude toward the experience he is relating but also show his "attempt *through language* to force the reader into a different attitude towards reading. An attitude which bars him from the complacent escape into the world of once-upon-a-time" (1975: 158).[23] In this way, the ignorance that our narrator enacts can be an ideologically valuable stance toward the future, like the *fides ficta libertatis*. No wonder he explicitly asks that men not be allowed to know the future: "Let the mind of men be blind to future fate; may it be allowed to the fearful to hope" (2.14–15). No wonder he looks forward to the time when Romans will refuse to believe that Pompey is actually dead and buried: "the proofs of your death will perish" (8.868–869). And it is not surprising that our narrator steps in once again to *enact* this open-endedness in his very syntax: as Pompey takes the fatal steps toward his death in book 8, leaving his ship for the Egyptian rowboat, Lucan ponders the law of fate drawing his hero to this tragic death—and never finishes his sentence, a rare ellipsis that seems to deliberately leave open the chance of escape and survival: "But if the laws of the fates and the proximity of a wretched death set by command of the eternal order were not drawing Magnus, doomed to death, to the shore . . . All his companions felt a premonition of the crime" (8.568–571). "Pompey would have esacaped (but did not)" is lacking from our text, as if in deliberate refusal to pin on the man an irrevocable end.

This procedure, of course, is an irrational one, since Lucan both points to the hopelessness of his cause and fights to make it a cause nonetheless. But what I hope to have made clear by the brief analogies to such thinkers as Pascal, James, and, more recently, Zizek and Rorty, is simply that where the potential for ideologically driven action is concerned, rationality is not everything. The most important of our decisions—those about religion, ethics, and sometimes politics—cannot always be based upon rational criteria, and so our engagement in the most fundamentally human aspects of life depends on our capacity to make decisions without a rational basis. Engagement, in other words, "implies commitment to the irrational, in which alone resolution and will are grounded" (Roth 1995: 49).[24] We could put the point another way by considering Gunnar Olsson's work contrasting logic and action; as he argues in *Lines of Power / Limits of Language,* logic enacts the preservation of sameness, whereas "the essence of action is not to be truth-preserving but to be truth-creating" (1991: 56).

> The moving force of deductive reasoning is in the desire of consistency. The accepted approach is to produce a chain of arguments which is so constructed that the truths of the premises are preserved in the conclusion. Truth-preservation is the name of the game. One proposition is perfectly translated into another such that whatever follows is parasitic on whatever went before. The logician and causal reasoner is thus trained not only to anticipate the future but to control it. (Ibid., p. 55)[25]

Not only does logic, then, not allow for innovation, but it makes no allowance for the potential of action itself to escape logical analysis, to be irrational in origin and unpredictable in outcome, like Cato's decision to side with Pompey and like the outcome of this choice, however brief, in book 9's fight between Caesar and *libertas*. Such a criticism of logic, however, in no way works as a rehabilitation of paradox, although we might wonder if Lucan's emphasis on the ravages of paradox as an effect of empire could not be positively construed as a rebellion against the straitjacket of rationality; but it cannot. Paradox itself is parasitic upon the logical system it destroys, and relies on it to overturn it; logic and paradox are counterparts, and the latter, too, denies the possibility of action rather than stasis. But narrative practices freedom of interpretation, and thus fosters freedom of action. As Arendt would put it, interpretation leads to natality, "the capacity of beginning something anew, that is, of acting."[26]

In sum, storytelling as Arendt describes it and as Lucan practices it repudiates disinterestedness, rules out the invocation of absolute authorities, and treats itself as not being *outside* history and thus privileged in some way, but *in* history, implicated in all the narrowness of an embedded perspective. Lucan's storytelling sets up the possibility for new beginnings, and does so with itself as a participating impetus and as an example, itself, of how such a new beginning might work. Lucan's goal, like that of Arendt's storyteller of history (1953: 389), is to reveal "an unexpected landscape of human deeds, sufferings and new possibilities which together transcend the sum total of all willed intentions and the significance of all origins."[27] And so he has recently been read by Quint, for whom the *Civil War* is the quintessential example of an open-ended text, a text that refuses to put the stamp of finality on the history it tells of (1993: 151):

> The political hope-against-hope of the *Pharsalia* lies in this insistence upon historical open-endedness at a time when the hated imperial regime had long been confirmed in power. The very fact that the poem continues rambling along after the battle of Pharsalia denies a sense of an ending to Caesar's victory. The struggle between Liberty and Caesar goes on and on, and the epic projects no goal or teleology for its narrative.

Quint's picture is perhaps rosier than I would paint; the despairing Lucan, the Lucan who seems to encourage belief and action *despite* themselves, is absent from his text. But in depicting the poet as a willful creator of open-ended history he has done a great service in redefining the old vision of Lucan as liar, cynic, hothead, rhetorician. The changes that Lucan would foster, if effective, should in the end eliminate the need for narratives such as his; but this is the task of the political ironist extraordinaire, the excavator of Rome's history. As Michael Roth (1995: 79) has remarked of such kinds of history, "The genealogist's act of interpretation is an act of will to foster change. The notion of *effective* history becomes more concrete when we see that the desired effect of interpretation is (at least in part) the disintegration of the structures of our discourse."

In this case, I have been arguing that the discursive structures Lucan is willing to eliminate from the repertoire of his times are precisely those he uses with such consistency in his own work. His implication in the language of boundary violation, horror, paradox, despair; the nods toward Stoicism, the black cynicism, the unthinking partisanship—all of these are revealed as unsatisfactory stances toward the world by the poem's careful juxtaposition of skepticism *and* ideology, and yet at the same time they *are* the poem, provide the body for its message. This kind of "tarring" with his own brush, the use of discursive structures he does not seem to endorse, may be inevitable for the ironist critic; Richard Gilman (1975: 107) puts it well when analyzing the late nineteenth-century poets of the so-called decadent style: "They are the victims of the age as much as they are its critics or defiers. But there is a sense in which the true critic or prophet has to carry in himself the infection of the time, holding it in solution, so to speak, perhaps even being its first or chief carrier in this way." So, too, Lucan seems to carry in himself the "infection of the time," and many of his critics have puzzled over (for example) his apparent enthusiasm for describing the mutilation of the human body—had he been so enthralled a spectator at the arena? Jamie Masters (1992: 211–212), discussing the poet's treatment of the Erictho scene, identifies precisely this tendency:[28]

> There is a basic difficulty in resolving Lucan's professed horror with his apparent willingness to continue writing, in such detail, in such depth . . . Lucan is tarring himself with his own brush; by denouncing the necromancy and at the same time displaying such obvious, (pseudo-)knowledgeable relish in his treatment, he is in effect denouncing himself. More profoundly, the author of the necromancy will inevitably be tainted by the evil he describes.

But for Masters, the solution lies with the poet's "fractured voice," his double identification with the forces of good and of evil. Masters' two Lucans—the one like Pompey, pious and dilatory, the other like Caesar, bloodthirsty and driven, and relishing "the *nefas* of describing the ultimate *nefas*" (1992: 148)—explain for him this "infection" of the poetic voice.[29] I would argue, however, that the explanation lies elsewhere, in Lucan's role as ironist critic. The product of his times, he would alter the world that created him; and yet, like all theorists willing to throw away their ladder once they have reached their goal, Lucan must first use that ladder to reach the position from which he can let it fall to the ground.[30]

Interpretation not only sets up one version of history; it leaves behind the fingerprints of the interpreter. It thus functions in a curiously symbiotic way, reflecting its author's persona as much as it casts light upon an angle of history. Like a lens through which, if we look backward, we see the eye of the gazing subject, the product of interpretation lets us construct the nature of its creator, gives outlines to a subject. But I am assuming in these few comments the priority of the subject over the story he creates, and this is too facile a procedure, especially when the story is a story about the past. For narratives of the past (whether personal or political) are a crucial ingredient among the elements that go into our self-conception:

> To be without a sense of the past is to lose one's self, one's identity, for who we are is revealed in the narratives we tell of ourselves and of our world shared with others. Even when tradition has crumbled, narrativity is constitutive of identity. Actions, unlike things and natural objects, only live in the narratives of those who perform them and the narratives of those who understand, interpret, and recall them ... The narrative structure of action and of human identity means that the continuing retelling of the past, its continued reintegration into the story of the present, its reevaluation, reassessment, and reconfiguration are ontological conditions of the kinds of beings we are ... Who we are at any point is defined by the narrative uniting past and present. (Benhabib 1990: 187–188)

History can thus provide an answer to the questions moral philosophy poses of us: "Who are we, how did we come to be what we are, and what might we become?" (Rorty 1989: 60). But historical accounts can also attempt to enact the answers to these questions by contributing to the formation of the new "us," or by spurring us to create new criteria by which we might then judge ourselves.[31]

There is a sense, then, in which I am arguing that one project of the *Civil War* is to reestablish criteria for that sense of self which the other side of the *Civil War* shows to be so insidiously under siege. The poet's answer to the facts of pervasive boundary transgression, including the assaults upon the boundaries of the self, seems to be the modeling of a new source of self-identity in the subjective, invasive, and impassioned voice of the narrator supporting his ideal. The setting up of such an ideal (again, despite its unworthiness and despite the cynical and pointless environment Lucan is *also* careful to construct), the positing of goals, the sense of being able to act upon one's world, the bold assertion of self (Lucan literally emerges as an "I" to match Caesar in "me teque legent," 9.985; we are reading *him*, the subject he has made of himself), and the refusal to go quietly, Stoically, into that dark night: *all* these aspects of the narrator's persona militate against the collapsing world of the *Civil War* and the fragmentation of its bodies and souls. Elizabeth Grosz (1992: 92), echoing many a philosopher before her, has commented: "Religion wrests the subject away from the abyss of abjection"; political ideology *is* Lucan's religion, and here it wrests *his* subject away from the abyss of abjection and the cult of the Same. "In a world in which the Other has collapsed, the aesthetic task—a descent into the foundations of the symbolic construct—amounts to retracing the fragile limits of the speaking being," argues Julia Kristeva (1982: 18). And this is precisely Lucan's project: To retrace the fragile limits of the speaking being at a time in which, as he so graphically demonstrates for us through the world of his poem, those limits are under assault.

I have been invoking throughout this chapter the idea of story and interpretation as leading to the capacity for a new beginning, for some kind of action based on the adoption of "belief before belief." If this notion is to be anything more than a cerebral fancy based on my reading of an ancient text, it seems only fair to take the bold step of moving out of that text and into history itself, of doing justice to my poet, Lucan, by entering the contested and problematic ground of biographical criticism and trying to forge a new beginning for him as well. This move from text to biography partially echoes some of the critical approaches to the poet I abjure. Nonetheless, in some small measure this is my willful attempt to make meaning out of the fragments of a life not always charitably interpreted: I invite the reader to think of it as a possibility that opens up for us the idea of Lucan's own engagement, *malgré soi,* with his times.

For we could say of Lucan that he, too, followed the prescriptions of his own epic and plunged into the chance to create something new. This, despite the problems involved in this attempt and the fact that it (like Cato's choice) bore little resemblance to any untarnished ideal.[32] I am referring, of course, to Lucan's participation in the Pisonian conspiracy, attested to by all the historical sources on the poet and apparently never driven by hope for the restoration of the Republic.[33] Critics invoke the sources' negative versions of Lucan's role in the Pisonian conspiracy to strip the poet of any potential for political idealism: for Tacitus as for Suetonius, it was merely Lucan's pique at Nero for insulting his poetry that spurred him to join the conspiracy: the ideology-free act, then, of a spoilt versifier who met a sorry end—even if Lucan was briefly (for Suetonius) "practically the ringleader" of the plot. The poet's character is still more besmirched by their gossipy assertions that Lucan implicated his innocent mother, Acilia, while under torture, apparently to curry favor with the matricidal emperor.[34] We hear nothing more of Acilia; indeed, it is not beyond Tacitus to hint at disaster and conceal the reality.[35] But this is not the point, really. Critics of the *Bellum Civile* consider our information on the poet's life and shrink from attributing even a passing political activism (in poetry or in conspiracy) to this pontificating coward: rhetoric is easy, life hard. I cannot understand this stance. Lucan's endorsement of a life enriched by ideals we can create for ourselves even in the face of an existence that seems manifestly devoid of all such ideals has little to do with his behavior under torture, even if the sources' tales are true; I for one have no idea whom I might drag down with me in the (unlikely, I hope) event of torture. Instead, I insist upon one simple fact: Lucan too, "coward" or not, opted for Cato's choice. Recognizing that no kind of choice, given the circumstances of his placement in history, could represent an ideal, he participated in the life of the state even though this participation, like apathy and detachment, might involve guilt of one form or another:[36] the guilt of a bad choice, the guilt of supporting an unworthy claimant to power, the guilt of self-interest.

As I end this book, the figure who comes to mind is that of the great god who prophesies at Delphi. Apollo—if it is he—may merely predict the future, but he may also create it; it is not for us to know (5.88–93):

> What god of heaven bears the weight of earth, holding all the secrets of the eternal process and knowing the world's future . . . great and powerful, whether he only predicts fate or whether what he pronounces becomes fate, because he has predicted it?

Lucan is no stranger to the question of fate or chance. But while his poem, too, seems to waver between fatalism and open-endedness, he lets the confrontation of these two stances beget something new: he chooses to believe that it is possible that what *he* pronounces can become fate, because he has predicted it.[37] If ideology can be seen as "a form of social philosophy that aspires to merge description and prescription" (Olsson 1991: 18–19), the merging of description and prescription, detachment and engagement, in this poem is the curious blend from which the *Civil War,* in the end, draws its own character as ideology. It is the self-conscious irony with which it does so that lets us praise Lucan, rather than condemn him, for being the first practitioner of his own poem's message.

Notes

One. The Subject under Siege

1. See further Douglas (1966) 114–128 and (1970) 65–81; Newbold (1979) 93–94; Ricks (1961); Stallybrass and White (1986) 26, 90.

2. Arist. *Poetics* 7; Plato *Phaedrus* 264c, 265e; Cic. *De orat.* 2.325. See the excellent discussion of Quint (1993) 140–141 and the list of metaphors in E. Fantham, *Comparative Studies in Republican Latin Imagery* (Toronto: 1972) 164–175.

3. Bibby (1993) 35 and passim.

4. Favazza (1987) 23. Favazza's whole study includes examples of such significant self-mutilation in different cultures and in psychiatry. See also Charles Segal's interesting discussion of Seneca's *Oedipus:* he suggests that the playwright dramatizes alienation from the central values of the culture "as the inflicting or suffering of physical violence, the most obvious form of violating the self" (1983, 173).

5. See also Douglas (1970) 70.

6. As Douglas (1966) 122 remarks, "Just as it is true that everything symbolizes the body, so it is equally true (and all the more so for that reason) that the body symbolizes everything else."

7. See esp. Henderson (1987) 139, 152; Masters (1992) 1–5, 64, 72; Wanke (1964) 111–112.

8. For a more detailed discussion, see Richard J. A. Talbert, *The Senate of Imperial Rome* (Princeton: 1984), esp. 341–491. Julius Caesar curtailed senatorial oversight of foreign policy and military and financial affairs.

9. *BC* 1.223. Cf. also the imagery of 1.253: Ariminum as the *Latii claustra.* Masters (1992) 1–5 well discusses the narrator's delaying tactics and

reluctance to narrate at this crucial point. Rosner-Siegel (1983) 168–169 emphasizes Caesar's portrayal as a boundary-crosser; like lightning, he can pass through anything (1.155–156).

10. On the Rubicon and other breached boundaries, see the list of Henderson (1987) 152.

11. On Romulus and Remus, see Livy 1.3.10 ff.; Plut. *Rom.* 3 ff.; Dion. Hal. *Ant. Rom.* 1.76 ff.; in the secondary material, T. P. Wiseman, *Remus: A Roman Myth* (Cambridge and New York: 1995); Matthew Fox, *Roman Historical Myths: The Regal Period in Augustan Literature* (Oxford and New York: 1996).

12. As Fantham (1992a) notes ad loc. In general, Lucan is fond of this conceit: see "cruor imperii" and "viscera rerum," 7.579. Armies, too, are figured as the body of their general: see 5.310, 252 (Caesar is mutilated, *truncus,* by the loss of his "hands" as his soldiers mutiny); and 8.608 with Postgate (1913) ad loc.; to some degree also 1.362–363, 369, 376–378, with the comments of George (1988) 337: Laelius "thinks of himself as the body to Caesar's will." Similar imagery is used of the Senate: see "membra [senatus]," 5.36–37; "sparsum senatus corpus," 7.239; possibly 9.1043. Hardie (1993) 7–8 has a good discussion of this imagery.

13. That the head of the world is a headless trunk (or a trunkless head?) is driven home mercilessly in books 8 and 9: in only 250 lines, there are seven references to Pompey as a *truncus*—at 8.674, 608, 722, 753, 774; and 9.14 and 53.

14. Most (1992) 398 compares the relative frequency of wounds in Lucan with that in Homer, Vergil, Silius Italicus, and Statius. Lucan, of course, tops the list, and especially so with amputations. Most (1992), Narducci (1979) 51, Fuhrmann (1968), and many others have commented on the strange excesses of Lucan's scenes of mutilation and his interest in the contortions of the human body.

15. Other sources for the civil war identify this character as one of Caesar's soldiers, Acilius; see Val. Max. 3.2, Suet. *Caesar* 68, Plut. *Caesar* 16. Herodotus 6.114, however, has a similar story about one Cynegeirus (who loses only one hand, not two). See Bonner (1966) 281–282; Metger (1970) 434; Hunink (1992) ad loc.

16. Quint (1993) 146 notes appositely of such mutilation of features that

"loss of identity is the final effect of almost all of Lucan's scenes of violence."

17. See Most (1992) 397 and Quint (1993) 143–144 for further examples along these lines, while Jal (1961a) and (1963) 420 ff. notes the special cruelty associated with all civil wars at Rome. Hardie (1993) 4 points out Lucan's taste for metaphorically filling one body with another, à la Thyestes—for example, in the combatants' guilty sleep after Pharsalia.

18. Newbold (1979) has an interesting discussion of barrier and penetration language in late Latin texts. He computes the number of references to clothing, body protection, barriers, etc., over against the references to wounding, body openings, fragmentation, etc., and concludes that the texts of late antiquity score higher in both kinds of usage than his test group of Horace, Vergil, Tacitus, Suetonius, and Seneca. However, it is perhaps significant that *within* his test group, the later three authors score higher than Horace and Vergil in penetration language and lower in barrier language.

19. Note *inter alia* the following significant uses of boundary vocabulary: *limen:* 1.62, 2.106, 6.200, 10.459; *limes:* 1.216, 1.404, 1.623, 2.11, 2.487, 7.298, 9.862; *finis:* 1.333, 2.381, 2.441, 5.68, 7.811; *confinis:* 2.435, 3.275, 6.649, 9.677; *modus:* 1.562, 2.131, 2.142, 2.381, 7.532, 8.799, 9.191, 9.794, 9.804; *misceo:* 1.271, 1.320, 3.194, 3.354, 3.518, 4.104, 4.190, 5.636, 6.101, 6.458, 6.754, 6.806, 7.815, 8.408, 9.793, 9.1077; *permisceo:* 2.152, 3.138, 3.577, 4.196, 7.101.

20. See Henderson (1987) 13, on this passage, and note too the *apo koinou* construction.

21. For the usage of *limes* here, see Fantham (1992a) ad loc.: "Like *finis* and *terminus* it denotes a sanctional limit that cannot/should not be moved."

22. It is worth noting Lucan's taste for *apo koinou* constructions just where he is talking about the failure of boundaries: in book 1, for example, 38–43 (*sanguine* with both *impleat* and *saturentur*), 72–73 (both *compages* and *hora* both *mundi*), 80 (both *machina* and *foedera* with *mundi*), 93 (*erit* with *fides* and *potestas*). Similarly with the crowd that tears apart Baebius, 2.119–121: does *carpentis* go with *manus* or *coronae*?

23. See similarly Boyle (1993) 154: "Lucan dismembered epic. His subject-matter demanded it," and his list of the elements of such literary dis-

memberment: "Discontinuous narrative, constant poetic intervention and apostrophe, descriptive set-pieces, verbal lists, declamatory structure, epigram, hyperbole, paradox, the summoning of the reader into the text, prosaic language and discordant rhythm, negative formulation." Lucan's literary fragmentation of epic is also discussed by Syndikus (1958) 24–29.

24. Conte (1968) 234 applies the idea of literary fragmentation to individual passages in which humans come to pieces, and finds that asyndetic phrases often parallel unconnected limbs. He adduces 2.182 ff.: "Ad ogni membro asportato dal corpo corrisponde nella struttura sintattica una proposizione a cui la seguente si coordina per asindeto: una semplice, lineare costruzione fatta di singoli elementi accostati di seguito l'uno all'altro con la stessa freddezza con cui in successione sistematica ogni mutilazione è compiuta." See also Fantham (1992a) at 2.119–121: "A tortured and elliptical sentence representing the swift brutality of action . . . The extraordinary hyperbaton between te (19) and its verb and the dislocated phrasing mirror the fragmentation of the victim." On hyperbaton, see also below, note 51.

25. See also Favazza (1987) 123.

26. For a similar thought in Seneca, see HF 624–625, where Amphytrion recognizes Hercules by his body; as Rosenmeyer (1989) 121 comments, "The man is identified by his muscles and his viscera."

27. See also Kristeva (1982) 3–4, where she waxes eloquent on the corpse: "Refuse and corpses *show me* what I permanently thrust aside in order to live. These body fluids, this defilement, this shit are what life withstands, hardly and with difficulty, on the part of death. There, I am at the border of my condition as a living being . . . If dung signifies the other side of the border, the place where I am not and which permits me to be, the corpse, the most sickening of wastes, is a border that has encroached upon everything. It is no longer I who expel, 'I' is expelled. The border has become an object. How can I be without border? . . . The corpse, seen without God and outside of science, is the utmost of abjection. It is death infecting life." See also Thomas (1980) 98–121, a section titled "Cadavre chose ou cadavre personne." And on Lucan specifically, see Aumont (1968b) 109: "Ce qui lui a plu, semble-t'il, c'est cette putréfaction du vivant, ou mieux: la vie, pendant quelques moments encore, de cette putréfaction"; and Fauth (1975), who sees a

pathological tendency to relish the details of putrefaction and physical disintegration.

28. As Thomas (1980) 179 remarks, "La crémation . . . est moins axée sur la destruction que sur la conservation car le feu ne fait que hâter et parfaire la dissolution des chairs molles pour aboutir plus vite au substitut immuable du mort: des restes purifiés, un corps transfiguré qui atteste la liberation de l'âme et symbolise sa permanence dans le monde invisible où elle peut désormais s'installer."

29. Segal (1983) 181 follows a similar track in his analysis of Seneca's *Hippolytus,* seeing evidence of "what psychologists call primary boundary-anxiety, the concern with the autonomy of our physical being, our corporeal integrity in its most fundamental sense"; this plays itself out in the imagery of both entrapment and dismemberment.

30. Serv. ad Verg. *Aen.* 3.61; Dion. Hal. *Comp.* 3; but cf. Cic. *Orat.* 27.93 and Quint. *IO* 8.6.23, where it is identified as a form of metonymy.

31. Wanke (1964) 134 also notes Lucan's fondness for hypallage. Hübner's studies of this odd distortion have focused especially on the rivers and tributaries of the *Civil War,* where Lucan reverses the common notion that large rivers take over the name of their smaller tributary; instead, we find that the smaller body "steals" the name of the larger, as at 4.24, where the Hiberus steals the name of the Cinga. Hübner's comments on Lucan's treatment of the Hellespont are especially insightful: not only is the mythological figure Helle said to steal ("abstulit") their original name from the straits she fell into, but this original name never even appears in the text (9.955–956); the subject Helle "behaves as a usurper [*Besitzergreifende*], who forces the earlier name into obscurity, in order to make her own name alone valid and dominant" (1975, 203; a subtle critique of the rhetoric of imperialism thus seems to emerge here; the suggestion that naming is not innocent dovetails with the epic's exposure of the way power warps political and ethical terminology). Nor are rivers an innocent topic where this kind of theft is concerned: T. Murphy's analysis of their function in the ethnography of Pliny the Elder, for example, well illustrates the way they can represent the expanding grasp of Roman domination as conducts for trade, culture, and power alike; see his outstanding dissertation, "Ethnography in the *Naturalis Historia* of Pliny the Elder" (University of California at Berkeley, 1997), pp. 104–114. Hübner (1975) 210 also notes the fre-

quency of Lucan's reversals of point of view, which has something of the same effect as the reversal of subject-object relations. See also pp. 204–205 for Caesar as both besieger and besieged at 10.490–491; and Fantham (1992a) at 2.190–191, 704–705.

32. My comments in what follows borrow much from Henderson's brilliant treatment in (1987) 136–141.

33. As Henderson [1987] 141 translates "viros, quod tela vacabunt." Similarly, shipwrecked Massilians grab onto a friendly craft only to have their arms lopped off; rather than the arms falling, the men fall from their severed limbs, leaving a row of arms hanging on the ship (3.667–669). Henderson (1987) 140 sums it all up nicely: "In Lucan's text these tropes are pushed into self-defeat: the mass of *personified* weapons, those *signa, aquilae,* and *pila* of his Proem, takes shape in all the *gladii* and *enses* surrounded with properties and epithets, governing verbs, dominating their lines *more than* you can disavow, and the tropes are twisted into *absurd* relations between agency and object-world, typified by Vulteius' scene where 'the sword is punctured by the chest.'"

34. The point is not, of course, the historical accuracy of this representation but that fact that Lucan uses the image repeatedly in expressing his horror of such war.

35. Hardie (1993) 31 makes a similar observation for Cato's projected suicide.

36. Even Pompey's decapitation is refigured as a kind of suicide, since Lucan complains that the man's head was cut off with his own sword (the assassin Septimius had once served in Pompey's army, and if general and army are one, Septimius is a limb of Pompey even as he kills him; 8.607–608). Saylor (1982) 176 well discusses the intrusion of suicide imagery at Massilia and Dyrrachium, as well as at Curio's defeat at Juba's hands in North Africa: "Significantly for the idea of suicide, no one can move in this mass without either stabbing or being stabbed by fellow Romans. Meanwhile, and also significant for the idea of suicide, the forces of Juba have little to see, much less do, to help this catastrophe along. Rather, Juba's soldiers, who might more reasonably be the object of Roman aggressions, stand untouched on the periphery, as if external or incidental to a process which is determinedly self-generated and self-destructive." See also Masters (1992) 42 on suicidal-seeming deaths in general.

37. For the elaboration of this idea in Roman literature see Dutoit (1936).
38. Rosenmeyer (1989) 65, who cites A. A. Long and David N. Sedley, *The Hellenistic Philosophers* I (Cambridge: 1987) 272–274. See also Long and Sedley pp. 333–343.
39. F. Nietzsche, *The Will to Power* §547. I quote from Oscar Levy's edition of the complete works, vol. 15: 53. See similarly §§ 488 and 546.
40. See, e.g., Sall. *BJ* 1.4, 31.1–2, 95.3 (quoted in Barton 1995, 5 n. 12). In Tac. *Agr.* 6.3, *inertia* is the opposite of the political involvement from which so many upper-class Romans derived their identity—a safe choice but a foreign one. (It is perhaps interesting that a common meaning of *agere,* "to act," is simply "to live"; *OLD* s.v. 35).
41. On this slippage between weapons and the body parts they wound, see further Conte (1988) 73; Henderson (1987) 140–141; Hübner (1972) and (1974) 350–357. Similarly, *volnera,* wounds, can refer to the *arma* that caused them (3.314–315); see Hübner (1974); Hunink (1992) ad loc. with further parallels; and Henderson (1987) 141. At 7.517, arrows are named for the death they cause ("mortes").
42. *Transmittere* can mean "to let pass through" (a person through a territory, light through a window), but Lucan's usage of the verb with the object, not the subject, of an act of wounding is catachrestic. Note that even Pompey's stake-borne head, the *ora ducis,* is not "impaled loftily on a stake" ("transfixa sublimia pilo") but "lofty on an impaled stake" ("transfixo sublimia pilo," 9.138), as if the head had impaled the stake! (After our double take, we might decide to take *transfigere* in the rarer meaning of "to allow impaling" or of "to drive *x* through *y*" instead of "to pierce *x* with *y*," as the *OLD* does for this case; but such an inversion is not beyond our narrator).
43. The ruins of Carthage "raise" Marius to office (8.269); the souls of the dead "rout" the light of day (6.713); the horse's mouth irritates the bit (4.751).
44. Mayer lists examples in Lucan: 2.259, 2.499, 7.260, 7.488, and 8.484. Another oddity is the use of *frangere,* "to shatter or ruin," which occurs in the active when the meaning is "allow to be shattered" (for example, if the Isthmus of Corinth were removed, this now absent land barrier would "shatter" the Ionian sea against the Aegean, 1.103–104). Other examples of this use of *frangere, rumpere,* etc., occur at 3.485, 5.606, 8.74 (Mayer 1981 ad loc.). Unlike other Lucanian idiosyncrasies, it is

not particularly rare in Latin poetry. Mayer at 8.698 claims that *litora* refers not to the shore but to the water on the shore's edge, obviating the need to see the syntax of the sentence as reversed. Again, in view of the frequency of this figure, such an argument is completely unnecessary. It is worth noting that Postgate (1913) at 8.74 identifies this last example and others like it as usages that are "not strictly actives but rather what we may call 'inverted passives' inasmuch as the effect is not produced by an action but only by a failure to act. The Stoic notion that *to mē kōluon* (non-prevention) was a cause, *aition*, is similar." In other words, what is at stake is precisely the notion of agency or its lack. (He remarks at 8.269: "A feature of artificial poetry is the freedom with which it turns a 'relation' into a 'subject.' It makes a principle of the fallacy 'quod *post* hoc, ergo *propter* hoc,' and in the same way of 'quod *cum* hoc' (or '*in* hoc'), 'ergo *ab* hoc.' In this way we get an 'inverted passive.' " This is true enough, but I think most critics today would recognize that there is more going on here than the rococo preciosity of "artificial poetry.") More examples still: 3.738–739 (if you accept Hunink 1992 ad loc.), 6.756, 9.332, 9.681 (with Kubiak 1985 ad loc.). Finally, the usage extends even to nouns and adjectives: *laetus* as "bringing joy to" (8.89, with later parallels adduced by Postgate 1913 ad loc.); *fatum* as the "power of inflicting death" (e.g., 9.753–754); *difficilis* used in the sense of "making difficult" (e.g., 1.511); *mors* taken as the *cause* of death (9.767). For a discussion of many of these individual words, see Nisard (1849) vol. 2, 235–245. Elsewhere Lucan observes that if the war had gone differently, life would never have "lacked" Cato ("nec sancto caruisset vita Catone," 6.311).

45. As Hübner (1972) 577 remarks, hypallage often represents dead and motionless objects in living and independent motion, and vice versa. Metger (1970) 432 likewise sees Lucan's dismembered body parts as working on their own; they seek "sich noch zu bewähren." See also Fantham's interesting discussion of the Medusa episode in book 9 (1992b: 100: "Lucan's Medusa narrative will oscillate between the active and passive hazard: did she kill by the act of looking, or merely by being seen full face? Since the whole Perseus tale traditionally hung on this distinction it bears observation").

46. Another example of his play with the animate and the inanimate is provided by Scaeva's last stand in book 6, where he becomes a human

wall against Pompey's forces. See the excellent discussion of Saylor (1978), esp. p. 252. For parallels in Rabelais, see Bakhtin (1968) 313: "The grotesque image of walls turned into flesh."

47. As Hunink (1992) comments ad loc., "the resulting impression is one of extreme isolation of body parts and depersonalization"; similarly, at 3.646 we see "death struggling with part of a human body which has already become anonymous and depersonalized." This trait in Lucan is also well discussed by Fuhrmann (1968) 55 and Metger (1970). See further Opelt (1957) 444 for the idea of bodily motion frozen in death: "das Motiv der durch den Tod jäh abgebrochen und auf immer fixieren, unvollendeten Bewegung." Note also *morientia membra* at 4.650 and 5.728, and *morientia ora* at 7.609.

48. Another living human, Marius Gratidianus, is similarly described at 2.177.

49. Note again the way *nobilis* is potentially shared between *irae* and *truncus*.

50. Once again, it is no surprise to see Lucan's interest in these issues playing itself out in unusual syntax and choice of figures. He has a tendency to make one noun predicate to another when one is a person and the other an abstract noun; see 1.343 (an old man/old age), 2.152 (flight/the fleeing), 2.708 (Pompey/victory), 5.344 (a soldier/ horror), and so forth. See further Barratt (1979) at 5.58–71; Burck (1971) 93; Wanke (1964) 132. He also makes unusual use of the partitive genitive with personal pronouns, as in "aliquid tui," "some part of you," 9.75, or, equally unusually, puts a person in apposition to the noun *pars,* as at 5.40, 5.757, and 6.593, so that the living human being is literally equated with a "part." Finally, his epic is particularly rich in synecdoche—*pars pro toto*—especially the variety that substitutes a part of the body for the human agent; see, e.g., Fantham (1992a) 37; and rich, too, in well-placed examples of hyperbaton, as immediately at 1.14, "hoc . . . sanguine," and elsewhere where bodies are bleeding or otherwise coming apart.

51. However, see also Ahl (1976) 268–271, where he suggests that Cato's representation here functions against a backdrop of the mythological, and serves to associate him "with the mythical conquerors of the bestial and subhuman—including Hercules himself." For other negative assessments, see Aumont (1968b); Morford (1967) 125, 127–128. The same

criticism can be applied to the common interpretation that Cato's march is an allegory for the Stoic sage's *durum iter ad leges;* see the discussion later in this chapter.

52. Note the emphasis on what happens to the body's *limit* (*modum* is used twice).

53. See Aumont (1968) and Cazzaniga (1957). Lucan sometimes attributes the characteristics of one kind of snake to another; more importantly, he exaggerates the effect and rapidity of each snake's venom, so that "l'observation est juste à l'origine; l'imagination macabre a fait le reste" (Aumont 1968, 107).

54. For the seps, see Arist. *Mir.* 846b11, Theophrastus *HP* 9.11.1, Aelian *NA* 16.40, Pliny *NH* 23.152. Comparisons of Lucan's snakes and what we know of their counterparts in his sources may be found in the detailed studies of Aumont (1968b) and Cazzaniga (1956) and (1957).

55. For a full bibliography, see Kebric (1976) 380 n. 1.

56. On this topic, see the excellent points of George (1988) 339–340.

57. Of course, I am being somewhat disingenuous here; as George (1988) 340 chooses to stress instead, "Lucan brings Cato the binder into sharper contrast with Caesar the destroyer by means of the marriage itself . . . At the very moment *(iam)* at which Caesar is dissolving the bonds which unite humanity and Romans, Cato is binding the bond which gives rise to the state."

58. When Cato offers his ambivalent assessment of Pompey's merits after his death, the idea of limit is once again the focus: Pompey is said to be far inferior to his ancestors in recognizing the limits of the law ("nosse modum iuris," 9.191).

59. Newbold (1979) 96–97 recognizes this and so includes mention of snakes—along with wounds, decay, fragmentation, body openings, and so forth—in his tally of "penetration" in late Latin texts.

60. See also the comments of Camporesi (1988) 276 on St. Augustine: the worm and Christ are conflated as the product of self-reproduction, not copulation. Note too that Pliny the Elder tells us that serpents can be born *ex putri,* from the spinal marrow of a human being (*NH* 10.188); this belief must have its origin in the real-life appearance of worms in carrion.

61. See also Camporesi (1988) 90.

62. Medusa's riven neck is described in unusual terms that stress its erstwhile status as the border, now severed, between head and body: Per-

seus severs the "lata colubriferi ... confinia colli," 9.677. *Confinium* is rarely employed of the human body and usually designates a geographic boundary.

63. Camporesi (1988) provocatively links the Roman fear of *animacula* generated in the body to anxieties about the undermining of Rome by immigrant populations, no longer confined in the Roman imagination to the edges of the known world. See also Calvert Watkins, *How to Kill a Dragon: Aspects of Indo-European Poetics* (Oxford and New York, 1995), 297–300 and passim, on the serpent as the symbol of chaos.

64. See Friedrich (1938) 87; Lausberg (1990); Martindale (1976); Schröter (1975) 104; Viarre (1982).

65. Morford's view, however, is based on his misreading of Aulus' death at 9.737–760. According to Morford, Aulus dies "with the courage of a Stoic, opening his veins to drink his own blood. He would have failed in his agony had Cato not been present: thanks to him Aulus died master of his fate" (1967, 128). In fact Aulus drinks first seawater and then his own blood in a frenzy of lost self-control, and all Cato does when he sees this is march away in a panic lest anyone learn "hoc posse sitim."

66. See, however, Thomas (1982), who emphasizes the ethnographic tradition behind Lucan's portrayal and well isolates those aspects of the narrative that have their roots in ethical philosophy's praise of the primitive way of life.

67. Hardie (1993) 11 is more disturbed by this than Quint is: "There is something megalomaniac in Cato's altruism . . . the narrative is taken up with a catalogue of the deaths of members of the rank and file, as vulnerable as the companions of Odysseus."

68. It is dangerous here, as always, to try to generalize about the responses readers have had or may have to a specific text. I base my comments about the *Civil War* here on the recorded responses of previous critics and the classroom reactions (giggles and disgust) of students in my undergraduate and graduate classes.

69. See Kayser (1981) 185–186 and Thomson (1972) 11. For a history of the term "grotesque," which has its roots in art history, see Barasch (1971) 17–52 and Kayser (1981) 19–28.

70. McNeil (1990) 171 and Thomson (1972) 20–27. Carroll (1990) 43–53 has much the same to say of the horror genre.

71. Carroll (1990) 175, in his discussion of the horror genre, puts it well: as

a subset of fantasy, it "establishes or dis-covers an absence of separating distinction, violating a 'normal,' or common-sense perspective which represents reality as constituted by discrete but connected unities. Fantasy is preoccupied with limits, with limiting categories, and with their projected dissolution."

72. Critics usually react to this by blaming Lucan's taste for excess; see, e.g., Conte (1968) 234–238 on the resultant "freddezza" that undoes all striving for pathos.

73. As Most (1992) 400 points out, "Lucan lingers on mutilation; yet it is striking that ... the mental sufferings of the physically wounded are scarcely if ever mentioned." See also Brown (1992), who notes the lack of any facial expression as a characteristic of the gladiators and *damnati* represented in Roman mosaics; and, for the medieval dismemberment of unfeeling saints, Bynum (1992) 290.

74. See Burck (1971) 14–15, 93–95; Fraenkel (1964); Fuhrmann (1968) 27, 51, who emphasizes the absurd and the "widerlich-undefinierbare Mischung"; Lefèvre (1970); Tucker (1969); Vessey (1970); and Segal (1984) 321, who notes Seneca's "baroque fluidity between animate and inanimate, reality and fantasm, movement and stasis." For a history of critical evaluation of Lucan as "baroque" (and often "decadent"), see Schrijvers (1990) and Wanke (1964) 146–154.

75. See also Fuhrmann (1968) 27 and Johnson (1987) 52. Johnson (esp. in his chapter on Cato) is right on the mark with his analysis of the disgusting yet funny death scenes in Lucan; I would disagree only with his pessimistic conclusion.

76. For the lack of parallels between Lucan's version of Massilia and the accounts by Caesar and Dio Cassius, see Opelt (1957).

77. Quint is also insightful on Pompey's apotheosis; as he comments of Pompey in book 9, laughing from above at his headless trunk, "the distance that wit creates upon Lucan's horrific scenes of bloodshed has here become literalized" (1993, 144).

78. See Kristeva (1982) 138 similarly on Céline: His narratives "cause horror to exist and at the same time take us away from it, grip us with fear and by that very fright change language into a quilt . . . a work of lace, a show of acrobatics, a burst of laughter and a mark of death."

79. Such alienation from the text is accounted for by yet another theory of aesthetics that leaves us with much the same conclusion. The gro-

tesque aside, we could explain our reaction by applying Lessing's concept of the "pregnant moment" and its violation. The pregnant moment is what lends pathos and beauty to art: it is the moment at which we see the object of representation in a state of suffering that throws fuel on our imagination and suggests worse to come, but does not try to represent it, so that a space is left for thought. Aesthetics, in other words, imposes a law that limits the object of representation, a "sacrifice" that the artist must make to beauty to avoid advancing into the disgusting and ridiculous (Lessing 1984, 132; Lessing felt that painting more than poetry had to observe the limits of decorum, but his own list of disgusting examples in *Laocoön* chapters 22 and following somewhat negates his point). Lucan, of course, goes too far, violating this moment by going beyond it in the graphic detail of his descriptions, so that the result is revulsion rather than pity. See similarly Roland Barthes, *The Eiffel Tower and Other Mythologies,* trans. Richard Howard (New York: 1979) 71. In an interesting take on Lessing's theory, Richter (1992) 72 suggests that the disgusting image decomposes before the viewer like a corpse.

80. As Conte (1968) 233 stresses, the lexical and syntactic complexity of many of these passages adds to the effect.

81. See Tac. *Hist.* 3.83 and Alain Malissard's essay "Tacite et le théatre ou la mort en scène," in J. Bländsdorf, ed., *Theater und Gesellschaft im Imperium Romanum* (Tübingen: 1990) 213–222.

82. Pompey at *De fin.* 2.18.57 is "cui recte facienti gratia est habenda; esse enim quam vellet iniquus poterat impune"; cited in Barton (1993) 49–50 n. 144. For the expression *finis legis,* the "boundary of the law," see, e.g., Cic. *Ver.* 3.220; for *dominatio* as the form of government lacking all *fines,* Tac. *Hist.* 4.8.

83. Douglas' theories are of course more complex and nuanced than I am suggesting, and her observations change according to cultural particulars; see, e.g., her discussion of "grid" and "group" in (1970) viii–x.

84. See chap. 13 of Nussbaum (1986) on Euripides' *Hecuba.*

85. Tacitus devotes long passages of the *Annals,* for example, to describing the rise of informers, or cases of servants turning in their masters; his description of Agrippina lurking behind her curtain at a Senate meeting early in Nero's reign is similar (*Ann.* 13.5). Newbold (1979) 93–94 suggestively compares being threatened with a knife to learning of an in-

vasion of one's country or "seeing a former slave wearing the insignia of high office."

86. Opelt (1957) 443 thinks Lucan's rendition of the battle at Massilia may have been influenced by actual *naumachiae*. For the influence of gladiatorial games on Lucan more generally, see Ahl (1976) 86–88.

87. Fuhrmann (1968) 27–30 sums up these influences as "die Stichworte Cäsarenwahnsinn, Gladiatorenspiele, Rhetorenschule und raffinierter Luxus," and goes on to include the contemporary interest in magic and ecstatic cult, the ever-present spectacle of death, and the popularity of declamation.

88. See Barton (1993) 35, 56, 61–65, 68, 106; Solimano (1991) 64 ff.

89. See also Sen. *De clem.* 1.25.2–3; *EM* 7.3–5.

90. See, e.g., Sen. *De const. sap.* on the impossibility of physical or emotional injury for the wise man.

91. E.g., Aumont (1968b), Fuhrmann (1968), Most (1992). See also Rosenmeyer (1989) 126 on Senecan drama.

92. See also Sen. *Cons. ad Marc.* 11.1 on "putre . . . fluidumque corpus."

93. See Shaw (1985) 18–19, stressing Stoicism's nature at Rome as a flexible background to daily realities.

94. Of course, I am not analyzing here the tenets of Stoic philosophy, but merely discussing a few implications of its general influence, perhaps in somewhat bastardized form, among Romans of a certain class. Hence the emphasis on Seneca.

95. For a fuller discussion of this aspect of the Stoic wise man, see Rist (1978b: 260): the wise man is "passionless *(apathes),* but not without rational feelings."

96. See Barton (1993) 62. More philosophically, we find in Stoicism the generalization of the idea of determinacy to the point that (as Postgate 1913 at 8.74 has already noted) nonprevention is seen as a cause, and every event is seen as the result of external and/or internal causality. On causality, see Shaw (1985) 32. For a discussion of moral responsibility in Stoicism, see Stough (1978).

97. Philo *De incorrupt. mundi* 48 (*SVF* 2.397); cited in Most (1992) 406, who directs the reader to the discussion in Long and Sedley, *The Hellenistic Philosophers,* vol. 1, 175–176.

98. Again, the truth of this representation is hardly at issue; and as Caesar

himself would have us know, most of the blood spilled at Pharsalus was not in fact Roman (7.269–270).

99. Shay (1994) 169 cites hopelessness, estrangement, and the destruction of previous personality traits as some of the results of such war.

100. "Combat trauma destroys the *capacity* for social trust . . . Lies and euphemisms by the soldier's own military superiors and civilian leaders of course undermine social trust by destroying confidence in language. Perversion of language and destruction of the trustworthy meaning of words by official lies were not new to the Vietnam war . . . When ruptures are too violent between the social realization of 'what's right' and the inner *thémis* of ideals, ambitions, and affiliations, the inner *thémis* can collapse" (Shay 1994, 33–34, 37).

101. "Reflections upon War and Death," trans. E. Colburn Mayne, in *Sigmund Freud: Character and Culture*, ed. Philip Rieff (New York: 1963) 122; quoted in Fussell (1975) 192. For the doubling of the individual in the theater of war, see Fussell (1975) chap. 6.

102. Norman Mailer's 1939 short short story "It" is a perfect capsule vision of the irony of the doubled person: "We were going through the barbed-wire when a machine-gun started. I kept walking until I saw my head lying on the ground. 'My God, I'm dead,' my head said. And my body fell over." In Norman Mailer, *Advertisements for Myself* (1968) 318; quoted in Fussell (1975) 319–320.

103. Barton (1995) 19 n. 54 further suggests that anxiety over boundaries points in fact to their tenuousness, and even goes on to make a Nazi analogy: "Compare the Nazi's obsession with *Ordnungsgemäss*."

104. It is precisely under these conditions at Rome that we find Stoicism thriving; and Stoicism starts to appear more and more an attempt to reestablish boundaries for the self, or at least find replacements for them; its popularity can be seen as a response to the ever more tenuous sense of a divide between the self and others. Quint (1993) 144 suggests that Lucan's violence is "an acting out, carried to a sensational extreme, of the Stoic's contempt for the body." But this would align such violence with a philosophy (as I will argue) that Lucan ultimately rejects. I see the degradation of the body in the *Civil War* not as an endorsement of any doctrine but as a condemnation of a process that was stripping the idea of the person of any positive meaning.

105. Burck (1971) 14, 93–95; Wanke (1964) 190.
106. See also Thomson (1971) 11.
107. This is related to Scarry's point that "at particular moments when there is within society a crisis of belief—that is, when some central idea or ideology has ceased to elicit a population's belief . . .—the sheer material factualness of the human body will be borrowed to lend that cultural construct the aura of 'realness' and 'certainty' " (1985: 14).
108. "To form subjects is . . . to form bodies, especially to redraw the boundaries of the body" (Olsson 1991, 138).
109. Is it a coincidence that Lucan's epic has a high incidence of the figure *emphasis:* the identification of oneself, in the third person, with one's rank, name, or other form of identity bestowed from the outside? See, e.g., 8.80, with the comment of Mayer (1981) ad loc.: "Lucan's Pompey is rather given to the figure."

Two. Paradox, Doubling, and Despair

1. See Maoz (1990) 11, 14 on the paradox's threat to logic and system, and in general W. V. Quine, *The Ways of Paradox* (London: 1965), according to whose classification we are discussing "antinomies," contradictions that cannot be resolved within their own logical systems.
2. As acknowledged by almost all his critics: see, e.g., Bonner (1966); Conte (1988) 43–46; Lefèvre (1970); Marti (1966); Martindale (1976); Moretti (1984); Thierfelder (1934–35); Wanke (1964) 126–133.
3. The Latin verb form here is impersonal and passive: "there is a flight, a fleeing, into war"—so that even the action of fleeing is somehow divorced of agency during this rush toward the front.
4. For examples such as these (e.g., *velle mori*), see Moretti (1984).
5. Conte (1988) 43–46 discusses how Lucan creates material for paradoxical manipulation by first turning every difference into an opposition; even the description of the *res gestae* of the civil war falls prey to this process.
6. Marti (1966) discusses this episode in depth. See also Henderson (1987) 125–128 and Johnson (1987) 57–60. There are similar analyses of the suicide of Vulteius and his men in book 4: see Ahl (1976) 118–121; Deratani (1970) 145–146; Rutz (1960) 466–468; Thompson and Bruère (1970) 164–167.

7. For Lucan's sources, see Bonner (1966) and Marti (1966).

8. Many such paradoxes depend on plays with the temporal aspect of the two poles. For example, "Massive brutality with impunity is not possible—except while you are brutal" ("facere omnia saeve / non inpune licet, nisi cum facis," 8.492–493) relies on the reader's ability to distinguish between the temporal distinction inherent in the two uses of the verb *facere*, one aorist, the other present duration.

9. The full quotation runs as follows: "gentesne furorem / Hesperium ignotae Romanaque bella sequentur / diductique fretis alio sub sidere reges, / otia solus agam? procul hunc arcete furorem, / o superi, motura Dahas ut clade Getasque / securo me Roma cadat" (2.292–297).

10. Fantham (1992a), for example, chooses "pudorem," which is the emendation suggested by Håkanson (1979); among other editors, Housman, Duff, and Luck retain "furorem." Fantham argues ad loc. that the mss. reading "would repeat *furorem* from 292, where it has the normal Stoic associations, but with a paradoxically opposite reference to indifference." Exactly. Note, however, that she contradicts herself later at 2.523–524, apparently reading *furorem* instead of *pudorem*: "Like Cato, [Brutus] embraces the *furor* of war, seeing neutrality as a worse madness."

11. J. D. Duff, in the Loeb edition, takes the second occurrence to refer not even to dead Roman leaders but to dead Parthian ones—even more "vexing"!

12. Nor will we point to "a lapse of sensitivity in the poet" (Fantham 1992a) when we find *tollere* repeated at 2.222 and 2.229 but with completely different meanings, one for Sulla's tomb, the other for his acts of murder; Henderson' reading is fully aware of the play here (1987, 129). Other examples occur at 8.625 and 631, where the repetition of the adjacent words *prospera* and *vita* heightens the contrast between a life of steady good fortune and one of change; at 8.796 and 799, where Pompey's *tumulus* is first a humble pile of dirt, then the bounds of the Roman Empire; at 6.443 and 444, where *gens* means first those whom the gods ignore, next those whom the gods obey; at 10.229 and 234, where the Nile swells *(tumet)* not in winter but in summer; at 8.574 and 575, where *classis* is first the Egyptian fleet, then the Roman one. For a complete list of all repetitions in Lucan, see Mayer (1981) at 574–575; for other comments on this tendency in Lucan, see Gagliardi (1989) at 1.93;

Housman's introduction to his edition, p. xxxiii; Heitland's introduction to Haskin's edition, pp. 81 ff.

13. Paradox is often seen as a means of creating pathos: see Fraenkel (1964) and Thierfelder (1934–35) 56–62. Such views, however, rely on the elision of the grotesque element in Lucan, since more often our pathetic response is corrupted by the comic unnaturalness the paradoxes serve to illustrate.

14. For further thought on paradox at Rome, see Barton (1993) 119–120.

15. See Harpham (1982) 19–20, 195 n. 31; Kayser (1981) 53. Harpham, who quotes Rosalie Colic, *Paradoxia Epidemica: The Renaissance Tradition of Paradox* (Princeton: 1966), to the effect that "the implications of any particular paradox impel that paradox beyond its own limitations to defy its categories," sees this process as a positive one, but in Lucan its effect is hardly the creation of a cheerful new world of possibilities.

16. On these lines, see Gagliardi (1989) ad loc. and Jal (1963) 324–326. *Signa,* of course, is multiply determined: the military standards, the tokens given to soldiers to enable recognition of their own side, and linguistic signs as well. Hellegouarc'h (1963) 553–565 and Jal (1963) 82–146, 322–326, well discuss the historical sources' similar stress on the resemblances between the two sides, their propaganda, their offices. Each claimed to be restoring *libertas* and opposing *servitus,* and accused the other of aspiring to *regnum* or *dominatio.*

17. I am tempted to include among these doublings Lucan's fondness for the figure of *interpretatio,* wherein the same idea is reexpressed with an exegetical phrase or synonym, and for pleonasms more generally; see Barratt (1979) at 5.102–104 and 5.533–535; Fantham (1992a) 38; Wanke (1964) 139–140. Note too his tendency to group speakers in pairs, with only one exception, as Basore (1904) xiv notes.

18. As Hunink (1992) comments at 3.670, "The poet no longer gives any indication as to the nationality of the victims." And at 3.728, "Only now do we learn that Argus' father is a Massilian. From here we can reconstruct the nationality of the preceding fighters." See also his comments at 3.667.

19. See Rosner-Siegel (1983) on the similes that compare Caesar and Pompey: they are paired, symmetrical, and equal in length.

20. On *par,* see Feeney (1991) 297; Henderson (1987) 136; Masters (1992)

108 ff.; although note 1.129 on their military ability: "nec coiere pares." On the gladiatorial connotation, see Ahl (1976) 86–88 and Jal (1963) 341–343.

21. On the apparent change in Lucan's ideological stance toward the two protagonists as the poem progresses, see Chapter 3.

22. As noted by Gagliardi (1975) ad loc. That the two *pars* reflect the two sides is confirmed by 7.501–503.

23. Justly emphasized by Grimal (1970) 63 and Pavan (1970) 408–409; for a different perspective, see Narducci (1976) 128. Thompson and Bruère (1970), in discussing the Vergilian background to Lucan's fourth book, stress the parallels set up between the pairs Aeneas-Turnus and Pompeians-Caesarians, which they argue has the effect of bringing out the "civil" aspect of the conflict.

24. Several of Lucan's contemporaries shared this view that both sides were equally to blame; see, e.g., Sen. *Cons. ad Marc.* 20.6; *Ep.* 95.70, 104.29–32; *De ben.* 2.20.2: The question was not whether men were fighting "an servirent, sed utri." For similar statements in Cicero, Valerius Maximus, and the Elder Seneca, see Lintott (1971) and note esp. Sen. *Contr.* 10.3.3: "Utrae meliores partes essent, soli videbantur iudicare di posse." For further discussion on the imperial attitudes to Caesar and Pompey, see Alexander (1946); Grenade (1950); and A. Dyroff, "Caesars Anticato und Ciceros Cato," *RhM* 63 (1908) 587–604.

25. It is not by chance that the extispicy that announces the horrors to come unearths an organ that is unnaturally doubled: the seer Arruns exclaims in horror as he slices open the sacrificial bull to reveal two lobes on the animal's liver (1.625–628; Gagliardi 1989 at 1.627–628 sees the two *capita* of the inauspicious liver as "un segno infallibile del conflitto" and adduces a parallel at Sen. *Oed.* 357–360. Note, too, the myth of the doubled flame of Eteocles' and Polyneices' pyre—again, kin in civil war).

26. Lucan's senior citizen wasn't the only one who was worried; the thought had occurred already to many of Caesar and Pompey's contemporaries. Cicero's letters of 50 and 49, for example, suggest that Pompey was seen as a second Sulla. See *Att.* 7.7, 9.7, 9.10, 9.14; Fantham (1992a) 19: "Pompey's slogan was said to be 'Sulla potuit: ego non potero?' (*Att.* 9.10)"; and Gagliardi (1989) at 1.580–83. For more on this topic, see Chapter 3.

27. The *Commentariorum de bello civili libri III*, or, more simply, *Commentarii*.

28. See Ahl (1976) 328–332; Häussler (1978) 56 ff.; Housman (1927) ad loc.; Kubiak (1985) ad loc; Postgate (1913) xc; and Schrijvers (1990) 32–36, who discusses the absence of parallels in earlier and later poetry. Postgate produces the diluted translation "the memory of Pharsalia in which you and I, Caesar, have a share, shall never die" (he also takes *saecula* here to refer not to the verdict of posterity but to the spirits of the unborn thronging the air); Schrijvers, like Kubiak, takes the apostrophe to refer to Caesar, not his work, and argues that Lucan gestures here toward his readers' eternal hatred of Caesar. On a different tack, Ciechanowicz (1982) somewhat implausibly argues for Nero as the addressee here, adducing the emperor's "Troica" as the comparandum. Griset (1954) agrees with the reading of "te" as Caesar's commentaries, but argues that Lucan wants to cancel it, not compare it to his own epic. In any case, it is worth noting that Lucan was well aware of the preceding account against which he was writing, to the extent of sometimes neatly reversing the Caesarian version: see Lounsbury (1975) and Rambaud (1955).

29. I thus disagree with Johnson (1987) 120, who reads the passage as a parody "of the vatic affirmation of the power of poetry and the immortality it confers," so that future readers will see Caesar for what he is—a mouther of drivel, basking in fake glory and real stupidity.

30. Scarry also links a culture's focus on the body in all its materiality precisely to the problems with discourse we are exploring above: "The body tends to be brought forward in its most extreme and absolute form only on behalf of a cultural artifact or symbolic fragment . . . that is, it is only brought forward when there is a crisis of substantiation."

31. The two and the one, in other words, are themselves the same in Lucan's strange rendition of the world in civil war. I think this is another perspective on the point made by Masters (1992) 64: "It is certainly the case that the *transgression* of boundaries is one of the most insistent themes in the poem, and there is a case to be made for saying that a definition transgressed is a definition destroyed. But civil war creates as many boundaries as it destroys: its keynote is *division*, and it is itself a *discrimen*." See further Hardie (1993) 10–11 on Roman epic's preoccupation with one and two, based on the binaries inherent in myth (Romulus and Remus), government (the two consuls), war (civil war),

and the prevalence of brothers in line for power in the imperial house-holds of the first century A.D. I have not been able to obtain P. Hardie's article "Unity and Division in Latin Epic," in *Nottingham Classical Literature Studies*, ed. J. H. Molyneux, vol. 1, 57–71.

32. Loraux (1987) 110 has noted, of a number of attempts in antiquity to represent civil war, that every formulation of the phenomenon "equalizes [the two sides] as a matter of principle, to the point of rendering interchangeable their language and their existence. As with Thucydides analyzing the language of those in civil war (3.82), a single description is felt to be enough for the two sides." Lucan is of course no exception here, and this has important implications for the way in which the poem can be read.

33. Saylor (1986) and Masters (1992) 65 and 71–73 are excellent on manipulation of this theme during the fraternizing at Ilerda. See also Saylor (1978) on the strangely one-sided wall at the siege of Dyrrachium, and Batinsky (1992) on the catalogue of Caesar's troops, which "implicitly identifies the Roman legions with the barbarous Gauls."

34. See Henderson (1987) 151–152: "The structured process that is War: duality leading through binarism to self-cancellation and the unitary." Masters (1992) 65 and Loraux (1987) 108—"la guerre civile ferait de l'un avec du deux"—make a similar point.

35. Fontanille (1993) 85, writing on Céline. For this collapse into the unitary in his writings, see also Bernheimer (1992) 55, where the confrontation between barbarians and civilization turns out to be a duplication of the same. Henderson (1987) 124 and Quint (1993) 145–147 make the same link between the torture of human flesh and the collapse of differences into one: "In the fearful terror of human minds and the ghastly torture of human tissue you are shown the spectacle of . . . One, caved-in, World" (Henderson).

36. Fittingly, Lucan repeats this collapse on the cosmic scale: the civil war is Rome's collapse upon herself, "sub pondere lapsus / nec se Roma ferens." 1.71–72, and this imagery is followed by an evocation of cosmic dissolution at the universe's end. On the repeated imagery of cosmic dissolution in the *Civil War* and its origins in Stoic cosmology, see Lapidge (1979).

37. For similar points of view, see Barton (1993) 107; Hardie (1993) 10–11 and chap. 2 passim.

38. Henderson (1987) 124: "When Victim is Victor, when the differences

constructed and confirmed by war have shrunk toward zero, when there is only one side . . . You have, you find, no way to tell the story. This is not what narrative *can* narrate."

39. Conte (1988) 35 puts it nicely: "La giornata di Farsàlo 'chiude' l'opposizione virgiliana tra distruzione e fondazione perchè riassume nella sua importanza catastrofica l'intero senso della storia di Roma."

40. Barton (1995) 55, speaking of the effects of the empire in general, comments that "as a result of the collapse of the rules of the game, immobility and stupor were almost as frequently depicted as violence in the literature of the great heterogeneous Roman Empire. The absence of clear rules made it hard to act and speak." In the note that accompanies this comment she narrows in on Lucan's representation of the stunned Roman civilians as the perfect victims of this paralysis: "The shock of civil war is described by Lucan in terms of the hiding, emotional paralysis, impotence, speechlessness and dishonor it engendered in the community and the individual."

41. Saylor (1982) analyses the narrative of Curio's defeat in North Africa and finds that here, too, standing and forms of *stare* are thematically linked with the fighting and even with the arbitrariness of the side Curio has picked.

42. So given in *OLD*, s.v. Lewis and Short, however, suggest a derivation from *sed* as *sine*, and *-itio*, though noting that Cicero offers it as a translation of the Greek *stasis*. And Robert Maltby, *A Lexicon of Ancient Latin Etymologies* (Leeds: 1991) s.v. cites Cic. *Rep.* 6.1 and other sources for a derivation from *seorsum ire.*

43. Hunink (1992) at 3.566 notes that Lucan uses *stare* unusually with *bellum* to mean "be stuck, stop," rather than the usual meaning of "last, continue." This is an odd little coincidence, give the dual etymology latent in *stasis*, and not at all beyond Lucan's capacity as poet, although his usage of *seditio* for one at 5.323 has nothing to distinguish it.

44. Saylor (1986) 150 comments of the narrator's treatment of Ilerda: "With this imagery Lucan creates an allegory whose essential idea is that personal loyalty is illusory, partisan loyalty is on inspection foul, unnatural, a recipe for being mixed up continually in civil war, and thus one should choose detachment which is represented as pure and natural." Saylor's 1982 study of Curio's defeat in North Africa comes to a similar conclusion. For the indebtedness of this passage to Verg. *Georgics* 2.458–

540, see Bruère and Thompson (1970). The best discussion of this episode is Masters (1992) 70–90; see note 33 above.

45. My colleague Ronald Stroud has kindly pointed out to me a curious precedent for Lucan's stance in Solon's so-called Law of Stasis. The law, if it is authentic, mandated participation in the event of civil war for all Athenian citizens—on either side, apparently!—on pain of *atimia,* and was perhaps intended to force Solon's more passive supporters into service. See Arist. *Ath. Pol.* 8.5 and, for general discussion, Jal (1963), 431–433; Loraux (1987); Manville (1980) and (1990). On its authenticity, which was not doubted by ancient authors, see recently E. David, "Solon, Neutrality, and Partisan Literature of Late 5th-Century Athens," *MH* 41 (1984) 129–138 (anti); and V. Bers, "Solon's Law forbidding Neutrality and Lysias 31," *Historia* 24 (1975) 507–508. There is further bibliography in Manville (1980) 217–218 and (1990) 147–148.

46. The bibliography on this issue is huge. Scholars arguing for the sincerity of the prologue include Brisset (1964); Dilke (1972) 75–76; Grimal (1960); Haüssler (1978) 76–80 (the proem as a *speculum principis*); Jenkinson (1974); Lebek (1976) 81–107; Levi (1949); Paratore (1982); Pfliegersdorffer (1959); Thompson (1964); Williams (1978) 163–165. Their arguments rely on some or all of the following theses: (1) there are parallels between the wording of the proem and Vergil's praise of Augustus at the beginning of *Georgics* 1 (other parallels can also be found in the apotheosis of Hercules in Sen. *Herc. Oet.*); (2) the proem's contents reflect the political program of the so-called *quinquennium;* (3) the proem can be dated to 62 A.D. on the basis of internal references to Nero's foreign policy, and this was too soon for hostility to have developed between poet and emperor; (4) if the proem was meant to be ironic, surely Nero would have punished the poet? Scholars arguing for an ironic reading include Conte (1966); Croisille (1982); Ebener (1984); Gagliardi (1970) 74–80; Griset (1955); Marti (1945); Morford (1985) 2014 n. 37; Schönberger (1958); also I. Lana in *Il proemio di Lucano* (Turin: 1971) 131–47. Here we find some or all of the following reasons: (1) the flattery of Nero is too excessive to be taken seriously by anyone; (2) the medieval scholiasts interpreted several of the proem's lines as references to Nero's obesity, squinting, baldness, and clubfoot; (3) Lucan is hostile to the Julio-Claudian line in the rest of the poem. Obviously, none of the arguments in either group is decisive. Sup-

porters of the "nod to convention" theory are Béranger (1966); Bohnenkamp (1977); Dewar (1994); Nock (1926); Syndikus (1958) 93. Finally, those who believe that the proem is *deliberately* a problematic
text include Ahl (1976) 47 ff. and Due (1962) 93–95, who points out the
fallacy of reason 4 in the "sincere" camp (*obvious* sarcasm would sound
the poet's death knell). Barton (1984) 111–127 questions the structural
assumptions that provide ballast for the notion of "sincerity" in the
first place.

47. Even punctuation contributes to this process. At 1.41 the presence or
    absence of a comma before "Caesar" makes all the difference. "The
    punctuation must make it clear that this word is vocative and antici-
    patory of *tibi* (45), else, if it is taken as nominative and the commas
    are removed, Lucan is made to reckon Julius Caesar among the disasters
    to Rome and the sense is spoiled." Or rather completed (Getty 1940 ad
    loc.). Due (1962) 97–98 draws attention to this and other ambiguities.
    See also Gagliardi (1970) 93–94 and (1989) at 1.670 for a similar problem
    with the referent of "domino" in "cum domino pax ista venit"—who's
    the *dominus?* For Gagliardi and Bruère (1950), it is Augustus. Bibliog-
    raphy on this question is provided by Häussler (1978) 77 n. 28.

48. For a discussion of the related phenomenon of literary doublespeak,
    see Bartsch (1994) chaps. 4 and 5.

49. See, e.g., 1.70, "invida fatorum series," and passim.

50. On this figure, see Canovan (1992) 11–27.

51. Barton (1984) 239–240 advances a similar reading: "Lucan questions the
    possibility of setting things aright from the outset. There is operating
    concurrently in Lucan . . . an inexpiable civil war, an inconquerable
    chaos."

52. On Lucan's definitively non-Stoic depiction of fate, providence, and
    the gods, see Feeney (1991) 283–285; Le Bonniec (1970) 178–182; Jal
    (1963) 170 ff.; Johnson (1987); Liebeschutz (1979); Schotes (1969) 105–
    110, 116–129 (who stresses the difference between Lucan's treatment of
    the natural world and of human affairs). As Due (1962) 119 rightly
    emphasized long ago, "The protest against the cruelty of destiny un-
    derlies the whole poem." It is important to understand, with Feeney
    (1991) 279–283, that Lucan "uses the language of destiny and random-
    ness more or less interchangeably," rendering attempts at detailed anal-
    ysis somewhat pointless. The reader with a taste for such discussions,

especially on the roles of Fortuna, Fate, and the gods, may consult Ahl (1974); Dick (1967); Friedrich (1938); Le Bonniec (1970); Liebeschutz (1979); Soria (1972). Feeney's treatment is the best summation of the various positions.

53. "The Stoics do not recognize a causeless change; the continuum hypothesis guarantees that everything that happens, and everything that is done and thought and enunciated, is both effect and cause of another effect" (Rosenmeyer 1989: 66). As Rosenmeyer notes (pp. 64–65), in *EM* 65 Seneca traces the unitariness of the causal principle back to God; no wonder Lucan sees fit to take it apart.

54. Syndikus (1958) 32 on 1.469–522: "Die Kausalzusammenhang wird unbedenklich zerrissen, und zwischen die zusammengehörigen Abschnitte wird eine Reihe von Partien eingefügt, die nicht die geringste Handlungsfunktion besitzen."

55. Grimal (1970) 106 was surely reading another epic by another Lucan when he suggested that Lucan's practice is to change "le contingent en rationnel ... Du moment qu'une finalité humaine est imposée aux événements, ceux-ci deviennent intelligibles, ils s'ordonnent, et l'historie devient poésie." And Brisset (1964) 77 was reading it with him: for her, Lucan "croit que l'ordre du monde—et par conséquent l'ensemble des événements humains—a été reglé pour le bien des hommes: pour lui, le caractère providentiel du Destin n'est pas douteux."

56. For an interesting discussion of the connections between causality, narrative, and tragedy, see Rosenmeyer (1989) 64.

57. See Dick (1963); Feeney (1991) 291; Makowski (1977). Note, however, that the death Lucan prophecies at 5.206–208 (and elsewhere) is Caesar's.

58. Viansino (1974) 145–162 notes Lucan's uncommonly heavy usage of the future participle to give away to readers the future events of the epic, almost as if *everything* must somehow be predetermined in its hopelessness, even for the reader. Cf. 5.57 ff., 5.200 ff. This causes Narducci (1979) 70 to wonder at Lucan's wish "liceat sperare timenti," 2.15; for the explanation, see Chapters 4 and 5.

59. Jal (1963) 170 makes a similar point when he notes that Lucan now blames the Romans, now the gods, for the onset of civil war: "D'une part, en effet, la guerre civile est condamnée comme une impiété, une faute comise par les hommes envers les dieux et, par suite, exigeant

une réparation. Mais on constate par ailleurs une certaine irritation, voire indignation, contre les même dieux, que les contemporains accusent d'être restés passifs devant les crimes de la guerre civile, parfois même de les tolérer avec une certaine complaisance."

60. It makes a difference, of course, what we believe the projected ending of the poem to be. I am in agreement with the majority of the scholarship, reviewed in Ahl (1976), that Cato's death at the end of book 12 was the epic's most likely conclusion; this view is based on the poem's tetradic structure, with deaths at books 4, 8, and 12, and on the darkness of Lucan's vision of Roman history—so far. For further bibliography on this question, see Häussler (1978) 257–258; Rutz (1985) 1467–70; and the extensive discussion in Masters (1992) 216–259. Masters himself, preceded by Buchheit (1961) and Haffter (1970), argues that the epic is complete as it is.

61. The analogy is common enough; see, e.g., Lifton (1986) 448 for the comments of a prisoner doctor.

62. On this impossibility of description and the dangers of narrative encapsulation of the unspeakable, see especially Braun (1994) and Kellner (1991). Arendt brings it up in (1968) and in (1958) 444: "There are no parallels to the life in the concentration camps . . . It can never be fully reported for the very reason that the survivor returns to the world of the living, which makes it impossible for him to believe fully in his own past experiences."

63. See, e.g., Thomas (1980) 101.

64. H. Voss and R. Harrlinger, *Taschenbuch der Anatomie,* 10th ed., vol. 1 (Stuttgart, 1961) 23, 29; quoted in Aly (1994) 147.

65. See Lewin (1993) and Stein (1993).

66. Doubling is also Lifton's term for the coping mechanisms developed by SS doctors to deal with their dual role as killers and "healers"; see (1986) 419 ff. For a detailed discussion of the Nazi negotiation of selfhood in response to the camps, see Lewin (1993) 299–303.

67. See also Arendt (1958) 468: "What totalitarian rule needs to guide the behavior of its subjects is a preparation to fit each of them equally well for the role of executioner and the role of victim. This two-sided preparation, the substitute for a principle of action, is the ideology."

68. This is not only Domitius, forced willy-nilly to call Caesar's pardon a "gift," *munus;* it is the whole of Lucan's epic, caught up in the very language it would curse as contaminated.

69. For recent bibliography on most of these issues, see Lewin (1993). On personality disintegration and destruction of autonomy, see the accounts of Bettelheim (1952) 105–111, Lewin (1993), and Stein (1993).

70. Disch (1994) 111, citing Hannah Arendt, *Eichmann in Jerusalem* (New York: 1963) 86.

71. And further: "One misses the horror of German and Jewish selfhood during the Holocaust if one does not realize how the death camps . . . were at once the symbolic gastrointestinal tract, the anus and toilet of Germany-as-a-body, through which the 'bad objects' would be disposed" (Stein 1993, 491).

72. On *Muselmänner,* see also Bettelheim (1952) 106.

Three. Pompey as Pivot

1. See Macaulay's final scribble in his own text of Lucan, quoted in Duff (1928) xiv.

2. See, famously, Marti (1945). Those who agree with her reading are Brisset (1964) 114 ff.; Conte (1968) 239–241; Menz (1952) 86; Narducci (1979) 125–130; Rimbaud (1956).

3. E.g., Due (1962) 106; Rose (1966) 388–390; Schönberger (1970) 537 actually comments of Pompey's improvement that "Vielleicht hat Lucan dabei Züge seiner eigenen Entwicklung widergespiegelt." See notes 46–50 below.

4. I have not included the hypothesis of Green (1994), which stands alone; Green argues that this and other inconsistencies are due to Lucan's use of "a religious paradigm of combat and murder for kingship that had once been practiced by Latin communities" (p. 204). Such a structure would explain the aloofness of the gods, the character development, and the imagery of lighting, groves, and sacrifice owed to the gods. It is an intriguing suggestion, but can hardly bear sole responsibility for the existence of the entire epic, as Green would have it do.

5. The double simile works to offset the inequality between the two in age and ability, which lies behind Lucan's "nec coiere pares," 1.129.

6. On this topic, see Pavan (1970) and the discussion of *par* in the preceding chapter.

7. In northern Italy, a large area is "pronior in Magnum" (2.543), although these towns are characterized in general as "vario favore ancipites."

8. Dio Cassius 41.54.1—"either carelessly or because this corresponded to

his view of the two personalities": Lintott (1971) 494. Or perhaps from reading Lucan? Before the *Civil War* the comparison remains unchanged. See Caesar *BC* 1.4.4; Vell. 2.33.3; Sen. *Cons. ad Marc.* 14.3 and *Ep.* 94.5. Further parallels are cited in Barratt (1979) at 5.662–663.

9. Livy *Per.* 89; Plut. *Pomp.* 10.1–4; Appian *BC* 1.94. See *contra* Fantham (1992a) ad loc.: Lucan "has suppressed this story of Pompey's brutal lack of support for a fellow Roman." A strange kind of suppression, to bring it in when it could have been omitted.

10. As Postgate (1913) comments at 7.25, "*Sullanus* usually has a sinister sense in Lucan, and Pompey is represented as being his apt pupil in cruelty."

11. As Fantham (1992a) at 2.30 aptly comments, Lucan here "offers no indication . . . that Pompey's actions are honorable or justified. Instead by abandoning Rome (and soon Italy) Pompey has separated his political cause from the city, and deprived himself of his best claim on men's loyalty." At 2.32 she argues that Lucan is showing Pompey at his weakest in this address to the troops. See her comments also at 2.41 (the comparison of Pompey to a defeated bull) and 2.277–279 *duce privato*: Pompey was not in fact a *privatus* in 49, but held proconsular *imperium* as well as the authority conferred upon him by the Senate's emergency decree of 7 January. "It suits Lucan's argument to ignore this special authorization."

12. Masters' interpretation of the episode is very different; he argues that Lucan here enacts a "fractured voice," a splitting of narratorial authority that imitates the effects of civil war and validates both parties. "This paradox, this internal discord which aligns the poet with each party and with both simultaneously and with neither, is one of the fundamental premises of the poem's violent logic" (1992: 10). His view is an important one, but my reasons for disagreeing with it should become clear from the progression of this and the next chapter.

13. This reaction on the narrator's part is not contradicted by his earlier wish that the two sides might not fight at all, and civil war thus come to an end (4.186 ff.): throughout, civil war is the ultimate *nefas*, despite his growing preference for Pompey's side.

14. Note the traditionality of Lucan's other uses of *devotio*. Cato in book 2 wants to die as a scapegoat for Rome, to pay with his blood for the redemption of the nation (2.306–313). See also 4.272 and 533.

15. Gagliardi (1975) complains ad loc. that Lucan's desire to explain Pompey's flight as a *devotio* leaves us unconvinced. The comments of Ahl (1976) 167–168 are apt.

16. Notoriously, book 8 opens with Pompey in terror and trembling, jumping at his shadow as he makes his way through Thessaly. Once again, a rude reminder of the "other" Pompey: the reader is simply not allowed to remain comfortable with either view for long.

17. Johnson (1987) 72 opines quite acridly that "Pompey's *katasterism*, whose slim claims to poetic plausibility Cato's malicious eulogy leaves in shreds, is ridiculous by design," and I am tempted to agree.

18. On this passage, see Masters (1994) 158–161. I address his interpretation later in this chapter. For the lack of literary parallels, see Albrecht (1968) 275.

19. Nisard (1849) vol. 2: 64. Cizek's wording in (1972) 176 suggests a similar mistake: "Le poète *oublie* entièrement les défauts qu'il mettait auparavant au compte de Pompée" (my emphasis).

20. Ahl (1976) 172 comments: "To restore himself to power, Pompey is ready to do everything Caesar does and more . . . But Pompey's contemplated action is worse than what Caesar does; at least Caesar would not subjugate Rome with the troops of Rome's great enemy." Whether this action is indeed worse is not my concern here: the point is that Pompey's words are Caesar's.

21. On this episode, see Ahl (1976) 170–173.

22. Ahl (1976) 171 attributes the absence of criticism from the narrator to a literary borrowing: "The poet, it appears, would rather let the condemnation come from another of his dramatis personae, just as Vergil allows the censure of Aeneas to come from Fama, Iarbas, Jupiter, Mercury, and Dido, in *Aeneid* 4."

23. On the negative aspects of Pompey's portrayal in the later books, see Gagliardi (1970) 90–91 n. 49. Gagliardi uses this evidence to bolster his argument that Pompey's character is mixed throughout the epic, a suggestion I find unsatisfactory because it does nothing to explain the narrator's growing favoritism.

24. For further discussion of Pompey's death scene, see Bell (1994); Flume (1970) 354–359, with whose comments on Pompey's internal development I do not agree.

25. Holliday (1969) 34 acknowledges the use of Cato here precisely to say

the things that the narrator won't: "Lucan, in Book 9, primarily through Cato, clearly stated the tyrannical objectives of both Pompey and Caesar."

26. On Cato's "eulogy," see Johnson (1987) 71; Kierdorf (1979).

27. The echo of the content of the early books should be sufficient to disarm the argument that Cato is just haranguing the troops with whatever insults he thinks will be effective.

28. Or by not even addressing the erratic quality of the apologia.

29. See, e.g., Ahl (1976) 150–189; Gagliardi (1970) 90–91; Kierdorf (1979); Narducci (1985) 1553–56; Newmyer (1983); Rosner-Siegel (1983); Schröter (1975); Syndikus (1958) 101–105.

30. Marti (1970) 31 still holds this opinion: "Bien que mûri par les épreuves et progressivement libéré de son ambition arrogante et despotique, Pompée n'attient la vraie grandeur qu'au moment de la défaite et de la mort." Similarly, Conte (1968) 240 would have us believe, "Following the eighth book of the *Pharsalia* his pilgrimage from evil to good, from Caesar's blameworthiness to Cato's sanctity, is completed."

31. See Schotes (1969) and above, Chapter 2, note 52.

32. E.g., Cattin (1965).

33. For further arguments against the view of Pompey as *proficiens,* see Ahl (1976) 170; Deratani (1970); Dilke (1979); Gagliardi (1975) 16–17; Kierdorf (1979); Lintott (1971) 504–505. But critics do not always distinguish between growing support for Pompey and growing hatred of Caesar, so that discussions of the one sometimes merge with analyses of the other, as in Dilke (1972).

34. Lucan is said to exonerate Pompey at Pharsalus for the following reasons: he invents the sympathetic dream of the eve of the battle; he transfers responsibility for the decision to fight to Cicero; he alters the battle plan used by Pompey; and he suggests Pompey's flight was intended to prevent further slaughter of the nobility. Lounsbury (1976) 229 concludes that "Much has changed from the poet's acrid assessment in book one: Pompey now is a hero against whom no hostile imputation is allowed."

35. See also Narducci (1979) 125–126.

36. Basing her arguments on Malcovati (1953).

37. For example, "Lucan's description of the 1st triumvirate is essentially the same as that of Cicero. In the opening lines of the *De bello civili,* he called it an alliance of tyranny, *foedus regni*" (Holliday 1969: 31). And

similarly with the crediting of Rome's downfall to three *domini* and the idea that both Caesar and Pompey were after *regnum.*

38. See, e.g., *Fam.* 8.4.4, 8.11.3, 8.14.3.

39. Not that negative evaluations too were not available in 60 and 59.

40. *Att.* 8.11.2 baldly states that "Tyranny [*dominatio*] is sought by both of them [Caesar and Pompey]"; see similarly 10.4.4.

41. There is more on Sulla and Pompey: see *Att.* 9.10.6 and the list of letters given by Fantham (1992a) 91; Lintott (1971) 498; and Malcovati (1953); all of which (as Fantham says) "bear witness to contemporary fears that Pompey would imitate Sulla ... Pompey's slogan was said to be 'Sulla potuit: ego non potero?' (*Att.* 9.10)." The perception of Pompey as a second Sulla is repeated in Appian *BC* 2.35, 2.41; Dio Cassius 41.5, 41.8, 41.16; Sen. *Contr.* 10.1.8; Val. Max. 6.2.4 ff.

42. Holliday (1969) 66 does acknowledge the existence of these letters, even pointing out the specifics of Cicero's criticisms: "In the letters of 49 and 48, Cicero repeatedly charged Pompey with cowardliness and fear ... Cicero feared Pompey's ambition for sovereignty and the bloodthirsty threats of many of the Pompeians. He wrote to Atticus that Pompey had decided to imitate Sulla's reign. He feared lest he win, for not a roof would be left in Italy (*Att.* 9.7.3, 9.7.5)." She must therefore explain away this stumbling block for her thesis of Ciceronian dependence by arguing that "Lucan recorded this criticism, [but] rejected it and called the various allegations unsound, *invalidae causae*" (p. 67); this is from 7.67, the narrator's response to Cicero's urgings for battle *only.* But why record it at all?

43. Caesar: 1.330, 7.307; Curio: 1.326, 1.335; Roman citizens: 2.171, 2.228, 2.232; Cato: 9.204; Pompey: 2.582.

44. See similarly Sen. *Cons. ad Marc.* 20.6. It is also worth noting that Plutarch's *Life of Pompey* records that Pompey's contemporaries compared him to Alexander the Great (§§2, 46), to whom Caesar is assimilated in *Bellum Civile,* book 9. Even Pompey's cavalry were critical of his lust for power, while Domitius Ahenobarbus (cos. 54) was calling him "Agamemnon" and "king of kings" (§67). Tacitus is also negative on Pompey, and seems to see the principate as much a continuation in some ways of the civil war; see Keitel (1984).

45. See, as well as the bibliography in note 46, B. W. Henderson, *The Life and Principate of Nero* (London: 1903) 264 ff.

46. On Lucan's life, politics, and poetic production, see Ahl (1971) and

(1976) 333–353; Due (1958) 90 ff.; Gresseth (1957); Griffin (1984) 157–159; Martindale (1984); Pfligersdorffer (1959); Rose (1966; his long study situates Lucan's change in book 7); Schönberger (1958) and (1970); Sullivan (1985) 458–460. The ancient sources are the Vaccan and Suetonian *Lives*, as well as the later medieval *Life* of the Codex Vossianus II; Tac. *Ann.* 15.49; Dio 62.29.4;

47. On the manner of Lucan's death, see Tucker (1987), suggesting execution; Wilson (1990), supporting suicide.

48. Based on the evidence of the Vacca life, 335.25 Hosius: "Quippe et certamine pentaeterico acto in Pompei theatro laudibus recitatis in Neronem fuerat coronatus et ex tempore Orphea scriptum in experimentum adversum complures ediderat poetas et tres libros, quales videmus. Quare inimicum sibi fecit imperatorem. Quo ambitiosa vanitate, non hominum tantum, sed et artium sibi principatum vindicante, interdictum est ei poetica, interdictum est etiam causarum actionibus." But Statius' chronology is different in *Silvae* 2.7.54–74, and in general opinions vary. Ahl (1971) suggests it was in fact the *De incendio urbis* that provoked the ban.

49. "Plerique Vestini quoque consulis acre ingenium vitavisse Pisonem crediderunt, ne ad libertatem oreretur, vel delecto imperatore alio sui muneris rem publicam faceret"; *Ann.* 15.52.5. In support of the view that by Lucan's day genuine belief in the potential of a republican restoration was dead, see Wirzubski (1950) 124–171 and K. Rauflaub, "Grundzüge, Ziele und Ideen der Opposition gegen di Kaiser im 1. Jh. n. Chr.: Versuch einer Stand orthestimmung," *Entretiens* 33 (1987) 1–64. However, the presence of at least some believers even at this late date is suggested by the very fact that the exclusion of Vestinius was necessary. Some critics go so far as to argue that Lucan (and the *Bellum Civile)* is not republican-minded at all, just dabbling in fashionable literature and/or urging Nero to be a better *princeps* on the Stoic model; see Béranger (1966) 103 ff.; Brisset (1964) 171–223; Griffin (1984) 156–159; Lebek (1976); Mayer (1978) 85–88; Pavan (1954–55); Schrijvers (1990) 15 ff.; Syndikus (1958) 90–92; and, *contra*, Martindale (1984). It seems to me one can simultaneously claim that the *Bellum Civile* is a republican poem and accept that belief in the restoration of the Republic was largely dead.

50. Of course, we could argue against this by accepting (as Tacitus and

Vacca claim) that Lucan's only reason for joining the conspiracy was poetic pique about the ban and that belief in the possibility of change had nothing to do with it. (See also Tac. *Ann.* 15.44 on Afranius Quintianus, goaded into joining by a dirty poem about him.) But it seems to me that if we are using the *Lives* to provide information about the *Bellum Civile* in the first place, we are accepting the link between Lucan's life and his literature, and cannot suddenly disown this link ("the fervent partisanship and anti-Julio-Claudianism of the poem means nothing") when it is convenient to do so. See also the cautions of Ahl (1976) 343–346 against accepting the frivolous view of Lucan's motivation.

51. The same criticism can be made of the less commonly advanced argument that the narrator eventually favors Pompey precisely because he has lost and, by losing, is cast in a new, more dignified role; see Burck (1970) 156: "nur nach der Niederlage von Pharsalus wächst er zu menschischer Größe empor." Similarly Cizek (1972) 176; Due (1958) 108–110; Fantham (1992a) 33; Viansino (1974) 130–133. Feeney (1986a) has a more interesting take on Pompey's change as the evolution from man to *nomen,* an idea that expands on Johnson (1987) 71: "Pompey remains for Cato ... merely the lesser of two evils, even though his *name* has become a slogan, a symbol of the new stages of the struggle against Caesar." On this idea, see Chapter 4.

52. Masters does acknowledge the presence of this voice at (1992) 168–169, but his interpretation of the poem does little to explain its presence.

53. For a different view of apostrophe as deflecting attention *away* from the narrator, see Rosenmeyer (1989) 179–182.

54. According to Hampel (1908), Lucan's use of apostrophe is more than triple the Vergilian incidences.

55. For comments (or criticism) on Lucan's extensive use of this device, see Ahl (1976) 151; Albrecht (1970) 289–292; Endt (1905); Henderson (1987) 135–136; Marti (1975) 82–89; Martindale (1993) 67–68; Mayer (1981) at 8.827; Narducci (1979) 115–119; Syndikus (1958) 39–43; Viansino (1974) 45–75, 97–101; Williams (1978) 234. On apostrophe in general, see Culler (1981) 135–154.

56. Block (1982) 8, who bases her description on Quint. 4.1.63 and other ancient sources; apostrophe is a " 'turning' from one stance to another, from objective to subjective narration, or from one audience to another

... [which] brings about a complementary change in the stance of the audience."

57. For convenient (but incomplete) lists of Lucanian apostrophes and their addressees, see Endt (1905) 111–116; Marti (1964) 180–181; Viansino (1974) 45–75.

58. See Endt (1905) 125–129, who notes that many of Lucan's apostrophic forms are the same in the vocative and nominative (e.g., "Caesar"); others are placed so that the short final syllable is lengthened through position anyhow. He concludes that "somit kann der Vokativ die Apostrophe nicht herbeigeführt haben. Diese Tatsache wird durch die Beobachtung gestützt, dass in manchem Verse, der die zweite Person enthält, überhaupt kein Vokativ enthalten ist."

59. Cf. "non gemitus, non fletus erat, salvaque verendus / maiestate dolor, qualem te, Magne, decebat / Romanis praestare malis. non impare voltu / aspicis Emathiam ... iam pondere fati / deposito securus abis" (7.680–687) and "pavet ille fragorem / motorum ventis nemorum, comitumque suorum / qui post terga redit trepidum laterique timentem / exanimat" (8.5–8). Some readers might quibble, saying that Pompey is unafraid as he flees Pharsalus but fearful later as he continues his flight. But my point is that these apparent changes in the epic's presentation of Pompey are somewhat startling, and seem to call for such rationalizing-away on a regular basis. The Pompey we see does not live up to the narrator's high expectations.

60. For examples of this attitude, see, 1.8 ff.; 4.788 ff.; 4.799–905; 5.297–299; 7.440 ff. I am clearly not taking *libertas* here in Wirszubski's sense of *senatoria libertas,* i.e., respect for the laws and for the views and role of the senate on the part of the *principes.* Lucan's freewheeling use of terms like *tyrannus* for anyone grasping at the role of "first citizen" and his laments for a bygone era in book 7 seem to rule out so tepid a view. See *contra* Pavan (1970).

61. On the narrator's *indignatio,* see Seitz (1965). Marti (1975) 84 notes the introduction into epic, with Lucan, of "authorial narrator's invective."

62. Epic narrators usually apostrophize the gods in a context of praise or the dedication of gifts; see Endt (1905) 117–119.

63. As Culler (1981) 150 puts it, "Apostrophes displace this irreversible structure [of temporality] by removing the opposition between presence and absence from empirical time and locating it in a discursive

time. The temporal movement from A to B . . . becomes a reversible alternation between 'A' and 'B.' "

64. See, e.g, 4.110–120; 4.182–185; 5.297 ff.

65. Endt (1905) 112–113 similarly notes the narrator's willingness to give away the future in apostrophe, as at 5.49 ff. in his address to Ptolemy.

66. See Ahl (1976) 570. For comparison to Homeric exclamations such as *nepios* ("fool!"), which are, however, never included in a narratorial address to any character, see Endt (1905) 122.

67. Viansino (1974) 66 ff. provides a more or less complete list of narratorial addresses to Pompey and Caesar, but it is marked by a few errors of addition and omission; for example, 1.330–331 is not a narratorial apostrophe, and 7.803–824, which is, does not figure in his list (perhaps because some mss. omit one of the two vocative forms of Caesar in this passage (at 7.820–822).

68. The relevant apostrophes are: to Caesar, 1.123–124, 4.254–259, 5.310–316, 7.721–723, 7.803–824, 9.1046–63; to Pompey (always as "Magne"), 1.121–123, 2.725–734, 5.472–475, 5.728–731, 7.29–44, 7.213, 7.233–234, 7.583–585, 7.679–681, 7.689–711, 7.726–727, 8.607–608, 8.804–806, 8.846–872, 9.1043–46, 10.6–8, 10.347–348, 10.413–414, 10.524–526. Note the increase from four addresses to Pompey in the first six books to fifteen in the last four.

69. As Endt (1905) 112 remarks of the narrator's apostrophes, "Der Dichter nimmt die Gelegenheit wahr zu sagen, dass er auf Seite der Feinde Caesars stehe. Dieser Zug lässt sich fast bei jeder Apostrophe an Pompeius erkennen."

70. Block (1982) 17–20 has an excellent discussion of these lines, setting up the narrator in opposition to his text in a way that seems to anticipate Lucan's manipulation of his narrator: "The narrator's response [to Nisus' and Euryalus' death] . . . clashes with the response triggered by the narrative itself, and demands that the audience see and consider this difference. It is perhaps not an exaggeration to say that the discrepancy is a shock that leads the audience to question the perceptions not only of itself but of the narrator upon whom it relies for its access to the poem. This is the unreliable, the idiosyncratic narrator of fiction . . . The apostrophe to Nisus and Euryalus in Book 9 emphasizes the persistent presence of a tension arising from the need on the part of the audience to accept responsibility for synthesizing disparate points

of view." On the comparison of Lucan and Vergil here, see also Endt (1905) 121.

71. The address to Magnus at 7.233–234, in which the narrator urges him to deprive Caesar of subject peoples to rule after his victory by spilling all their blood at Pharsalus, is not negative; it is a last, crazy prayer on the narrator's part that Caesar's triumph should in fact be meaningless.

72. The presence of "nostra" at 9.14 seems to suggest here, too, the subjective stance of the narratorial voice rather than a detached authorial account, but these distinctions are not always completely clear. Nor do I claim they are: my point is merely that in those instances in which the narrator's voice is clearly discernible as such, Pompey emerges as the hero we hate to love.

73. On the essential hopefulness of these lines, see Quint (1993) 150–151; Schröter (1975) 104.

74. This is all the more surprising if we recall the reservations about Pompey voiced in Cicero's letters.

75. See also Culler (1981) 152–153: "Apostrophe is not the representation of an event; if it works, it produces a fictive, discursive event."

Four. The Will to Believe

1. Such people understand that "moral principles (the categorical imperative, the utilitarian principle, and so forth) only have a point insofar as they incorporate tacit reference to a whole range of institutions, practices, and vocabularies of moral and political deliberation. They are reminders of, abbreviations for, such practices, not justifications of such practices" (Rorty 1989, 58–59).

2. See similarly Canovan (1992) 198 on Hannah Arendt: She "was at one and the same time sure of her own convictions *and* sure that no one's personal convictions can be authoritative for politics. Such convictions are subjective, which does not make them any less demanding for the subject in question, but does mean that they cannot simply be generalized to produce authoritative moral rules."

3. For example, the narrator repeatedly uses the hollowed-out term *virtus* in its nonironic sense; see, e.g., 3.475, 7.383, 9.371, 9.882; contrast 1.668, 6.148. Saylor (1978) 253 well discusses the adjacent and opposite usages of *pius* in book 6 to characterize both Pompey and Scaeva, although

he goes on to argue that one *pius* is "true," the other not. Brouwers (1989) and Wanke (1964) 177 have discussions of such terminology.

4. When I use the term "ideology" or its derivatives here and elsewhere, I am doing so in three of the possible meanings laid out by Eagleton (1991) 2: as "a socially necessary illusion," an "action-oriented set of beliefs," and "the indispensable medium in which individuals live out their relations to a social structure" (definitions [i], [l], and [o] in Eagleton). This is in essence a restatement of Martin Seliger's definition in *Ideology and Politics* (London: 1976) 11: "Sets of ideas by which men posit, explain, and justify ends and means of organized social action, and specifically political action, irrespective of whether such action aims to preserve, amend, uproot or rebuild a given social order" (quoted in Eagleton 1991, 6–7).

5. For deliberate self-contradiction in Roman epic, see the suggestive article on Vergil of O'Hara (1994).

6. For Masters' other argument, that "Lucan's poem is a *reductio ad absurdum* of politically committed writing" (1994, 168), see the previous chapter.

7. From the perspective of the "curable" universe, and in the passages involving *piacula, inferiae,* and *devotiones,* "Lucan expresses the necessity and desire to expiate, and expiation implies the power of humans to effect their own salvation. It also implies the existence of a contractual relationship to the *superi* and the adherence of the *superi* to that contract. This is the aspect of Lucan which appears to and appeals to those who give the *Bellum Civile* an essentially Stoic interpretation" (Barton 1984, 239).

8. For Barton, too, there is a temporal aspect to this development: "From Book One, however, these patterns of thought coexist in Lucan's mind . . . with patterns based on a perception of the forces outside of one's control as being hostile, arbitrary, and humiliating" (1984, 150–151). While her perspective is more closely focused on Lucan's attitude to the divine, and while her arguments are more complicated than the brief sketch I have given above (our views on the proem, for example, are quite different), I find the similarities in our points of view well worth noting.

9. Nor have I anything to say here about Rorty's further distinction between private irony and liberal hope, between the goals of literature

and the goals of philosophy. I am interested purely in his concept of the ironist.

10. Although one does not lack for sources ready to attest to our own societal oscillation between meaning and nonmeaning, moralism and cynicism: we are "plagued by the embarrassing discrepancy between the two" (Eagleton 1991: 39).

11. William James, *The Varieties of Religious Experience* (New York: 1936) 519.

12. For James, what would be irrational would be the refusal to harbor a beneficial belief only because its truth could not be proved: "We are supposed to gain, even now, by our belief, and to lose by our non-belief, a certain vital good" (1979: 30).

13. There are perhaps similarities here with the phenomenon of "doubling," the splitting of personhood that I discussed briefly at the end of Chapter 1—the sense that the person doing the suffering or (on the other side) the torturing is not the same person as oneself. As Lifton (1986) 420 explains, "Doubling is part of the universal potential for what William James called the 'divided self'; that is, for opposing tendencies in the self . . . To James . . . the potential for doubling is part of being human, and the process is likely to take place in extremity, in relation to death." In its application to the murderer-doctors of the Nazi concentration camps (see Lifton 1986, 420), this theory has not found universal acceptance; for one rebuttal, see the introduction to Aly (1994). For the association of doubling with situations of extreme stress, see also Fussell (1975) 191–196.

14. All quotations of Pascal are from A. J. Krailsheimer's translation of the *Penseés* (Harmondsworth: 1966).

15. This is not to be confused with P. Sloterdijk's thesis in *The Critique of Cynical Reason* (1983), where he suggests that the cynical subject knows well the dissembling nature of official ideology but finds reasons to act according to that ideology and to maintain its mask. For a discussion of the contrast between Sloterdijk and Zizek, see Eagleton (1991) 40: "Zizek, by contrast, suggests a critical adjustment: 'they know that, in their activity, they are following an illusion, but still, they are doing it.' "

16. For an excellent discussion of the gods in Lucan in general (and the relevant bibliography), see Feeney (1991) 269–301, with whom I am in

essential agreement. Häussler (1978) 96–97 is also worth consulting for secondary sources.

17. For this, see Ahl (1974); Dick (1967); Friedrich (1938); Le Bonniec (1970); Schönberger (1958); Wanke (1964) 163–166. Barratt (1979) 95–96 has further bibliography.

18. "This supposedly godless poem is actually obsessed with the gods, crammed with references to their plans and deeds, with prophetic scenes, with the poet's addresses to the ones above. As has been noted many times, it is specifically the mimesis of divine characters in action which is missing" (Feeney 1991, 270).

19. This address is very similar to that at 5.297–299. See other citations of such "unknowing" apostrophes in Chapter 3.

20. Due (1970) 216 calls "la jalousie des dieux" and "la cruauté des destins" the fundamental experience that, for Lucan, constitutes the tragedy of Roman history.

21. I cannot therefore agree with Ahl (1974) 569, who claims that "at no point during the Pharsalia does Lucan go so far as to say that the gods do not exist. He argues, rather, that they no longer wield any power in human affairs." Ahl seems to be looking only at "mentimur regnare Iovem," which one might translate as "Jupiter exists but does not rule over us"; however, the phrase that precedes rules out this interpretation.

22. "Cladis tamen huius habemus / vindictam, quantam terris dare numina fas est: / bella pares superis facient civilia divos" (7.455–457). See Due (1962) 101–102 on this absurdity, and Le Bonniec (1970) 200 on its relation to the proem.

23. Lucan affects a similar doubt about the reasons for various natural phenomena, and often offers his readers a choice between a divine aetiology and a naturalistic or scientific one. See Dick (1965); Häussler (1978) 60–68; Hunink (1992) at 3.198; Le Bonniec (1970) 167–168; Malcovati (1940) 46–51; O'Hara (1994). The device is common in Lucretius.

24. "Even if it is *fors incerta* that determines what does and does not occur," as Johnson (1987: 8) points out, "then Jupiter cannot reasonably be called upon to predict a future that he is ignorant of (an ignorance that the ironic *paras* underscores)."

25. Or with Nature rather than Jupiter, who cannot be assumed to exist in

the background. See Fantham (1992a) at 2.7 on *parens rerum:* "perhaps Mother Nature (cf. *TLL* 10.364.iii.b) rather than the Demiurge or even Jupiter (ibid. iii. 1.2a). The use of *parens rerum* for Nature is found in Stoic writing (cf. 10.238; Cic. *Tusc.* 1.118, 5.39," etc.

26. See Fantham (1992a) ad loc.; Gagliardi (1989) at 1.642–644; Schotes (1969) 16–18; Viansino (1974) 81–82. On this passage in general, see Johnson (1987) 7–9; Le Bonniec (1970) 177–178. For a parallel passage in Seneca, see *EM* 16.4.

27. As Johnson (1987) 9 would have it, "The alternatives that Lucan posits in his ironic prayer to Jupiter are precisely what he rejects from his poem. His universe is not divine or rational. It is demonic and sub-rational."

28. Of course, the most common response to the contradictions here and elsewhere has been to remove one of the offending sides, usually by identifying it as an emotional outburst that has no basis in the poet's *real* opinion. Hutchinson (1993) 254 remarks on "sunt nobis nulla profecto numina": "We should not make this passage the key to the theology of the poem ... The line of argument looks strange and futile when the gods have positively and persistently promoted the cause of wrong." Malcovati (1940) puts the contradictions down to the different religious tendencies present in Lucan's environment and to his youth.

29. Häussler (1978) 52–53 suggests that Lucan's religious inconsistencies represent an active and ongoing struggle in the poet's mind.

30. Viansino (1974) 101, commenting on the combination of hope and illusion characteristic of this epic, has it exactly right: "Con l'alternarsi di speranze e di certezze, la teatrale dinamicità del 'Bellum civile,' pur illusoria nella sua dialettica, vale quindi a liberare autore e lettori dalla disperazione implicita in un presente irrimediabile."

31. It is interesting, though not necessarily significant, that the idea of believing in one's own fiction crops up at least twice among the terrified denizens of Lucan's text: see 1.484–486 and 502–503. *Fingere* is of course the activity of the composing poet *and* the manner of *libertas'* continued existence until Pompey's death; on this, see Chapter 5.

32. Note his equation of civil war with *ekpurōsis,* emphasized by George (1991) 252.

33. Again, see Johnson (1987) 71: "Pompey remains for Cato ... merely the lesser of two evils, even though his *name* has become a slogan, a symbol

of the new stages of the struggle against Caesar." See also Boyle (1993) 156 on "the gap between Pompey and his name."

34. Recalling, of course, Lucan's famous description of the man early in the epic as "magni nominis umbra," 1.135. For further plays on "Magnus," especially during Pompey's death scene ("the 'nomen est omen' . . . is reversed here"), see Hunink (1991) at 3.5.

35. On the further connotations of *nomen* as the name of the dead, see Postgate (1913) at 8.803.

36. *Contra* Narducci (1979) 68–69, who thinks that Lucan's outlook is fundamentally Stoic despite its inconsistencies and that the outbursts are spurred by youth and emotion. Due (1970) 220, on the other hand, notes that Lucan "fait usage de la langue stoïcienne, des catégories stoïciennes, de la physique stoïcienne; mais en décrivant ce qui à ses yeux est la destruction finale et irrévocable de la patrie idéale, il se refuse à y voir la main du dieu bon." See further Gagliardi (1970) 123. The view of Brisset (1964) 77–78 that Lucan believes that the world and its events are all regulated for the ultimate good of mankind, and that he does not doubt the providential character of destiny, is flatly wrong.

37. On the Stoic elements in the *Civil War,* see Due (1970); Gagliardi (1970); George (1968) 331 n. 1; Lapidge (1979); Le Bonniec (1970); Malcovati (1940) 56 ff.; Schotes (1969); Syndikus (1958) 82–84; Viansino (1974). Schotes' careful study concludes that the poem's take on nature and ethics is derived from Stoicism, but not so its position on God, fortune, and the fates.

38. On this idea, see, e.g., Sen. *EM* 95.49; *De ira* 2.27.

39. As Due (1970) 212, contrasting Seneca's prescriptions in *De ira* 2.9.3–4, and Nisard (1849) at 2.134–135 already point out. Says Le Bonniec (1970) 68, "Aucun poète ancien n'est comparable à Lucain pour la véhémence et la constance dans l'invective blasphématoire."

40. On this topic, see Brunt (1975); George (1991); Shaw (1985).

41. Note that Lucan is negative on Alexander in 10.20–52, unlike Stoics, for whom Alexander was a model king. See George (1991) 241, 257; and J. Rufus Fears, "The Stoic View of the Career and Character of Alexander the Great," *Philologus* 118 (1974) 113–130.

42. Alexander (1946) specifically derives Lucan's portrayal of Cato from the influence of Seneca. But Seneca's was a changing view; see Narducci (1979) 135.

43. Croisille (1982) thus suggests that Lucan's Cato is actually a spokesperson for Seneca himself, with Lucan in the minor role of Brutus; Grimal (1970) 97–98 would see the discussion as a debate between the principles of the Academy (Brutus) and Stoicism (Cato).

44. For citations from *SVF* (Greek, not Roman Stoics) and general bibliography in favor of the wise man's participation in the state, see George (1991) 240 nn. 10–11. Note that George's (Greek) citations for the notion of the wise man as adviser to the monarch include no suggestion of the wise man fighting to help *make* the monarch (p. 241).

45. On the whole issue of the so-called Stoic opposition, see Brunt (1975); Griffin (1984) 171–177; Shaw (1985); Wirzubski (1950) 138–143. I am in agreement with their conclusion that the political circumstances of the Roman senators who were Stoic "took precedence over any philosophical views they might happen to espouse" (Shaw 1985: 47; for his modification of Wirzubski, see p. 48); for a different view, see Ramsay MacMullen's *Enemies of the Roman Order: Treason, Unrest, and Alienation in the Empire* (London and New York: 1966) 1–94. I would suggest, in fact, that Stoicism seems to have conveniently supplied senators with categories in which to voice their opposition; it provided the vocabulary to made dissent ideological—a different thing altogether from any "Stoic opposition."

46. Thus "Seneca's views on the propriety of a political career are self-contradictory, but the assumption that these contradictions can be explained simply by the hypothesis that he recommended *otium* only when his own political prospects were impaired and political activity only when himself engaged in public affairs, hardly fits the fact that we find the same antinomy in the sermons of Epictetus and the *Meditations* of Marcus. Seneca's advocacy of quietism reflects one important aspect of Stoic influence" (Brunt 1975: 19).

47. Brunt (1975) 10 n. 13 cites the texts in question: Quint. *pr.* 15, 12.3.12; Tac. *Ann.* 13.42.3; *Hist.* 4.5; *Agr.* 4.3; and adduces also Cic. *Fam.* 15.4.16: "Philosophiam veram illam et antiquam, quae quibusdam oti esse et desidiae videtur, in forum atque in ipsam aciem paene deduximus."

48. See Epict. 1.29, 3.24.103–107; 4.1.86–90; 4.7. Brunt continues: "Thrasea went no further, and perished on that ground alone. Under Domitian too Arulenus Rusticus, called an ape of the Stoics, is said to have suffered death merely for his laudation of Thrasea, Herennius Senecio for

his biography of the elder Helvidius and for failing to pursue the normal senatorial career, and Helvidius' own son for his withdrawal from politics and for alleged libels on the emperor; by what they did not do, and sometimes what they said, these men had indicated that Domitian was a tyrant, no more, but that was sufficient offense." Brunt also discusses the case of the Elder Helvidius, who went further, and locates his motivation as much in a desire to defend the constitution as in the enactment of a Stoic role.

49. George (1991) suggests that Lucan's presentation of Cato shows that there did still exist belief in the Republic; but Cato is not in fact possessed of such an opinion. So it is incorrect to argue that because "the Roman Republic was Zeno's ideal state in action . . . the Stoic ideal and the *mos maiorum* had become intertwined, [and] Cato could at once fight and die for both." Against this view, cf. also Lintott (1971) 495.

50. See Goar (1987) 24–25, with parallels referring to Cato in Cicero.

51. We find the same sentiment voiced by the narrator at 7.134 ff. George (1988) sees nothing inconsistent with Stoicism in these lines, and argues that Stoic *oikeiōsis*, feeling for his fellow man, in fact forces Cato to fight.

52. As Brunt (1975) 32 remarks, "If in politics success is the standard of judgment, there was little to commend in men who did not identify outward defeat with sheer futility" and who refused to admit "that there might be something unwelcome in the ruin of the world."

53. On the literary genealogy of this scene in the life of Alexander the Great, see Ahl (1976) 258–259; Rutz (1970a); and Steinberg (1990).

54. On Cato's decision in book 2, see Adatte (1964); Ahl (1976) 234–247; Brisset (1964) 151 ff.; Brouwers (1989); Croisille (1982); Fantham (1992a) 234–235; Goar (1987) 42–43; George (1991); Griffin (1968) 73; Grimal (1970) 91 ff.; Johnson (1987) 38–46; Lebek (1976) 178 ff.; Martindale (1984) 73; Narducci (1979) 130–144 and (1985) 1557–58; Pavan (1970) 409–411; Schotes (1969) 23; Schrijvers (1989) 73 f.; Soria (1972); Tasler (1972) 168–170.

55. Adatte (1965) 236–237, Ahl (1976) 240, and Schrijvers (1989) 73 also notice this inconsistency but explain it away in other terms; as Ahl would have it, "Cato follows but he disapproves." Note also Seneca's formulation in *De prov.* 5.4: "boni viri . . . non trahuntur a fortuna, sequuntur illam et aequant gradus." But Lucan's Cato *is* dragged.

56. This is not to suggest that Lucan's Cato is not capable of mouthing pieces of Stoic orthodoxy, especially in book 9.

57. This sentiment is echoed almost verbatim at Tac. *Hist.* 1.50.

58. And Fantham (1992a) 234–235 agrees, *contra* Griffin (1968): "Although . . . these words are the argument of Seneca's adversary, not his own argument, the Senecan text still does not suggest that Cato was right to join the Republican forces, or his decision necessary . . . The sentence at 104.30 shows his inability to produce a morally satisfactory analysis." George (1991) 244–245 voices similar disagreement with Griffin.

59. See similarly *EM* 14.11, 19.2, 22.5, 68.1–7, 73, 103.4–5.

60. Also in Cicero, even a hint of compromise from Cato garners criticism; see *Att.* 7.15.2: "Cato enim ipse iam servire quam pugnare mavult" (26 January 49 B.C.). Grimal (1970) 91–93 reads Cicero's comment as benignly as possible, pointing out that Cicero himself understood that Cato's compromise rested on Caesar's withdrawal first from the occupied parts of Italy and the return of the magistrates to Rome, and that his personal presence at the projected meeting of Caesar and Pompey would ensure against the emergence of a duumvirate.

61. Accepting "in servis se libertati addixisse" (Hense) against "inservisse dixisse" of Bf. For other readings, see the apparatus to L. D. Reynold's OCT edition.

62. On this Cato, see Grimal (1970) 102–103: "Caton croit fermement que sa sagesse a pour object, avant tout, le bien de la cité . . . Il pensait que sa qualité de Romain modifiait, en quelque sorte, la signification de sa sagesse, qu'elle qui donnait des responsabilités que ne pouvait avoir un homme d'école ou un simple particulier."

63. It is worth noting that Seneca in *EM* 71.8 puts Cato in Pompey's party but himself sides with that side, identifying it with the Senate and the optimates.

64. Adatte (1965) 235 calls this criticism unique in Seneca's oeuvre. The Seneca of *De otio* may prefer retirement to participation under certain circumstances (it is better to concern yourself with the world, through philosophy, than with the state, through political participation); but Adatte draws attention to the "souplesse des prémises" operating here: "S'il est vrai que le cosmopolitisme stoïcien fait placer l'intérêt de la communauté avant celui de l'individu, comme l'affirme Cicéron dans le *Des finibus*, Sénèque utilise ce point de doctrine à des fins opposées;

dans le *De tranquillitate animi,* le cosmopolitisme invite à l'action . . . Ainsi, qu'on en blâme l'opportunisme ou qu'on en apprécie la souplesse, la morale de Sénèque est trop flottante pour que la critique de la lettre 14 puisse être interprétée comme une condamnation de Caton." This is not really surprising; as Shaw (1985) 48–49 points out, Stoicism provided tools for argument "shared and used by various, even divergent, social groups . . . Stoicism was useful to everyone."

65. See, e.g., Mayer (1981) at 8.554–555; Haskins' 1887 edition at 1.77 and 2.355 ("the negative is carried on in Lucan's favorite manner"); Weise's 1835 edition at 2.355 ("more Lucani, de quo vide I.76"). Weise remarks at 1.76: "quem usum quoniam non animum advertere, plerique interpretes, et Bentleius quoque, frustra fuere."

66. E.g., *Cael. Fam.* 8.13.2: "rationem eius habendam, qui exercitum *neque* provincias traderet."

67. Bramble (1983) 49–61 calls the practice of describing an event by what did *not* happen "negation antithesis" but does not comment on the grammatical peculiarity it often entails in Lucan.

68. Interestingly, Lucan's ancient readers did not always get it "right"; the scholium in Usener (1869) ad loc., unlike Endt (1909) ad loc., reads the lines on Brutus exactly as they are written, and comments of Brutus: "quamvis esset pars lugentis populi, non tamen terrebatur. For the marriage ceremony, both texts have the same interpretation, and in Endt (1909) ad loc. the meaning is carefully spelled out: for *discurrit,* "hoc est non discurrit"; for *stat torus,* "id est non stat"; for *nudatos cingunt,* "id est non cingunt." In general, these passages are read by the scholia as by their modern translators, the exception being the line on Brutus.

69. Examples may be found at 1.76–77; 2.39–40; 2.234–236; 2.354–359; 2.372–373; 2.441–442; 2.567–568; 4.750–753; 6.306–313; 8.554–555. Is it significant that this forcing of readerly choice as to which meaning to pick is so predominant in book 2 in particular? Lucan's practice here well explains 1.76–77, a bugaboo for the scholarship, since it solves the problem that the negative force of *nolet* needs to continue into the next clause if we are to make sense of the verse. For a full discussion of these lines, see Hudson-Williams (1952). On *nec . . . aut,* which I have not discussed, see Mayer (1981) at 8.387, and *TLL* 2.1568.4–11.

70. Instances in which Lucan has us reading *nec* as a negative conjunction

and –*que* and *et* as positive ones even after a preceding *non* or *nec,* a far more natural practice than the one I have just described, occur throughout; for example, when Lentulus angrily refutes Pompey's suggestion that they apply for aid to the Parthian king (8.371–379): "The Parthian will not climb the harsh mountain ridges where the earth swells up, nor will he wage war in thick darkness, when incapacitated by his uncertain bow, nor will he stem a river's violent eddy by swimming, nor will he endure the summer sun under hot dust, when he is soaked with the blood of battle in all his limbs. They have no battering-rams, nor any war-engine, nor are they able to level ditches, *and* [*et*] whatever can block an arrow will act as a wall against the Parthian in pursuit." Martindale (1981) 72–73 discusses this feature as Lucan's fondness for dismissing the norm in a series of negative statements, "so that the rhetorical climax (the positive statement) is made to assume a surprising character."

71. A similar phenomenon whose presence in the text of the *Civil War* is more sporadic than Lucan's play with *et* and *nec* is catalogued by Dehon (1989), who has noted that certain lines in Lucan are susceptible to an interpretation that reverses their meaning; the selection of the "correct" interpretation is once again up to the reader's "common sense." Here there is no violation of the text itself, for Dehon's examples are characterized by an ambiguity that allows a double reading of the line with perfect syntactic justification. But it is an interesting parallel to our argument for readerly involvement in an unprecedentedly bare act of meaning-creation that Dehon's "amphibology" involves a similar act of intervention. For example, at 7.81, when Cicero nags Pompey to join battle and asks him, "Why do you hold back the swords of the world from the blood of Caesar?" ("Quid mundi gladios a sanguine Caesaris arces?"), we could just as well take *mundi* with *sanguine, Caesaris* with *gladios,* and thus have Cicero ask why Pompey holds back Caesar's swords from the blood of the world—a much more accurate prediction of the way Pharsalus actually turns out. We don't, because it makes no narrative sense for Cicero to ask that; but as Dehon (1989, 121) notes, "Pompey's reaction to Cicero's speech will be precisely to suspect some kind of divine trick and to suspect that destiny is definitely opposed to his plan: 'Ingemuit rector sensitque deorum/ esse dolos et fata suae contraria menti' (7.85–86), and here *contraria* well and truly invites us to

reverse the terms of verse 81's interrogation." In other words, Pompey—perhaps like us—suspects it might be the opposite reading that will prevail. See similarly Dehon's discussion of 7.23–34, 7.350, and 5.194–196.

72. See similarly Martindale (1993) 73: "Interpretation is not something we can choose to do or not to do; to read is to interpret, and to read in one way is inevitably not to read in some other(s)." But I have to disagree with his analogy of the reading experience with Wittgenstein's duck-rabbit, "which can be seen either as a duck or as a rabbit but not as both at precisely the same time." For Lucan's request of us is exactly this.

73. Pavan (1970) 414–415 also makes the interesting suggestion that for Lucan freedom lives wherever someone is willing to fight for it: "für ihn lebt die Freiheit solange, wie man für sie kämpft; man weiss sich verplichtet, sich diesem Versuch bis zum Ende zu stellen, damit sich das Bewusstsein ohne Furcht vor der Niederlage über die Wechselfälle des Geschicks, über das Spiel der geschichtliche Kräfte erheben kann."

74. This discussion elides the question of Cato's suicide at Utica, with which I believe (with the majority of the scholarship; see Chapter 2, note 60) Lucan ended the *Civil War*. Should the epic, on the interpretation given above, have concluded on a more upbeat note? Not at all. What Cato chose to do here made *his nomen* the beginnings of a legend that spurred later generations to action. For the Cato legend, see Goar (1987).

75. George (1991) 254 agrees: "Cato did affect the nature of the conflict. The wise man taught the followers of Pompey to be partisans of *libertas*." See pp. 256–257 for his comments on the rejuvenation and transformation of the war.

Five. History without Banisters

1. Ormand (1994) 50 raises both possibilities and decides that "the apostrophe here is intelligible only if we take it as addressed to the guide." But he goes on to read the passage much as I do.

2. Not to mention the evocations of Verg. *Aen.* 8.337–361, where Aeneas treads on what *will* be Rome, and the interpreter of the humble huts and underbrush is Vergil himself, who interweaves his observations with Evander's. The association is made all the stronger by Caesar's promise, in Lucan, to restore Pergamum to its former glory and make it a *Roman Troy:* "Date felices in cetera cursus, / restituam populos;

grata vice moenia reddent / Ausonidae Phrygibus, Romanaue Pergama surgent" (9.997–999). Ahl (1968) 136 suggests that "Lucan dedicates his epic to Julius Caesar in the midst of the ruins of Troy, and, for a suspended moment, the head of Pompey and the head of Priam become one and the same. The gap between myth and history, past and present is bridged in the desolate ruins of Troy."

3. Ormand (1994) 52 sees this as a *negative* quality of the text: "We, as much as Caesar, are dependent upon the guide/poet to see what would normally, and should, be passed over. Through Caesar, Lucan has created a model of reading that is creative, subjective, and doomed to miss the point by its own selectivity." But what I am arguing for is a *positive* evaluation of this selectivity and subjectivity.

4. Again, this cannot happen without the reader's meaningful intervention and choice: "Hic situs est Magnus," as Malamud (1995) 178 correctly points out, could just as easily mean "Here is great decay" or even "This is a great spot."

5. See 9.619–623, where Lucan prefaces his aetiology of the snakes with the assertion that the tale is not true.

6. Malamud goes on to attribute this sensitive reading of Lucan to Statius *Silvae* 2.7, where, she argues, Statius does for Lucan what Lucan is doing for Pompey, and equally self-consciously.

7. For an excellent reading of Libya's unreliable desert sands as a metaphor for Lucan's poetic project, see O'Gorman (1995) 126–127: "Lucan's construction is a castle *deliberately* built on sand, a self-undermining, self-sustaining project."

8. Is it a coincidence that several decades later, Pliny, too, would thank his emperor for making possible the *liberae civitatis simulatio* (*Paneg.* 63.5)? A telling expression, indeed. See Bartsch (1994) 186–187.

9. *Fingere,* like *nomen,* seems to have both a positive and a negative meaning in Lucan's usage; contrast 5.392 to 6.577, where Erictho, like Lucan maybe, "carmen novos fingebat in usus." Certainly Lucan's Romans can believe in what they make up: "quae finxere timent," 1.486.

10. See 9.359–360. For relevant discussions of Lucan's varying attitudes to myth, see Fantham (1992b) 98 and Häussler (1978) 60–68.

11. Lucan, in other words, is like Ormand's version of Pompey, an *auctor vix fidelis;* see Ormand (1994) 43–44.

12. See similarly Arendt's protests against the idea of history as represent-

able by a single account with a rational, predictable "plot," in *The Human Condition* (Chicago: 1958) 184–186.

13. But we should not confuse marginality itself with truth-telling: "To the extent that proponents of marginal voice assert a naive expectation that the stories of the oppressed are inherently truthful and authentic and so can be taken literally, they provide little defense for storytelling" (Disch 1994: 7).

14. Arendt's perspective on historiography provides illuminating tools with which to analyze Lucan's opus. I hope the following arguments will justify the analogy themselves, but it is worth remembering that much of Arendt's philosophy was rooted (like Lucan's) in her response to totalitarianism, including her own nostalgic-seeming analyses of the Greek polis; see Canovan (1992) 2.

15. "What totalitarianism accomplished was to shatter the single most important 'pillar' of Western humanism: the reasonable individual" (Disch 1994, 207).

16. Disch (1994) 70, discussing Benhabib (1990). See also Arendt (1972) against the "mastery" of history.

17. Lucan also makes a gesture in the direction of the *unnarratability* of traumatic events when during the battle of Pharsalus he starts to eschew narration altogether: "Hanc fuge, mens, partem belli tenebrisque relinque / nullaque tantorum discat me vate malorum, / quam multum bellis civilibus, aetas" (7.552–554). On the dangers of a successful narrative of trauma and the threat of its integration into "normative" explanation, see Braun (1994) 172; Davidoff (1995); Kellner (1991) 292–293; Roth (1995) 205–209.

18. See similarly Rorty (1989) 99.

19. As Hutchinson (1993) 251 remarks of this effect in the narrator's relation to the gods, "In form and feeling, the narrator's handling of the gods stands close to his characters', far more so than in ordinary epic. There is no 'objective' description to make the gods vivid. The poet like the characters prays, protests, and condemns . . . Subjectivity and objectivity cannot readily be sundered."

20. E.g., 4.110–120, 4.181–188. See Chapter 4 for a fuller discussion.

21. See also Quint's excellent observations on 7.695–696 ("sed par quod semper habemus, / Libertas et Caesar erit"): "The confusion of tenses—present and future describing a past event—again spells out

the message. Precisely at the moment of crushing republican defeat, the poem announces a sequel of ongoing resistance: this is the war we are still fighting, despite setbacks. Such assertions at the beginning and end of the narration of Pharsalia counterbalance the despairing declaration of finality that lies between them [viz., 7.640–647]."

22. Interestingly, an effect of the use of an affective historical present performance in general "when it overshoots its mark, i.e., is identified by the audience as affective, [is to] turn 'authentic' eyewitness report into its opposite (this may actually be the whole point of the performance)," notes Casparis (1975) 83. This dovetails well with the suggestion that Lucan's "affectivity" is deliberately *de trop.*

23. An emphasis on the present in narration also deemphasizes coherence and rational understanding in favor of "rendering experience as raw material in manifest concreteness" (Casparis 1975: 74).

24. Quoting Carl E. Schorske, *Fin-de-Siècle Vienna: Politics and Culture* (New York: 1980) 19.

25. Olsson (1991) 173 carefully distinguishes between causal relations and logical relations: "Whereas cause-and-effect involves time, power, and responsibility, logic is without time, without freedom, and without guilt." This is important, given the treatment of causality in Chapter 1.

26. Hannah Arendt, *The Human Condition* (Chicago: 1958) 9. The influence of Nietzsche is perhaps visible here: see *The Will to Power* § 767, ed. Oscar Levy: "The individual is something quite *new,* and capable of creating new things ... The individual in the end has to seek the valuation for his actions in himself: because he has to give an individual meaning even to traditional words and notions. His interpretation of a formula is at least personal, even if he does not create the formula itself: at least as an interpreter he is creative."

27. See also Canovan (1992) 213: "This sheer human spontaneity, this 'ability to initiate' which belongs to the individual, is pre-political. It becomes freedom in the full sense of the word only when it generates a 'mundane reality' that can actually be seen by all, and politics is, for Arendt, 'the place where freedom can manifest itself and become a reality.' "

28. See also Le Bonniec (1970) 186.

29. See also Barton (1993) 23 n. 43: "Seneca was, like Lucan ... fascinated

with the violence he often decries . . . It is a mistake to think that Seneca *simply* abhorred violence. The loathing does not preclude the loving or the need." And later: "The writers of the Neronian period . . . were at once both victims and spectators" (1993: 25).

30. As Roth (1995) 126 puts it, ironists "must use an inherited vocabulary in order to create a new one. They feel the impulse to throw off the past because they feel themselves to be a part of the past."

31. As Rorty (1989) 86 notes, in the absence of transcendent scenarios about redemption beyond the grave we need to tell ourselves secular stories about how things might get better.

32. Many critics have stressed a connection between the active partisanship of the *Civil War* and Lucan's eventual decision to join the Pisonian conspiracy: see, e.g., Croisille (1982) 79; Lounsbury (1971) 234–239; Marti (1945) 375–376; Pavan (1970) 419; Schönberger (1970) 545; Schotes (1969) 514.

33. For bibliography on the conspiracy and the question of Lucan's politics, see Chapter 3, note 49.

34. See Tac. *Ann.* 15.56; Suet. *Vita Lucani.*

35. A favorite trick; consider his treatment of the future emperor Vespasian at *Ann.* 16.5.3. There was no "ruin" threatening the man for falling asleep while Nero was singing.

36. This was also Arendt's experience: Despite the temptation to wash one's hands of an often bleak and violent world, "she had no doubt that there is a duty to resist political evil, even though this resistance may well involve guilt" (Canovan 1992, 187).

37. Martindale (1993) 51 notes that ideologies "may hammer together energizing 'contradictions,' which are not then felt as contradictions." I would argue that here Lucan does the opposite: he exposes and highlights contradictions, but insists on ideology nonetheless.

Bibliography

Adatte, J. 1965. "Caton ou l'engagement du sage dans la guerre civile." *Etudes de lettres* 7: 232–40.

Ahl, Frederick. 1968. "Pharsalus and the *Pharsalia*." *C&M* 29: 124–61.

———— 1971. "Lucan's *De Incendio Urbis, Epistulae ex Campania* and Nero's Ban." *TAPA* 102: 1–27.

———— 1974a. "The Pivot of the *Pharsalia*." *Hermes* 102: 305–320.

———— 1974b. "The Shadows of a Divine Presence in the *Pharsalia*." *Hermes* 102: 567–590.

———— 1976. *Lucan: An Introduction*. Ithaca.

———— 1984a. "The Art of Safe Criticism in Greece and Rome." *AJP* 105: 174–208.

———— 1984b. "The Rider and the Horse: Politics and Power in Roman Poetry from Horace to Statius." *ANRW* 2.32.1: 40–110.

———— 1993. "Form Empowered: Lucan's *Pharsalia*." In *Roman Epic*, ed. A. J. Boyle. Pp. 125–142. London and New York.

Albrecht, M. von. 1968. "Der Dichter Lucan und die epische Tradition." In *Lucain*, ed. M. Durry. *Entretiens de la Fondation Hardt* 15. Pp. 267–308. Geneva.

Alexander, W. 1946. "Cato of Utica in the Pages of Seneca the Philosopher." *Transactions of the Royal Society of Canada* 40: 59–74.

Aly, Götz. 1994. "The Posen Diaries of the Anatomist Hermann Voss." In *Cleansing the Fatherland: Nazi Medicine and Racial Hygiene*, ed. Aly et al. Trans. Belinda Cooper. Baltimore.

Arendt, Hannah. 1953. "Understanding and Politics." *Partisan Review* 20: 377–392.

———— 1958. *The Origins of Totalitarianism*. 2nd ed. London.

———— 1964. "Personal Responsibility under Dictatorship." *The Listener*, 6 August 1964, 185–187: 205.

———— 1969. "The Archimedean Point." *Ingenor* 6: 4–9, 24–26.

———— 1972. "Lying in Politics." In *Crises of the Republic*. Pp. 1–47. New York.

Auguet, Roland. 1972. *Cruelty and Civilization: The Roman Games*. London.

Aumont, J. 1968a. "Caton en Libye (Lucain, Pharsale, 9.294–949)." *REA* 70: 304–320.

———— 1968b. "Sur l'épisode des reptiles dans la Pharsale de Lucain (9.587–937)." *Bulletin de l'Association Guillaume Budé*, ser. 4, no. 1: 103–119.

Bakhtin, M. M. 1968. *Rabelais and His World*. Trans. Hélène Iswolsky. Cambridge, Mass.

Barasch, Frances K. 1971. *The Grotesque: A Study in Meanings*. The Hague.

Barratt, P. 1979. *M. Annaei Lucani Belli Civilis Liber V: A Commentary*. Amsterdam.

Barton, Carlin. 1984. "*Vis Mortua:* Irreconcilable Patterns of Thought in the Works of Seneca and Lucan." Ph.D. diss., University of California at Berkeley.

———— 1993. *The Sorrows of the Ancient Romans: The Gladiator and the Monster*. Princeton.

———— 1995. "The 'Moment of Truth' in Ancient Rome: Honor and Embodiment in a Contest Culture." Manuscript.

Bartsch, Shadi. 1994. *Actors in the Audience: Theatricality and Doublespeak from Nero to Hadrian*. Cambridge, Mass.

Basore, J. W. (1904) "Direct Speech in Lucan as an Element of Epic Technique." *TAPA* 35: xciv–xcvi.

Batinski, E. E. 1992. "Lucan's Catalogue of Caesar's Troops: Paradox and Convention." *CJ* 88: 19–24.

Bell, A. A., Jr. 1994. "Fact and Exemplum in Accounts of the Deaths of Pompey and Caesar." *Latomus* 53: 824–836.

Benhabib, Seyla. 1990. "Hannah Arendt and the Redemptive Power of Narrative." *Social Research* 57: 167–196.

Béranger, Jean. 1966. "Idéologie impériale et épopée latine." In *Mélanges d'archéologie, d'épigraphie et d'histoire offerts à Jerôme Carcopino*. Pp. 97–112. Paris.

Bernheimer, Charles. 1992. "The Decadent Subject." *L'esprit créateur* 32: 53–62.

Berthold, H. 1977. "Beobachtungen zu den Epilogen Lucans." *Helikon* 17: 218–225.

Bettelheim, Bruno. 1952. *Surviving and Other Essays*. New York.

Bibby, M. 1993. "Fragging the Chains of Command: GI Resistance Poetry and Mutilation." *Journal of American Culture* 16: 29–38.

Billerbeck, M. 1986. "Stoizismus in der römischen Epik neronischer und flavischer Zeit." *ANRW* II.32.5: 3116–51.

Block, E. 1982. "The Narrator Speaks: Apostrophe in Homer and Vergil." *TAPA* 112: 7–22.

Bohnenkamp, K. E. 1977. "Zum Nero-Elogium in Lucans Bellum Civile." *MH* 34: 235–248.

Bonner, S. F. 1966. "Lucan and the Declamation Schools." *AJP* 87: 257–289.

Boyle, A. J. 1993. *Roman Epic*. London and New York.

Bradford, D. T. 1990. "Early Christian Martyrdom and the Psychology of Depression, Suicide, and Bodily Mutilation." *Psychotherapy* 27: 30–41.

Bramble, J. C. 1983. "Lucan." In *Cambridge History of Classical Literature*, ed. E. J. Kenney. Vol. 2: 37–61. Cambridge.

Braun, Robert. 1994. "The Holocaust and Problems of Historical Representation." *History and Theory* 33: 172–197.

Brink, C. O. 1960. "Tragic History and Aristotle's School." *PCPS*, n.s. 6: 14–19.

Brisset, J. 1964. *Les idées politiques de Lucain*. Paris.

Brouwers, J. H. 1989. "Lucan über Cato Uticensis als *exemplar virtutis*." In *Fructus Centesimus: Mélanges offerts à Gerard J. M. Barthelink*. Pp. 49–60. Steenbergen.

Brown, Susan. 1992. "Death as Decoration: Scenes from the Arena on Roman Domestic Mosaics." In *Pornography and Representation in Greece and Rome*, ed. Amy Richlin. Pp. 180–211. New York.

Bruère, Richard T. 1950. "The Scope of Lucan's Historical Epic." *CP* 45: 217–235.

Brunt, P. 1975. "Stoicism and the Principate." *Papers of the British School at Rome* 43: 7–35.

Buchheit, V. 1961. "Lucans Pharsalia und die Frage der Nichtvollendung." *RM* 104: 362–365.

Burck, Erich. 1970. "Vom menschenbild in Lucans Pharsalia." In *Lucan*, ed. W. Rutz. Pp. 149–159. Darmstadt.

———— 1971. *Von römischen Manierismus. Von der Dichtung der frühen römischen Kaiserzeit*. Darmstadt.

Butrica, J. L. 1993. "Propertius 3.11.33–38 and the Death of Pompey." *CQ*, n.s. 43.1: 342–346.

Bynum, Caroline Walker. 1992. *Fragmentation and Redemption: Essays on Gender and the Human Body in Medieval Religion.* New York.

Camporesi, Piero. 1988. *The Incorruptible Flesh: Bodily Mutation and Mortification in Religion and Folklore.* Trans. Tania Croft-Murray and Helen Elsom. Cambridge.

Cancik, Hubert. 1970. "Ein Traum des Pompeius." In *Lucan,* ed. W. Rutz. Pp. 546–552. Darmstadt.

Canovan, Margaret. 1992. *Hannah Arendt: A Reinterpretation of Her Political Thought.* Cambridge.

Carroll, Noel. 1990. *The Philosophy of Horror, or Paradoxes of the Heart.* New York and London.

Casparis, C. P. 1975. *Tense without Time: The Present Tense in Narration.* Schweizer Anglistische Arbeiten 84. Berne.

Cattin, A. 1965. "Une idée directrice de Lucain dans la *Pharsale.*" *Etudes de lettres* 8: 214–223.

Cazzaniga, Ignazio. 1956. "Osservazioni a Lucano no. 1, 9.828–33: L'avventura di Murro col Basilisco." *Acme* 9: 7–9.

——— 1957. "L'episodio dei Serpi Libici in Lucano e la tradizione dei Theriaka Nicandrei." *Acme* 10: 27–41.

Ciechanowicz, Jerzy. 1982. "Das Problem der Apostrophe IX 980–986 in der Pharsalia von Marcus Annaeus Lucanus." *Eos* 70: 265–275.

Cioran, E. M. 1982. *A Short History of Decay.* Trans. Richard Howard. New York.

Cizek, E. 1972. *L'époque de Néron et ses controverses idéologiques.* Leiden.

Clover, Carol J. 1992. *Men, Women, and Chainsaws: Gender in the Modern Horror Film.* Princeton.

Conte, G. B. 1966. "Il proemio della *Pharsalia.*" *Maia* 18: 42–53.

——— 1968. "La guerra civile nella rievocazione del popolo: Lucano 2.67–233." *Maia* 20: 224–253.

——— 1988. *La Guerra Civile di Lucano. Studi e prove di commento.* Urbino.

Croisille, J.-M. 1982. "Caton et Sénèque face au pouvoir: Lucain, *Pharsale,* 2.234–235; 9.186–217." In *Neronia 1977,* ed. J.-M. Croisille and P.-M. Fauchère. Pp. 75–82. Clermont-Ferrand.

Culler, Jonathan. 1981. "Apostrophe." In *The Pursuit of Signs: Semiotics, Literature, Deconstruction.* Pp. 135–154. London and Henley.

Daube, D. 1972. "The Linguistics of Suicide." *Philosophy and Public Affairs* 1: 387–437.

Dawidoff, Robert. 1995. "History . . . But." *NLH* 21: 395–406.

Deferrari, Roy J., Sister Maria W. Fanning, and Sister Anne S. Sullivan. 1940. *A Concordance of Lucan.* Washington, D.C.

Dehon, Pierre-Jacques. 1989. "Une amphibologie de Lucain (B.C. VII, 81)?" *Latomus* 48: 120–126.

de Man, Paul. 1979. "Autobiography as Defacement." *MLN* 94: 919–930.

Deratani, Nikolaj F. 1970. "Der Kampf für Freiheit, Patriotismus und Heldentum im Gedicht Lucans 'Über den Bürgerkrieg.' " In *Lucan,* ed. W. Rutz. Pp. 133–148. Darmstadt.

Dewar, Michael. 1994. "Laying It On with a Trowel: The Proem to Lucan and Related Texts." *CQ,* n.s. 44: 199–211.

Dick, Bernard F. 1963. "The Technique of Prophecy in Lucan." *TAPA* 94: 37–49.

———— 1965. "The Role of the Oracle in Lucan's *De Bello Civili.*" *Hermes* 93: 460–466.

———— 1967. "Fatum and Fortuna in Lucan's *Bellum Civile.*" *CP* 62: 235–242.

Dilke, O. A. W. 1972. "Lucan's Political Views and the Caesars." In *Neronians and Flavians,* ed. D. R. Dudley. Pp. 62–82. London.

———— 1979. "Lucan's Account of the Fall of Pompey." In *Studi su Varrone, sulla retorica, storiografia e poesia latina: Scritti in onore di Benedetto Riposati.* Vol. 1, pp. 171–184. Rieti.

Disch, Lisa Jane. 1994. *Hannah Arendt and the Limits of Philosophy.* Ithaca.

Douglas, Mary. 1966. *Purity and Danger: An Analysis of Concepts of Pollution and Taboo.* New York.

———— 1970. *Natural Symbols: Explorations in Cosmology.* New York.

Due, Otto Steen. 1962. "An Essay on Lucan." *C&M* 23: 68–132.

———— 1970. "Lucain et la philosophie." In *Lucain,* ed. M. Durry. *Entretiens de la Fondation Hardt* 15. Pp. 203–232. Geneva.

Duff, J. D. 1928. *Lucan with an English Translation.* Cambridge, Mass.

Durry, M., ed. 1968. *Lucain. Entretiens de la Fondation Hardt* 15. Geneva.

Dutoit, E. 1936. "Le thème de 'la force qui se détruit elle-même' (Hor., *Epod.* 16,2) et ses variations chez quelques auteurs latins." *REL* 14: 365–373.

Eagleton, Terry. 1991. *Ideology: An Introduction.* New York.

Ebener, D. 1984. "Lucans Bürgerkriegsepos als Beispiel poetischer Gestaltung eines historischen Stoffes." *Klio* 66: 581–589.

Endt, J. 1905. "Der Gebrauch der Apostrophe bei den lateinischen Epiker." *WS* 27: 106–129.

———— 1909. *Adnotationes super Lucanum.* Leipzig.

Fantham, Elaine. 1985. "Caesar and the Mutiny: Lucan's Reshaping of the Historical Tradition in *De Bello Civili* 5.237–373." *CP* 80: 119–131.

———— 1992a. *Lucan, De Bello Civili, Book 2.* Cambridge.

———— 1992b. "Lucan's Medusa Excursus: Its Design and Purpose." *Materiali e discussioni* 29: 95–119.

Fauth, Wolfgang. 1975. "Die Bedeutung der Nekromantie-Szene in Lucans Pharsalia." *RM* 118: 325–344.

Favazza, Armando R. 1987. *Bodies under Siege: Self-Mutilation in Culture and Psychiatry.* Baltimore.

Feeney, D. C. 1986a. " 'Stat Magni Nominis Umbra': Lucan on the Greatness of Pompeius Magnus." *CQ,* n.s. 36: 239–43.

———— 1986b. "History and Revelation in Vergil's Underworld." *PCPS,* n.s. 32: 1–24.

———— 1991. *The Gods in Epic.* Oxford.

———— 1992. "*Si licet et fas est:* Ovid's *Fasti* and the Problem of Free Speech under the Principate." In *Roman Poetry and Propaganda,* ed. Anton Powell. Pp. 1–25. London.

Flume, Helmut. 1970. "Die Einheit der künstlerischen Persönlichkeit Lucans." Excerpted in *Lucan,* ed. W. Rutz. Pp. 296–298, 354–359. Darmstadt.

Fontanille, J. 1993. "The Diagram of Fear: Phobia, Anguish and Abjection in the 'Voyage au Bout de la Nuit.' " *Ars Semeiotica* 16: 83–99.

Fraenkel, E. 1964. "Lucan als Mittler des Antiken Pathos." In *Kleine Beiträge zur klassichen Philologie.* Vol. 2: 233–266. Rome.

Frank, E. 1970. "The Structure and Scope of Lucan's *De Bello Civili.*" *CB* 46: 59–61.

Freud, Sigmund. 1953. "Medusa's Head." In *Collected Papers,* ed. J. Riviere. Vol. 5: 105–106. London.

Friedrich, Hugo. 1936. "Pascal's Paradox: Das Sprachbild einer Denkform." *Zeitschrift für Römanische Philologie* 56: 322–370.

Friedrich, Wolf-Hartmut. 1938. "Cato, Caesar und Fortuna bei Lucan." *Hermes* 73: 391–423.

Fuhrmann, M. 1968. "Die Funktion grausiger und ekelhafter Motive in der lateinischen Dichtung." In *Die nicht mehr schönen Künste. Grenz-phänomene des ästhetischen,* ed. H. R. Jauss. Pp. 23–66. Munich.

Fussell, Paul. 1975. *The Great War and Modern Memory.* London.

Gagliardi, Donato. 1970. *Lucano: Poeta della libertà.* 2nd ed. Naples.

———, ed. 1975. *M. Annaei Lucani Belli Civilis Liber VII.* Florence.

——— 1985. "La letteratura dell'irrazionale in erà Neroniana." *ANRW* 2.32.3: 2047–65.

———, ed. 1989. *M. Annaei Lucani Belli Civilis Liber I.* Naples.

George, D. B. 1988. "Lucan's Caesar and οἰκείωσις Theory: The Stoic Fool." *TAPA* 118: 331–341.

——— 1991. "Lucan's Cato and Stoic Attitudes to the Republic." *CA* 10.2: 237–258.

Getty, R. 1940. *M. Annaei Lucani De Bello Civili Liber I.* Cambridge.

Gigliucci, Roberto. 1994. *Lo spettacolo della morte: Estetica e ideologia del macabro nella letteratura medievale.* Anzio.

Gilman, Richard. 1975. *Decadence: The Strange Life of an Epithet.* New York.

Goar, Robert J. 1987. *The Legend of Cato Uticensis from the First Century B.C. to the Fifth Century A.D.* Collection Latomus 197. Brussels.

Goebel, George H. 1981. "Rhetorical and Poetical Thinking in Lucan's Ha-rangues (7.250–382)." *TAPA* 111: 79–94.

Goldmann, Lucien. 1964. *The Hidden God: A Study of the Tragic Vision in the Pensées of Pascal and the Tragedies of Racine.* Trans. Philip Thody. London.

Gordon, R. 1987. "Lucan's Erictho." In *Homo Viator: Classical Essays for John Bramble,* ed. M. Whitby and P. R. Hardie. Pp. 231–241. Bristol.

Green, C. M. C. 1992. "*Stimulos Dedit Aemula Virtus:* Lucan and Homer Reconsidered." *Phoenix* 45: 234–249.

——— 1994. "The Necessary Murder: Myth, Ritual, and Civil War in Lucan, Book 3." *CA* 13: 203–233.

Greenblatt, Stephen. 1996. "Mutilation and Meaning." Manuscript.

Grenade, P. 1950. "Le mythe de Pompée et les Pompeiens sous les Césars." *REA* 52: 28–63.

Gresseth, Gerald K. 1957. "The Quarrel between Lucan and Nero." *CP* 52: 24–27.

Griffin, Miriam. 1968. "Seneca on Cato's Politics: Epistle 14.12–13." *CQ* 18: 373–375.

——— 1984. *Nero: The End of a Dynasty.* London.

Grimal, Pierre. 1960. "L'éloge de Néron au début de la Pharsale est-il ironique?" *REL* 38: 296–305.

———— 1970. "Le poète et l'histoire." In *Lucain*, ed. M. Durry. *Entretiens de la Fondation Hardt* 15. Pp. 53–117. Geneva.

Griset, E. 1954. "Lucanea I: Le due Farsaglie. II. I Proemi." *Rivista di studi classici* 2: 109–113, 185–190.

———— 1955. "Lucanea III: L'anticesarismo. IV: L'elogio Neroniano. V: L'universalismo." *Rivista di studi classici* 3: 56–61, 134–138, 203–238.

Grosz, Elizabeth. 1990. "The Body of Signification." In *Abjection, Melancholia and Love: The Work of Julia Kristeva,* ed. John Fletcher and Andrew Benjamin. Pp. 80–103. London.

Guillemin, A. 1951. "L'inspiration Virgilienne dans la Pharsale." *REL* 29: 214–227.

Gurrey, C. S. 1991. "Paradox, Will, and Religious Belief." *Philosophy* 66: 503–511.

Haffter, Heinz. 1970. "Dem schwanken Zünglein lauschend wachte Cäsar dort." In *Lucan*, ed. W. Rutz. Pp. 264–276. Darmstadt.

Håkanson, L. 1979. "Problems of Textual Criticism and Interpretation in Lucan's *De Bello Civili*." *PCPS* 25: 26–51.

Hampel, E. 1908. "De Apostrophae apud Romanorum Poetas Usu." Diss. Jena.

Hardie, Philip R. 1993. *The Epic Successors of Virgil: A Study in the Dynamics of a Tradition.* Cambridge.

Harich, Henriette. 1990. "Catonis Marcia: Stoisches Kolorit eines Frauenporträts bei Lucan (II.326–350)." *Gymnasium* 97: 212–223.

Harpham, Geoffrey Galt. 1982. *On the Grotesque: Strategies of Contradiction in Art and Literature.* Princeton.

Haskins, C. E. ed. 1887. *M. Annaei Lucani Pharsalia, Edited with English Notes.* London.

Häussler, R. 1978. *Studien zum historichen Epos der Antike II: Das historische Epos von Lucan bis Silius und seine Theorie.* Heidelberg.

Hellegouarc'h, J. 1963. *Le vocabulaire latin des relations et des partis politiques sous la république.* Paris.

Henderson, J. 1987. "Lucan: The Word at War." *Ramus* 16: 122–164.

Hermann, Léon. 1970. "Der Prolog der *Pharsalia*." In *Lucan*, ed. W. Rutz. Pp. 283–287. Darmstadt.

Holliday, Vivian L. 1969. *Pompey in Cicero's Correspondence and Lucan's Civil War*. The Hague and Paris.

Hosius, C., ed. 1985. *De Bello Civili Libri X*. Rev. ed. R. Badalì. Stuttgart.

Housman, A. E. 1927. *M. Annaei Lucani Belli Civilis Libri Decem*. Oxford.

Hübner, U. 1972. "Hypallage in Lucans *Pharsalia*." *Hermes* 100: 577–600.

——— 1974. "Eine übersehene Metonymie in Lucans Pharsalia." *RM* 117: 350–357.

——— 1975. "Studien zur Pointentechnik in Lucans Pharsalia." *Hermes* 103: 200–211.

——— 1976a. "Der Sonnenaufgang vor Pharsalus. Zu Lucan 7, 1–3." *Philologus* 120: 107–116.

——— 1976b. "Zu Lucan 7.566ff." *Philologus* 120: 302–307.

——— 1984. "Episches und Elegisches am Anfang des dritten Buches der 'Pharsalia.' " *Hermes* 112: 227–239.

Hudson-Williams, A. 1952. "Lucan 1.76–7." *CR* 66: 68–69.

Hunink, V. 1992. *M. Annaeus Lucanus: Bellum Civile, Book 3*. A Commentary. Amsterdam.

Hutchinson, G. O. 1993. *Latin Literature from Seneca to Juvenal*. Oxford.

Jacobson, Kenneth. 1994. *Embattled Selves: An Investigation into the Nature of Identity through Oral Histories of Holocaust Survivors*. New York.

Jakobson, R. 1990. "The Concept of Mark." In *On Language: Roman Jakobson*, ed. L. R. Waugh and M. Monville-Burston. Pp. 134–140. Cambridge, Mass.

Jal, P. 1961a. "Remarques sur la cruauté à Rome pendant les guerres civiles (de Sylla à Vespasien)." *Bulletin de l'Association Guillaume Budé* 20: 475–501.

——— 1961b. "La propagande religieuse à Rome au cours des guerres civiles de la fin de la république." *L'antiquité classique* 30: 395–414.

——— 1962a. "Les dieux et les guerres civiles dans la Rome de la fin de la république." *REL* 40: 170–200.

——— 1962b. "Bellum civile . . . bellum externum." *Les études classiques* 30: 257–267, 384–390.

——— 1963. *La guerre civile à Rome: Etude littéraire et morale*. Paris.

——— 1982. "Lucain dans la littérature antique des guerres civiles." In *Neronia 1977*, ed. J.-M. Croisille and P.-M. Fauchère. Pp. 83–91. Clermont-Ferrand.

James, William. 1979. *The Will to Believe and Other Essays in Popular Philosophy*. Cambridge, Mass.

Jenkinson, J. R. 1974. "Sarcasm in Lucan 1.33–66." *CR* 24: 8–9.

Johnson, W. R. 1987. *Momentary Monsters: Lucan and His Heroes*. Ithaca.

Kayser, Wolfgang. 1981. *The Grotesque in Art and Literature*. Trans. Ulrich Weisstein. New York.

Kebric, R. B. 1976. "Lucan's Snake Episode: A Historical Model." *Latomus* 35: 380–382.

Keitel, Elizabeth. 1984. "Principate and Civil Wars in the *Annals* of Tacitus." *AJP* 105: 306–325.

Kellner, Hans. 1991. "Beautifying the Nightmare: The Aesthetics of Post-Modern History." *Strategies* 4: 289–313.

Kierdorf, W. 1979. "Die Leichenrede auf Pompeius in Lucans Pharsalia (9.190ff.)." *Würzburger Jahrbücher*, n.s. 5: 157–162.

König, Fritz. 1970. "Mensch und Welt bei Lucan in Spiegel bildhafter Darstellung." In *Lucan*, ed. W. Rutz. Pp. 439–476. Darmstadt.

Koppenfels, W. von. 1975. " 'Our Swords into Our Proper Entrails': Aspeckte des Lucans-rezeption im elisabethanischen Bürgerkriegsdrama." *Antike und Abendland* 21: 58–84.

Kristeva, Julia. 1982. *Powers of Horror: An Essay in Abjection*. New York.

——— 1985. "The Speaking Subject." In *On Signs*, ed. Marshall Blonsky. Pp. 210–220. Oxford.

Kubiak, David. 1985. *Lucan Bellum Civile, Book 9*. Bryn Mawr.

Lapidge, M. 1979. "Lucan's Imagery of Cosmic Dissolution." *Hermes* 107: 344–370.

Lausberg, Marion. 1990. "Epos und Lehrgedicht: Ein Gattungsvergleich am Beispiel von Lucans Schlangenkatalog." *Würzburger Jahrbücher für die Altertumswissenschaft* 16: 173–203.

Lebek, W. D. 1976. *Lucans Pharsalia: Dichtungsstruktur und Zeitbezug*. *Hypomnemata* 44. Göttingen.

Le Bonniec, H. 1970. "Lucain et la réligion." In *Lucain*, ed. M. Durry. *Entretiens de la Fondation Hardt* 15. Pp. 159–200. Geneva.

Lefèvre, Eckard. 1970. "Die Bedeutung des Paradoxen in der römischen Literatur der frühen Kaiserzeit." *Poetica* 3: 59–82.

Lessing, Gotthold Ephraim. 1984. *Laocoön: An Essay on the Limits of Painting and Poetry*. Trans. Edward A. McCormick. Baltimore.

Levi, M. 1949. "Il proemio della 'Pharsalia.' " *Rivista de filologia e di istruzione classica,* n.s. 27: 71–78.

Lewin, Carroll McC. 1993. "Negotiated Selves in the Holocaust." *Ethos* 21: 295–318.

Liebeschutz, J. H. W. G. 1979. "The System Rejected: Lucan's *Pharsalia.*" In *Continuity and Change in Roman Religion.* Pp. 140–155. Oxford.

Lifton, Robert Jay. 1986. *The Nazi Doctors: Medical Killing and the Psychology of Genocide.* New York.

Lintott, A. W. 1971. "Lucan and the History of the Civil War." *CQ* 21: 488–505.

Lloyd-Jones, H. 1990a. Review of P. F. Widdows, *Lucan's "Civil War" Translated into English Verse. New York Review of Books,* 18 January 1990, pp. 39–41.

———— 1990b. "What Did Cato Mean?—Reply." *New York Review of Books,* 19 July 1990, p. 53.

Long, A. A., ed. 1980. *Soul and Body in Stoicism.* Center for Hermeneutical Studies in Hellenistic and Modern Culture. Protocol of the 36th Colloquy, 3 June 1979. Berkeley, Calif.

Loraux, Nicole. 1987. "Le lien de la division." *Le cahier du Collège international de philosophie* 4: 101–124.

Lounsbury, R. 1975. "The Death of Domitius in the *Pharsalia.*" *TAPA* 105: 209–212.

———— 1976. "History and Motive in Book Seven of Lucan's *Pharsalia.*" *Hermes* 104: 210–239.

———— 1986. "Lucan, the *Octavia,* and Domitius Nero." *Latomus Studies in Latin Literature* 4: 499–520.

Mackay, L. A. 1953. "Lucan 1.76–7." *CR* 3: 145.

———— 1961. "The Vocabulary of Fear in Latin Epic Poetry." *TAPA* 92: 308–316.

Makowski, J. F. 1977. "*Oracula mortis* in the *Pharsalia.*" *CP* 72: 193–202.

Malamud, Martha A. 1995. "Happy Birthday, Dead Lucan: (P)raising the Dead in *Silvae* 2.7." In *Roman Literature and Ideology: Ramus Essays for J. P. Sullivan,* ed. A. J. Boyle. Pp. 169–198. Bendigo, Victoria.

Malcovati, Enrica. 1940. *M. Annaeo Lucano.* Milan.

———— 1953. "Lucano e Cicerone." *Athenaeum* 31: 288–297.

Manville, Philip Brook. 1980. "Solon's Law of *Stasis* and *Atimia* in Archaic Athens." *TAPA* 110: 213–221.

———— 1990. *The Origins of Citizenship in Ancient Athens.* Princeton.

Maoz, Zeev. 1990. *Paradoxes of War: On the Art of National Self-Entrapment.* Boston.

Marti, Berthe. 1945. "The Meaning of the *Pharsalia.*" *AJP* 66: 352–376.

———— 1964. "Tragic History and Lucan's *Pharsalia.*" In *Classical, Medieval, and Renaissance Studies in Honor of Berthold Louis Ullman,* ed. C. Henderson Jr. Vol. 1: 165–204. Rome.

———— 1966. "Cassius Scaeva and Lucan's *Inventio.*" In *The Classical Tradition: Literary and Historical Studies in Honor of Harry Caplan,* ed. L. Wallach. Pp. 239–257. Ithaca.

———— 1970. "La structure de la Pharsale." In *Lucain,* ed. M. Durry. *Entretiens de la Fondation Hardt* 15. Pp. 1–50. Geneva.

———— 1975. "Lucan's Narrative Techniques." *Parola del passato* 30: 74–90.

Martindale, Charles A. 1976. "Paradox, Hyperbole, and Literary Novelty in Lucan's *De Bello Civili.*" *BICS* 23: 45–54.

———— 1977. "Three Notes on Lucan VI." *Mnemosyne* 30: 375–387.

———— 1980. "Lucan's Nekuia." In *Studies in Latin Literature and Roman History,* ed. C. Deroux. Pp. 367–377. Collection Latomus 168. Brussels.

———— 1981. "Lucan's Hercules: Padding or Paradigm? A Note on *De bello civili* 4.589–660." *Symbolae Osloenses* 56: 71–80.

———— 1984. "The Politician Lucan." *Greece & Rome* 31: 64–79.

———— 1993. *Redeeming the Text: Latin Poetry and the Hermeneutics of Reception.* Cambridge.

Masters, Jamie. 1992. *Poetry and Civil War in Lucan's Bellum Civile.* Cambridge.

———— 1994. "Deceiving the Reader: The Political Mission of Lucan's *Bellum Civile.*" In *Reflections of Nero: Culture, History, and Representation,* ed. Jás Elsner and Jamie Masters. Pp. 151–177. Chapel Hill.

Mayer, R. 1978. "On Lucan and Nero." *BICS* 25: 85–88.

———— 1979. "Pharsalica damna." *Mnemosyne,* 4th ser. 32: 338–359.

———— 1981 *Lucan Civil War VIII, Edited with a Commentary.* Warminster.

McNeil, David. 1990. *The Grotesque Description of War and the Military in 18th Century English Fiction.* Newark, N.J.

Menz, Walter. 1970. "Caesar und Pompeius im Epos Lucans: Zur Stoffbehandlung und Charakterschilderung in Lucans *Pharsalia.*" Excerpted in *Lucan,* ed. W. Rutz. Pp. 257–263, 360–379. Darmstadt.

Metger, Wilhelm. 1970. "Kampf und Tod in Lucans *Pharsalia.*" Excerpted in *Lucan,* ed. W. Rutz. Pp. 423–438. Darmstadt.

Miller, J. F. 1992. "The *Fasti* and Hellenistic Didactic: Ovid's Variant Aetiologies." *Arethusa* 25: 11–31.

Miller, J. Hillis. 1977. "The Critic as Host." *Critical Inquiry* 3: 439–448.

Momigliano, A. 1941. "Epicureans in Revolt." *JRS* 31: 151–157.

Moretti, G. 1984. "Formularità e tecniche del paradossale in Lucano." *Maia* 36: 37–49.

Morford, Mark. 1985. "Nero's Patronage and Participation in Literature and the Arts." *ANRW* 32.3: 2003–31.

Morford, M. P. O. 1966. "Lucan and the Marian Tradition." *Latomus* 25: 107–114.

———— 1967. "The Purpose of Lucan's 9th Book." *Latomus* 26: 123–129.

———— 1967. *The Poet Lucan: Studies in Rhetorical Epic.* Oxford.

Most, G. W. 1992. "*Disiecti membra poetae:* The Rhetoric of Dismemberment in Neronian Poetry." In *Innovations of Antiquity,* ed. R. Hexter and D. Selden. Pp. 391–419. New Haven.

Mudry, Philippe. 1991. "Le rêve de Pompée ou le temps aboli (Lucain, Pharsale VII, 1–44)." *Etudes de lettres* 2: 77–88.

Myers, Gerald E. 1986. *William James: His Life and Thought.* New Haven.

Narducci, E. 1973. "Il tronco di Pompeo (Troia e Roma nella *Pharsalia*)." *Maia* 25: 317–325.

———— 1974. "Sconvolgimenti naturali e profezia delle guerre civili: Phars. 1.522–695." *Maia* 26: 97–110.

———— 1976. "Allusività e autodemistificazione: Lucano 7.254–63." *Maia* 28: 127–128.

———— 1979. *La provvidenza crudele: Lucano e la distruzione dei miti augustei.* Pisa.

———— 1985. "Ideologia e tecnica allusiva nella 'Pharsalia.' " *ANRW* II.32.3: 1538–64.

Newbold, R. F. 1979. "Bodies and Boundaries in Late Antiquity." *Arethusa* 12: 93–114.

Newmyer, S. 1983. "Imagery as a Means of Character Portrayal in Lucan." In *Studies in Latin Literature and Roman History,* ed. Carl Deroux. Pp. 226–252. Collection Latomus 180. Brussels.

Nisard, Désiré. 1849. *Etudes de moeurs et de critique sur les poètes latins de la décadence.* Paris.

Nock, A. D. 1926. "The Proem of Lucan." *CR* 40: 17–18.

Nussbaum, Martha C. 1986. *The Fragility of Goodness: Luck and Ethics in Greek Tragedy and Philosophy.* Cambridge.

Nutting, H. C. 1932. "The Hero of the *Pharsalia.*" *AJP* 53: 41–52.

O'Gorman, Ellen. 1995. "Shifting Ground: Lucan, Tacitus, and the Landscape of Civil War." *Hermathena* 159: 117–131.

O'Hara, James J. 1993. Review of Jamie Masters, *Poetry and Civil War in Lucan's "Bellum Civile."* *CJ* 89: 83–86.

——— 1994. "They Might Be Giants: Inconsistency and Indeterminacy in Virgil's War in Italy." *Colby Quarterly* 30.3: 206–226.

O'Higgins, Dolores. 1988. "Lucan as *vates.*" *CA* 7: 208–226.

Olsson, Gunnar. 1991. *Lines of Power / Limits of Language.* Minneapolis.

Opelt, Ilona. 1957. "Die Seeschlacht vor Massilia bei Lucan." *Hermes* 85: 435–445.

Ormand, Kirk. 1994. "Lucan's *Auctor Vix Fidelis.*" *CA* 13: 38–55.

Paratore, Ettore. 1982. "Néron et Lucain dans l'exorde de la *Pharsale.*" In *Neronia 1977,* ed. J.-M. Croisille and P.-M. Fauchère. Pp. 93–101. Clermont-Ferrand.

Pavan, Massimiliano. 1970. "Das politische Ideal Lucans." In *Lucan,* ed. W. Rutz. Pp. 407–422. Darmstadt.

Pfligersdorffer, G. 1959. "Lucan als Dichter des geistigen Widerstandes." *Hermes* 87: 344–377.

Phillips, O. C. 1968. "Lucan's Grove." *CP* 63: 296–300.

Pichon, R. 1912. *Les sources de Lucain.* Paris.

Plass, Paul. 1995. *The Game of Death in Ancient Rome: Arena Sport and Political Suicide.* Madison.

Postgate, J. P. 1913. *M. Annaei Lucani De Bello Civili Liber VIII.* Cambridge.

Quint, D. 1993. *Epic and Empire.* Princeton.

Rambaud, M. 1955. "L'apologie de Pompée par Lucain au livre VII de la Pharsale." *REL* 33: 258–296.

Richter, Simon. 1992. *Laocoon's Body and the Aesthetics of Pain.* Detroit.

Ricks, C. 1961. "Sejanus and Dismemberment." *MLN* 75: 301–308.

Rist, John M., ed. 1978a. *The Stoics.* Berkeley.

Rist, John M. 1978b. "The Stoic Concept of Detachment." In *The Stoics,* ed. J. Rist. Pp. 259–72. Berkeley.

Roller, Matthew. 1994. "Ethical Contradiction and the Fractured Community in Lucan's *Bellum Civile.*" Ph.D. diss., University of California at Berkeley.

Ronnick, Michele V. 1991. *Cicero's "Paradoxa Stoicorum": A Commentary, an Interpretation and Study of Its Influence.* Frankfurt am Main.

Rorty, Richard. 1989. *Contingency, Irony, Solidarity.* Cambridge.

Rose, Herbert J. 1958. "The Dream of Pompey." *Acta Classica* 1: 80–84.

Rose, Kenneth F. C. 1966. "Problems of Chronology in Lucan's Career." *TAPA* 97: 379–396.

Rosenmeyer, Thomas G. 1989. *Senecan Drama and Stoic Cosmology.* Berkeley.

Rosner-Siegel, Judith A. 1983. "The Oak and the Lightning: Lucan, *Bellum Civile* 1.135–57." *Athenaeum* 61: 165–177.

Roth, Michael S. 1995. *The Ironist's Cage: Memory, Trauma, and the Construction of History.* New York.

Rowland, R. J. 1969. "The Significance of Massilia in Lucan." *Hermes* 97: 204–208.

Rudich, Vassily. 1993. *Political Dissidence under Nero: The Price of Dissimulation.* London.

Rutz, Werner. 1960. "Amor Mortis bei Lucan." *Hermes* 88: 462–475.

———— 1963. "Der Träume des Pompeius in Lucans Pharsalia." *Hermes* 91: 334–345.

———— 1970a. "Lucan und die Rhetorik." In *Lucain,* ed. M. Durry. Pp. 235–265. *Entretiens de la Fondation Hardt* 15. Geneva.

————, ed. 1970b. *Lucan.* Darmstadt.

———— 1970c. "Studien zur Kompositions Kunst und zur epischen Technik Lucans." In *Lucan,* ed. W. Rutz. Pp. 160–216. Darmstadt.

———— 1985. "Lucans 'Pharsalia' im Lichte der neuesten Forschung." *ANRW* 2.32.3: 1457–1537.

Sanford, Eva M. 1931. "Lucan and His Roman Critics." *CP* 26: 233–257.

———— 1933. "Lucan and Civil War." *CP* 28: 121–127.

Saylor, C. 1978. "*Belli spes improba:* The Theme of Walls in Lucan, *Pharsalia* 6." *TAPA* 108: 243–257.

———— 1982. "Curio and Antaeus: The African Episode of Lucan *Pharsalia* 4." *TAPA* 112: 169–177.

———— 1986. "Wine, Blood, and Water: The Imagery of Lucan *Pharsalia* 4.148–401." *Eranos* 84: 149–156.

———— 1990. "Lux Extrema: Lucan *Pharsalia* 4.402–581." *TAPA* 120: 291–300.

Scarry, Elaine. 1985. *The Body in Pain: The Making and Unmaking of the World.* Oxford.

Schönberger, O. 1958. "Zu Lucan. Ein Nachtrag." *Hermes* 86: 230–239. Reprinted in *Lucan,* ed. W. Rutz. Pp. 486–497. Darmstadt.

——— 1970. "Ein Dichter römischer Freiheit, M. Annaeus Lucanus." In *Lucan,* ed. W. Rutz. Pp. 525–545. Darmstadt.

Schotes, H. A. 1969. *Stoische Physik, Psychologie und Theologie bei Lucan.* Bonn.

Schrijvers, Pieter H. 1989. "Interpréter Lucain par Lucain: La Pharsale, I, 1–82, II, 234–325." *Mnemosyne* 42: 62–75.

——— 1990. *Crise poétique et poétique de la crise: La reception de Lucan aux XIXe et XXe siècles.* Amsterdam and New York.

Schröter, Robert. 1975. "Die krise der römischen Republik im Epos Lukans über den Bürgerkrieg." In *Krisen in der Antike. Bewusstein und Bewältigung,* ed. G. Alföldy et al. Pp. 99–111. Dusseldorf.

Segal, Charles. 1983. "Boundary Violation and the Landscape of the Self in Senecan Tragedy." *Antike und Abendland* 29: 172–187.

——— 1984. "Senecan Baroque: The Death of Hippolytus in Seneca, Ovid, and Euripides." *TAPA* 114: 311–325.

Seitz, K. 1965. "Das Pathetische Erzählstil Lukans." *Hermes* 93: 204–232.

Shackleton-Bailey, D. R. 1987. "Lucan Revisited." *PCPS* 33: 74–91.

Shaw, B. 1985. "The Divine Economy: Stoicism as Ideology." *Latomus* 44: 16–54.

Shay, Jonathan. 1994. *Achilles in Vietnam: Combat Trauma and the Undoing of Character.* New York.

Shoaf, R. A. 1978. "*Certius exemplar sapientis viri:* Rhetorical Subversion and Subversive Rhetoric in *Pharsalia* 9." *Philological Quarterly* 57: 143–154.

Slater, Philip. 1968. *The Glory of Hera: Greek Mythology and the Greek Family.* Boston.

Solimano, Giannini. 1991. *La prepotenza dell'occhio: Riflessioni sull'opera di Seneca.* Genoa.

Soria, C. 1972. "Optimismo y pessimismo en Lucano." In *Actas del primer Simposio nacional de estudios clásicos, Mayo 1970.* Pp. 291–298. Cuvo.

Spurr, David. 1993. *The Rhetoric of Empire: Colonial Discourse in Journalism, Travel Writing, and Imperial Administration.* Durham, N.C.

Stallybrass, Peter. 1990. "Boundary and Transgression: Body, Text, Language." *Stanford French Revew* 14: 9–23.

Stallybrass, Peter, and Allon White. 1986. *The Politics and Poetics of Transgression.* London.

Stein, Howard F. 1993. "The Holocaust, the Self, and the Question of Wholeness: A Response to Lewin." *Ethos* 21: 485–512.

Steinberg, L. 1990. "What did Cato Mean?—Comment." *New York Review of Books,* 19 July 1990, p. 53.

Stough, Charlotte. 1978. "Stoic Determinism and Moral Responsibility." In *The Stoics,* ed. J. Rist. Pp. 203–231. Berkeley.

Sullivan, J. P. 1982. "Petronius' *Bellum Civile* and Lucan's *Pharsalia:* A Political Reconsideration." In *Neronia 1977,* ed. J.-M. Croisille and P.-M. Fauchère. Pp. 151–155. Clermont-Ferrand.

———— 1985. *Literature and Politics in the Age of Nero.* Ithaca.

Syndikus, H. P. 1958. "Lucans Gedicht vom Bürgerkrieg." Diss. Munich.

Tasler, W. 1972. *Die Reden in Lucans Pharsalia.* Bonn.

Thierfelder, A. 1934–35. "Der Dichter Lucan." *Archiv für Kulturgeschichte* 25: 1–20. Reprinted in *Lucan,* ed. W. Rutz. Pp. 50–69. Darmstadt.

Thomas, Louis-Vincent. 1980. *Le cadavre: De la biologie à l'anthropologie.* Brussels.

Thomas, Richard F. 1982. "The Stoic Landscape of Lucan 9." In *Lands and Peoples in Roman Poetry: The Ethnographic Tradition.* Pp. 108–123. Cambridge.

Thompson, Lynnette. 1964. "Lucan's Apotheosis of Nero." *CP* 59: 147–153.

———— 1983–84. "A Lucanian Contradiction of Virgilian *pietas:* Pompey's *amor.*" *CJ* 79: 207–215.

Thompson, Lynnette, and Richard T. Bruère. 1968. "Lucan's Use of Virgilian Reminiscence." *CP* 63: 1–21.

———— 1970. "The Virgilian Background of Lucan's Fourth Book." *CP* 65: 152–172.

Thomson, Philip J. 1972. *The Grotesque.* London.

Tucker, Robert A. 1969. "Lucan and the Baroque: A Revival of Interest." *CW* 62: 295–297.

———— 1970. "The Colors of Lucan: Anti-War Propaganda?" *CB* 46: 56–58, 64.

———— 1977. "Lucan and Libertas." *CB* 53: 81–85.

———— 1981–82. "Lucan's Tears." *CB* 58: 1–4.

———— 1983–84. "The Meaning of 'Gloria' in Lucan's 'Bellum Civile.' " *CB* 60: 4–9.

———— 1990. "Love in Lucan's 'Civil War.' " *CB* 66: 43–46.

———— 1991. "The Alleged Neronian Epitaph for Lucan." *Latomus* 50: 176–183.

Ullman, B. L. 1942. "History and Tragedy." *TAPA* 73: 25–53.

Usener, H, ed. 1869. *M. Annaei Lucani Commenta Bernensia.* Leipzig.

Verdaguer, P. 1988. *L'univers de la cruauté. Une lecture de Céline.* Geneva.

Vessey, D. W. T. C. 1970. "Lucan, Statius and the Baroque Epic." *CW* 63: 232–234.

Viansino, G. 1974. *Studi sul "Bellum Civile" di Lucano.* Salerno.

Viarre, S. 1982. "Caton en Libye: L'histoire et la métaphore (Lucain, Pharsale, 9.294–949)." In *Neronia 1977,* ed. J.-M. Croisille and P.-M. Fauchère. Pp. 103–110. Clermont-Ferrand.

Viljamaa, Toivo. 1992. *"Crudelitatis odio in crudelitatem ruitis:* Livy's Concept of Life and History." In *Crudelitas: The Politics of Cruelty in the Ancient and Medieval World,* ed. T. Viljamaa et al. Pp. 41–55. Krems.

Wagener, Anthony P. 1931. "Stylistic Qualities of the Apostrophe to Nature as a Dramatic Device." *TAPA* 62: 78–100.

Walbank, F. W. 1955. "Tragic History: A Reconsideration." *BICS* 2: 4–14.

———— 1960. "History and Tragedy." *Historia* 9: 216–234.

Wallach, Barbara Price. 1990. "Rhetoric and Paradox: Cicero, 'Paradoxa Stoicorum IV.'" *Hermes* 118: 171–183.

Walsh, G. B. 1991. "Callimachean Passages: The Rhetoric of Epitaph in Epigram." *Arethusa* 24: 77–105.

Wanke, Christiane. 1964. *Seneca, Lucan, Corneille. Studien zum Manierismus der römischen Kaiserzeit und der französischen Klassik.* Heidelberg.

White, J. B. 1994. *Acts of Hope: Creating Authority in Literature, Law, and Politics.* Chicago.

Williams, G. 1978. *Change and Decline.* Berkeley.

Willis, Sharon. 1987. *Marguerite Duras: Writing on the Body.* Urbana.

Wirszubski, C. 1950. *Libertas as a Political Idea at Rome.* Cambridge.

Zetzel, J. E. G. 1980. "Two Imitations in Lucan." *CQ,* n.s. 30: 257.

Zizek, Slavoj. 1989. *The Sublime Object of Ideology.* London and New York.

Zwierlein, Otto. 1990. "Unterdrückte Klagen beim Tod des Pompeius (Lucan 7,43) und des Cremutius Cordus (Sen. Consol. Marc. 1,2)." *Hermes* 118: 184–191.

Index